Creativity for Li ...
Career Advancement

Creativity for Library Career Advancement

Perspectives, Techniques and Eureka Moments

Edited by VERA GUBNITSKAIA *and* CAROL SMALLWOOD

Foreword by DEB BIGGS TENBUSCH

McFarland & Company, Inc., Publishers
Jefferson, North Carolina

ISBN (print) 978-1-4766-7401-8
ISBN (ebook) 978-1-4766-3636-8

LIBRARY OF CONGRESS AND BRITISH LIBRARY
CATALOGUING DATA ARE AVAILABLE

Front cover photograph and illustration © 2019 ImageFlow

Printed in the United States of America

*McFarland & Company, Inc., Publishers
Box 611, Jefferson, North Carolina 28640
www.mcfarlandpub.com*

Table of Contents

Part VII. Partnerships, Collaborations and Networking

Part VIII. Budget Matters

Foreword

DEB BIGGS TENBUSCH

Infusing creativity into your work is something that is not necessarily done consciously or considered essential when starting in a profession. Newly minted librarians are engaged in learning what is expected of them to do the job properly, and navigating the ebb and flow of professional waters. As the years go by, the importance of creativity becomes more apparent in order to sustain your interest in and continuing contributions to the profession. Some of us, like myself, have found a diverse palette of job opportunities within the library profession. I have been an academic and a public librarian, a marketing associate at a bibliographic database management company, a project specialist for building a special library, a director of an information clearinghouse for instruction librarians, a coordinator for a statewide digital library, an account manager for a library content provider, and now am at Gale, Cengage Learning. These different but closely aligned positions have enabled me to stay inspired within the profession by allowing me to develop diverse skill sets and opportunities thereby keeping my interests creative and ongoing.

Such is not the case for everyone. There may not be the option to move around or there may be a reason to stay—for example, tenure or a spouse/partner's job. That's where it becomes paramount to make sure that what you do professionally, what you do to ensure your livelihood, stays fresh, relevant, and continually interesting to you. In so doing, this becomes a way to enhance and advance in your career which is a realistic and the ultimate goal.

Incorporating a creative way of thinking into your career can be looked at as a methodology where you engage in thinking outside the box in the performance of your job. Managers' wish lists of desired employee characteristics often include creativity, ranking it high—right up there with integrity. The library profession clearly mandates integrity, but creativity on the job is also now frequently valued and expected for career advancement. Librarianship is exceptionally well suited for an individual who possesses an eclectic personality, and therefore, one could assume, has a creative mindset. Eclecticism, however, does not always equal creativity. As the clock ticks off the years, one needs to embrace or reinvent the creative streak in life to stay fresh and career focused.

The insightful collection of essays in this volume covers the wide spectrum of methods of cultivating the creative for career fulfillment and ultimate success; it also emphasizes the necessity of taking the time to explore ways to invigorate one's creativity. Starting with the first essay, readers will see the wisdom of relaxing, having fun, engaging

1

in play, listening to music, even daydreaming, so that they can open the door to their creative selves. From there, explore gaming, improv, tarot, makerspace, writing, research, publishing, and exhibit creation. Reinvigorate your teaching and consider incorporating music, photography, art, zines, and digital collection creation and management, staff accommodations and talents, support groups, networking outside the library, and much more, as unique ways of taking a creative approach to work and the responsibilities of becoming a true professional. Frankly, I was astonished at the depths the authors went to in sharing specifics on how they each embraced creativity in their work which ultimately both enhanced and helped define or redefine their careers. If you think that your library career path might need an inspiration infusion, this is the book for you!

Preface

Steve Jobs once observed that "creativity is just connecting things"—a very concise definition. You can find many and much longer descriptions, but the editors (one of the team is a published poet and the other a published and exhibited artist) believe Jobs expressed its essence. Librarians are surrounded with things to connect, and it is plain from the table of contents of *Creativity for Library Career Advancement* that they have the ability to recognize connections—and they do it well. In the About the Contributors section it is also evident that the authors' experiences, which they depict in their essays, echo this ability, like the highly successful diversified career of forewordist Deb Biggs Tenbusch. In today's job market as a whole, it is more necessary than ever that creativity is utilized as economics demand adaption, evolution, and renewal.

It has been a joy to read about the experiences of the contributors, who have all shared such vibrant work that is so relevant to the librarianship profession.

PART I

Nurture Your Mind

The Power of Incubation

Slowing Down to Speed Up Creativity

JIM JIPSON *and* KELLIE SPARKS

One might assume the life of a librarian is slow-paced and quiet. Images of leisurely days spent reading inside the hallowed halls of a brick-and-mortar library might be conjured up by those unfamiliar with such a vocation. As librarians, we know this is simply not the case. Librarians have become experts in the art of multitasking. We proudly move from one task to another while providing impeccable service to those who enter our library. Librarians are also prone to working long hours and bringing work home with us at the expense of our personal time.

But what does this have to do with our natural creative ability? Do we do a disservice to our patrons by not setting aside enough time for ourselves to find the spark of creativity that lies underneath the deadlines and endless meetings? Contrary to popular belief, can slowing down actually speed up the process of creative insight?

On my personal journey to answer these questions, I conducted secondary research and attended an Advanced Creativity course led by Professor Jim Jipson at the University of West Florida. Through this process, I learned a great deal about the creative process. I also discovered a powerful tool to fuel creative insight called incubation.

Daniel Kahneman in *Thinking Fast and Slow* describes the subconscious or unconscious minds as the thought processes that are fast, automatic, frequent, and emotional. These include completing a well-known phrase such as "war and…" or solving a simple equation like "1 + 1 = …" He describes the conscious mind as being responsible for the slower, more logical and calculated thoughts such as trying to remember a specific sound or looking for a specific person in a crowd (Kahneman 2011). Incubation refers to the part of the creative process where you let things "slow down" and take time to let ideas "marinate." Incubation is the period of time when one disconnects from the project at hand and lets the unconscious and conscious minds work together to create new insights and connections.

In 1926, social psychologist Graham Wallas introduced the idea of incubation through his seminal work on the subject of creativity, *The Art of Thought*. The book describes the four stages of the creative process which are preparation, incubation, illumination, and verification (1926).

As a librarian, I felt that incubation went against what inadvertently happens while working in libraries. Most projects are expected to be completed as quickly as possible—

without much time to mull over ideas about how a project or task can be expanded upon or approached from different perspectives. Concrete thinking and analysis has always been at the forefront of what is important during the completion of a library project—but I began wondering—what about creativity and incubation?

In this essay, we explore the neuroscience and art behind creative incubation. We examine practices such as "mushing," utilizing oblique strategies, fun and play, undertaking multiple tasks, relaxation, movement, sleep, listening to music, and daydreaming. These are just a few examples of how one can step away from focused mental control and activate the unconscious mind. We will also discuss the value of daily moments of incubation and introduce how one might change their brainwave activity to allow for opportunities of creative insight.

Before we delve into the science and techniques of incubation, it is important to note that incubation should take place within a judgment-free zone. Whether you are incubating ideas individually or with a group, fear has no place in the incubation phase. Ideas, no matter how unusual, need a space to flow freely with no fear of being criticized. Part of the incubation process includes creating the right atmosphere for creativity to flourish.

Neuroscience

Creativity research has found that humans are hardwired to reject new ideas. Our brains search out the comfortable rather than the uncomfortable as thoughts are created (Mueller, Melwani, and Goncalo 2011). But attaching oneself to what is comfortable and only utilizing concrete thinking when a problem arises can be detrimental to creativity. Having too much order and focusing only on the black-and-white options will diminish the chance of seeing the creative "gray" area that encompasses the natural chaos that is creative thought. The ability to let in the chaos of creativity without becoming overwhelmed is a key part of the creative process (Pillay 2017).

Recent research has debunked outdated perceptions of creativity and has shown that when creative insight happens in the brain, it is a result of the right and left hemispheres of the brain actively working together (Kaufman and Gregoire 2015). The study of the neuroscience of creativity has also shown that environmental factors can play an even larger role in creativity than intelligence.

For professionals, the need for a work environment supportive of creative incubation is important when we are involved in creative tasks. Dr. Rex Jung, a leading neuropsychologist from the University of New Mexico, has highlighted the importance of "downregulation," or more simply, downtime, in our daily lives. This downtime makes room in the brain for new ideas to form, as well as to "flow and bump into each other." Downtime is an important part of incubation that provides a mental space away from modern day distractions such as social media (Mehta and Mishra 2016).

The unconscious mind and certain brainwaves play a significant role in the incubation process. During incubation, we can choose to distract ourselves from the current creative problem and try to mentally relax so that we do not consciously think of the problem at hand (Sadler-Smith 2015). By creating mental space between yourself and the creative problem, you increase the ability of the unconscious mind to intervene. As we understand how the unconscious mind interacts with the creative process, it is also helpful to consider the role of brainwave activity during creative thought.

Harvard-trained psychiatrist Pillay compares brainwaves to music notes, going from low to high on a musical scale. There are five main sets of brainwaves, Beta, Alpha, Delta, Theta, and Gamma, that typically work together when you have a feeling or thought. Beta waves are considered the "focus waves"—the waves that are highlighted when your mind is rigidly focused on a task. Alpha can be considered the "VIP" brainwave when it comes to creative incubation—facilitating pure relaxation. Theta and Delta also promote deep relaxation and sleep within an unfocused mind. Gamma waves are the most energetic waves of the brainwave bunch and are known to link information from all parts of the brain (Pillay 2017).

It is interesting to note that certain daily practices can bolster specific brainwave activity and assist in turning your attention inward, further instigating creative thought. For example, activities as simple and routine as taking a shower, driving a car, or drawing, can promote the "Alpha" brain state that is present during creative insight (Pillay 2017). These activities can become a valuable tool during the creative process if one wants to consciously switch brain waves from the Beta waves required in the "preparation" stage to the Alpha waves required for incubation to occur.

Certain areas of the brain are correlated with creativity and incubation as well. The Default Mode Network (DMN), a network of interacting brain regions shown to be active during mental breaks, has been noted as an important component of the incubation process. The DMN is a driver in divergent, or non-linear, thinking; it is where many spontaneous thoughts occur within the brain. The DMN helps you develop unique associations between thoughts and fosters originality (Jung et al. 2013).

The DMN is part of a larger neural network which psychologist and leading creativity researcher Scott Barry Kaufman (2015) has termed the "Imagination Network." The "Imagination Network" consists of the DMN, as well as two additional neural networks called the Executive Attention Network, and the Salience Network. The Executive Attention Network is the area of the brain that controls focused attention and logical thinking. This particular area is necessary for creative thinking since we need mental focus to refine and implement our creative ideas. The Salience Network helps us switch back and forth between imaginative and practical thinking. All three of these work together when we think divergently and give birth to a new idea (Beaty et al. 2016).

Another part of the brain that has an essential role in creativity is the hippocampus. The hippocampus stores 'episodic memory' of experienced events and helps people imagine unique future possibilities by enabling the formation of creative associations (Vartanian, Bristol, and Kaufman 2013). When we take a creative "leap" by imagining and constructing ideas of the future, we pull from these stores of episodic memory in the brain (Creative Thinking Project 2015). Therefore, the hippocampus is essential to the incubation stage of the creative process.

Tools for Incubation

As we move to understand more about everyone's capacity to be creative, we want to highlight the tools that librarians can use every day to boost our chances of creative insight while incubating an idea or project. These simple tools can be used to help you become more self-reflective, lessen mental distractions, and connect with the unconscious mind. It can also be beneficial to allow for enough time in the day to practice these strategies without feeling rushed.

The goal is to allow the mind to create space for thought to flow freely and easily, without feeling overloaded by details or mental strain. You might even consider changing locations when practicing the art of creative incubation, to find what works best for you. Keep in mind, though, that the following tools are subjective and are intended to be adopted based on your own personal preference.

Mushing

This term, coined by Jim Jipson, is used to describe tactile action, such as knitting or washing dishes, undertaken during the incubation process. This "mushing" activity with your hands helps you access the area of the brain responsible for creative insight (Sparks 2017). A common example of this is doodling. Psychoanalyst Marion Milner (2010) found that doodling helps with bypassing the focus of the conscious mind and activates the connection with your unconscious mind. If you are already a librarian that likes to doodle in meetings, you are in good company. As of 2007, twenty-six of the forty-four U.S. Presidents were self-confessed doodlers, as was Russian writer Fyodor Dostoyevsky (Pillay 2017). "Mushing" is a great way to let the conscious mind know that it's time to move over and let the unconscious take the lead.

Oblique Strategies

Occasionally, a creative block can sneak up and halt the creative process. To combat this, two creatives, Brian Eno and Peter Schmidt, developed a tool called Oblique Strategies. Oblique Strategies is a set of cards that specialize in encouraging different ways of approaching your creative problem. They provide a series of prompts to help stimulate creative thinking. These prompts ask anything from "What would your closest friend do?" to "How can I use an old idea?" as a method of pushing one out of their comfort zone. They have been described as cards that provoke you "as if you are asking your blood to flow in another direction" (Harford 2016). They would certainly be an interesting addition to any librarian's creativity arsenal!

Fun and Play

George Bernard Shaw once wrote, "We don't stop playing because we grow old, we grow old because we stop playing" (Quotes.net 2018). Research shows that a mix of work and play provide the most optimal context for learning and creativity. Play is also about disconnecting from established patterns of thought and connecting actions in innovative ways. Even focusing on the mental "playground" by cultivating a more playful attitude in how you interact with the world and embrace change can influence creative thinking (Bateson 2015).

Increasing the level of fun and play in daily life allows the mind to naturally gravitate towards abstract thinking rather than to remain in a rigid mental state when tackling a creative problem. One way to achieve this is to surround yourself with others who inspire play, positivity, and laughter. Encourage play within your library team by planning fun activities to share with your colleagues, such as a lunchtime board game or video game hour. Cultivate laughter as a daily practice by making a rule of having a "laughter lunch." For example, try watching a fun YouTube video or comedy routine while taking your lunch break (Van Edwards 2017). The more you play, the easier it will be to access creative insight!

Multiple Tasks

Not to be mistaken for multitasking. Jim Jipson recommends working on at least three creative projects concurrently as this can be beneficial to the creative process. However, the timing of these projects is key. For example, while one project is actively being pursued, the mind can be contemplating the other two unconsciously. You may find that after mentally focusing on one project, your mind can turn to the other two with greater creative insight as a result. Since stress is ultimately toxic when it comes to creativity, make sure not to overwhelm yourself by actively working on too many projects. Three tasks are considered a manageable number when it comes to allowing yourself room to incubate (Sparks 2017).

Relaxation

An essential part of the incubation process is relaxation. Spending time in nature and active breathing are two tools that can help you relax while incubating. Many instinctively know that spending time in nature can help promote mental relaxation. In fact, the practice of spending quiet time in nature has been proven to increase creativity. Researchers sought out to determine if hikers could solve more creative puzzles by sending participants on a four-day excursion into nature. The study found that the hikers did forty-seven percent better than the control group when solving the creative puzzles (Atchley, Strayer, and Atchley 2012).

Breathing is another aspect of relaxation that can help stimulate creativity. Allowing the mind to temporarily "forget" the past and future while focusing on the present can help promote rest and relaxation when one is in a stressful state of mind. The process of actively becoming aware of your breath helps ground you in the present moment. You will want to leave room in the mind for creative thought rather than to fill it with thoughts of the past. At the very minimum, taking 5 minutes a day to shift gears away from a project can help accomplish the goal of creative incubation.

Movement

The fluid physical movement of walking can assist in the cognitive processing behind creative thought and improve creativity by as much as sixty percent (Opezzo and Schwartz 2014). Incorporating walking meetings into the work schedule is one example of how librarians can implement movement into their daily work life. Creating a library work culture that supports movement and exercise breaks throughout the day can help fight the creativity blocks that can occur during those sedentary moments.

Sleep

John Steinbeck (1954) once wrote, "It is a common experience that a problem difficult at night is resolved in the morning after the "committee of sleep" has worked on it." Sleep is another way of delving into creative insight. One example of this is the glimpse of creativity which sometimes occurs while the brain is coming out of the "alpha state" when first waking. Researcher M. Wieth (2011) has also found that some people may experience increased creativity when they are feeling sleepy. This indicates that it may be beneficial to plan creative work at a non-optimal time of day.

Most people are familiar with the advice of just 'sleeping on it' when they have encountered a creative block. This is good advice as sleep is an excellent way to disconnect from a lofty library project. However, be sure your slumber happens after the creative research and preparation that occurs at the beginning of the creative process, or you won't get much done!

Beyond the alpha waves that are present at waking moments, dreams can also be a window to creative problem solving. Research suggests that dreaming while in REM (rapid eye movement) sleep may boost creativity and improve memory. Dreaming allows the brain to recharge, reorganize memories, and collect new and old ideas at will. Dreams have also been known to inspire minds into action. For instance, Paul McCartney was reportedly inspired by a dream to compose the melody of his famous song, "Yesterday." Albert Einstein also let dreams be the inspiration for his theory behind the circularity of time (Pillay 2017).

Music

Listening to music is another excellent way to incubate during a creative library project. Recent research has shown that listening to happy music as opposed to silence can have a positive effect on creative cognition. This particular study demonstrated that upbeat classical music influenced participants to display greater cognitive flexibility and divergent creativity during tasks (Ritter and Ferguson 2017). Feel free to get lost in a powerful melody when trying to break free from the external world when in incubation mode. By getting lost, you return to the "Imagination Network" in the brain that loves to conjure up new and dynamic ideas.

Daydreaming

Allowing your mind to simply wander is another way to promote creative incubation. Daydreaming, also known as mind-wandering, gives your brain a chance to disengage from the present moment and engage in a range of thoughts not connected to the here and now. The Default Mode Network area of the brain is active during these times of creative daydreaming and mind-wandering. Research has shown that people spend approximately 25–50 percent of their waking hours engaged in mind-wandering (Kane et al. 2007; Killingsworth and Gilbert 2010). For librarians, allowing time and space for idle moments, especially after a long bout of focused analysis, can be beneficial in terms of creativity. By creating a workspace and culture that supports downtime, we can improve the chances for creative insight of all library professionals.

Conclusion

While it may be difficult for a librarian to find time in a busy work schedule to slow down and incubate, it is highly recommended as a pathway to generating better creative outcomes. By slowing down and taking the mind off the task at hand, you are consciously making room for new ideas to take shape. Librarians should ultimately schedule a period of "unfocus" as a priority within any project timeline (Pillay 2017). While this may go against the adage of "getting the job done," you should find that creative insight begins to come easier leading to new and unique solutions for every creative project.

REFERENCES

Atchley, Ruth Ann, Strayer, David L., and Atchley, Paul. 2012. "Creativity in the Wild: Improving Creative Reasoning Through Immersion in Natural Settings." *PLOS ONE* 12: Academic OneFile, EBSCOhost.

Bateson, Patrick. 2015. "Playfulness and Creativity." *Current Biology: CB* 25 (1): R12-R16. MEDLINE, EBSCOhost.

Beaty, Roger E., Benedek, Mathias, Silvia, Paul J., and Schacter, Daniel L. 2016. "Creative Cognition and Brain Network Dynamics." *Trends in Cognitive Sciences* 2 (87). Academic OneFile, EBSCOhost.

The Creative Thinking Project. 2015. "Creative Thinking." http://www.creativethinkingproject.org/creativity-and-the-brain/.

Harford, Timothy. 2016. *Messy: The Power of Disorder to Transform Our Lives.* New York: Riverhead Books.

Jung, Rex E., Mead, Brittany S., Carrasco, Jessica and Flores, Ranee A. 2013. "The Structure of Creative Cognition in the Human Brain." *Frontiers in Human Neuroscience* 7. Directory of Open Access Journals, EBSCOhost.

Kahneman, Daniel. 2011. *Thinking, Fast and Slow.* New York: Farrar, Straus, and Giroux.

Kane, Michael J., Brown, Leslie H., McVay, Jennifer C., Silvia, Paul J., Myin-Germeys, Inez, and Kwapil, Thomas R. 2007. "For Whom the Mind Wanders, and When: An Experience-Sampling Study of Working Memory and Executive Control in Daily Life." *Psychological Science* 7: 614. JSTOR Journals, EBSCOhost. http://dx.doi.org/10.1111/j.1467-9280.2007.01948.x.

Kaufman, Scott Barry, and Gregoire, Carolyn. 2015. *Wired to Create: Unraveling the Mysteries of the Creative Mind.* New York: Perigee.

Killingsworth, Matthew A., and Gilbert, Daniel T. 2010. "A Wandering Mind Is an Unhappy Mind." *Science* 6006: 932. JSTOR Journals, EBSCOhost.

Mehta, Rohit, and Mishra, Punya. 2016. "Downtime as a Key to Novelty Generation: Understanding the Neuroscience of Creativity with Dr. Rex Jung." *Techtrends: For Leaders in Education & Training* 6: 528. Academic OneFile, EBSCOhost.

Milner, Marion. 2010. *On Not Being Able to Paint.* New York: Routledge.

Mueller, Jennifer, Melwani, Shimul, and Goncalo, Jack. 2011. "The Bias Against Creativity: Why People Desire but Reject Creative Ideas." *Psychological Science.* 23 (1): 13–17.

Opezzo, Marily and Schwartz, Daniel L. 2014. "Give Your Ideas Some Legs: The Positive Effect of Walking on Creative Thinking." *Journal of Experimental Psychology: Learning, Memory, and Cognition* 4 (1142). Journals@OVID, EBSCOhost.

Pillay, Srini. 2017. *Tinker Dabble Doodle Try: Unlock the Power of the Unfocused Mind.* New York: Ballantine.

Quotes.net. 2018. "George Bernard Shaw." https://www.quotes.net/quote/404.

Ritter, Simone M., and Ferguson, Sam. 2017. "Happy Creativity: Listening to Happy Music Facilitates Divergent Thinking." *PLOS ONE* 12 (9): e0182210 DOI: 10.1371/journal.pone.0182210

Sadler-Smith, Eugene. 2015. "Wallas' Four-Stage Model of the Creative Process: More Than Meets the Eye?" *Creativity Research Journal* 27 (4): 342–352. Social Sciences Citation Index, EBSCOhost.

Sparks, Kellie. 2017. "Applying the Creative Process to Library Branding." *Marketing Libraries Journal* 1 (1): 30. http://journal.marketinglibraries.org/dec2017/5_Branding_MLJ-v1-i1-Fall2017.pdf.

Steinbeck, John. 1954. *Sweet Thursday.* New York: Viking Press.

Van Edwards, Vanessa. 2017. "Laughter Lunch." https://www.scienceofpeople.com/laughter-lunch/.

Vartanian, O., Bristol, A.S., and Kaufman, J. 2013. *Neuroscience of Creativity.* Cambridge: MIT Press.

Wallas, Graham. 1926. *The Art of Thought.* New York: Harcourt Brace.

Wieth, Mareike B. 2011. "Time of Day Effects on Problem Solving: When the Non-Optimal Is Optimal." *Thinking & Reasoning* 17 (4): 387–401. E-Journals, EBSCOhost.

TWO WORLDS, ONE OUTLET

ZINE MAKING AND CRITICAL REFLECTION FOR PROFESSIONAL AND PERSONAL DEVELOPMENT

SILVIA VONG

Critical reflection is a branch of reflection; often the phrase "critical reflection" is used interchangeably with the term "reflection." However, critical reflection is defined in the nursing and education literature as a form of reflection that focuses on power, oppression, and assumptions that favor one group over the other (Brookfield 1995). While much of the work in the library engages with patrons with diverse needs, our relationships between colleagues and staff warrant attention since power dynamics exist. Critical reflection is often not practiced due to lack of time, and lack of acknowledgment or resources. Zine-making can be a medium that helps encourage critical reflection with the appropriate prompts and strategies. In reference to research on zines and critical reflection, Deysallas and Sinclair write that "...as people began to let go of the traditional constraints, people began to have a voice—a voice they were willing to share—and stopped remaining silent about social injustices and the ways in which oppression and privilege has impacted their lives and the lives of others" (Deysallas and Sinclair 2014, 310). Critical reflection through zine-making can be helpful in reflecting on library professional practice as well as personal growth by raising one's own awareness of relationships and power.

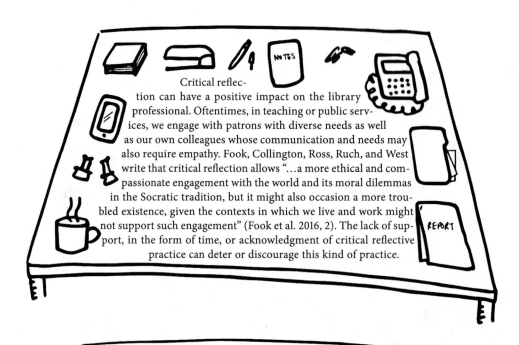

Critical reflection can have a positive impact on the library professional. Oftentimes, in teaching or public services, we engage with patrons with diverse needs as well as our own colleagues whose communication and needs may also require empathy. Fook, Collington, Ross, Ruch, and West write that critical reflection allows "…a more ethical and compassionate engagement with the world and its moral dilemmas in the Socratic tradition, but it might also occasion a more troubled existence, given the contexts in which we live and work might not support such engagement" (Fook et al. 2016, 2). The lack of support, in the form of time, or acknowledgment of critical reflective practice can deter or discourage this kind of practice.

In the personal realm, critical reflection in the form of zines can encourage thinking as well as set aside personal time for thinking about power dynamics that exist in our lives, building empathy for others, and social justice issues. Oftentimes the visual unpacking of these ideas can be helpful in uncovering any presuppositions. Activities such as concept mapping can be better facilitated and likely kept as a record in the form of a zine. The activity itself can help one explore multiple perspectives while the medium preserves or documents the process. While zines create a safe space to explore one's own thinking, critical reflection facilitates the conversation focused on building more awareness of social justice issues in one's own environment and personal relationships.

How to make a zine!

The current page shows you the basic steps to making a mini-zine. However, it is important to note that zines are not structured or confined by size requirements which means that zines can be made at any size, stapled, glued, or sewn together. The next page is an illustrated list of zine supplies and page five is a sample zine with critical reflection content. Simply photocopy the sample zine and practice folding the pages based on the instructions on the current page.

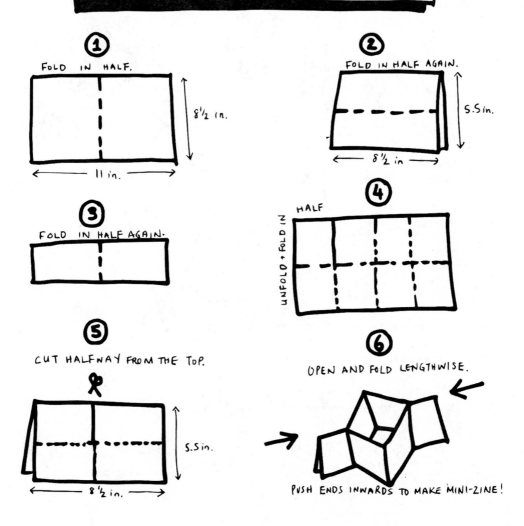

① FOLD IN HALF.

8½ in.

11 in.

② FOLD IN HALF AGAIN.

5.5 in.

8½ in

③ FOLD IN HALF AGAIN.

④ UNFOLD + FOLD IN HALF

⑤ CUT HALFWAY FROM THE TOP.

5.5 in.

8½ in.

⑥ OPEN AND FOLD LENGTHWISE.

PUSH ENDS INWARDS TO MAKE MINI-ZINE!

A
critical reflection
on

DEPARTMENT

MEETINGS

Tripp (2012) provides a valuable framework for critical reflection while Brookfield (1995) provides examples in applying the frame to teaching. This zine applies the frame to my experience as a manager of a department, specifically around department meetings.

my intended meaning:

I want to ensure staff in my department meet in-person to discuss and come to a consensus at a department meeting.

contradictions + omissions:

"Department meetings" have long been used to communicate news and discuss issues, however, the assumption is that <u>all</u> that attend will participate or are able to openly discuss issues.

who benefits or is harmed?:

Benefits: Those who talk aloud or are social learners.

Harmed: Those who struggle to speak in groups or are intimidated by dominant speakers.

an alternative:

I would like to provide alternative meeting type:
- online discussion boards allow everyone time to think
- Provide lots of notice on topic items so people have time to think.

BIBLIOGRAPHY:

Brookfield, Stephen Becoming a Critically Reflective Teacher. San Francisco: Jossey-Bass, 1995.

Tripp, David. Critical Incidents in Teaching. New York: Routledge, 2012.

E: silvia.vong@utoronto.ca

While the idea of reflection may seem like an everyday action, a meaningful reflection requires some structure to help with its focus. This is particularly important with a critical reflection as a model may guide the discussion more towards ideas of power in the classroom or social injustices in one's personal environment. There are several ways to frame a critical reflection; this chapter focuses on the following:

- Four Critically Reflective Lenses (Brookfield 1995, 29–39)
- The Critical Reflection Model (Fook and Gardener 2007, 75–126)
- Ideology Critique (Tripp 2012, 56–60)

It is important to note that these models are meant to provide guidance. These are not sets of questions you answer in succession. We can forget that learning is not a linear or restricted process and we need to watch out for old habits such as following a formula or method too closely, approaching new ideas and perspectives with preconceived notions, and trying to solve the problem rather than listening to the person (Fook and Gardener 2007, 96–97).

In the first model, Brookfield outlines four lenses to engage in a critical analysis of incidents and teaching experiences. The four lenses include the autobiography, feedback, collegial discussion, and research. Autobiography refers to the need of understanding one's own learning approaches and teaching methods as well as how each inform the other. This in-depth understanding provides insight into dominant practices that may include or exclude some students. The feedback lens refers to listening carefully to students' comments around one's teaching. The collegial discussion encourages the use of a mentor or trusted colleague to provide insight into our own practice through observation or modelling. Finally, the research lens refers to the importance of continually conducting research on teaching to ensure different perspectives and new information to be considered in one's own practice. While Brookfield's work is aimed at teaching, the four lenses could be applied to one's own personal experiences (see facing page).

The benefit of Brookfield's approach is that it encourages the exploration of different perspectives through various channels and people. This approach ensures that the critical reflection accounts for various perspectives.

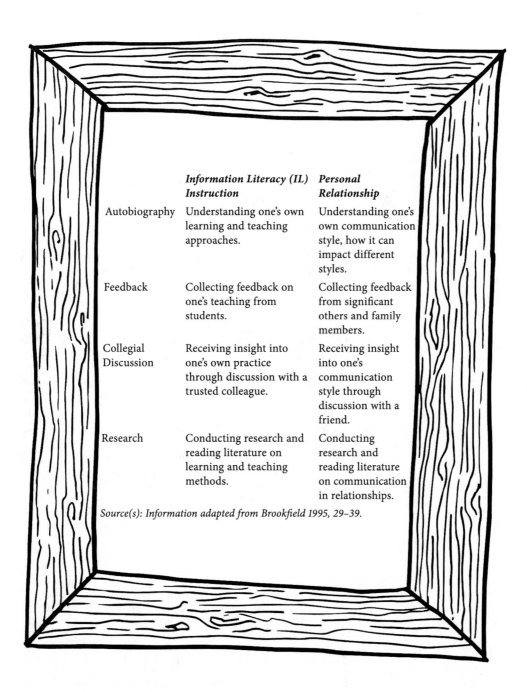

	Information Literacy (IL) Instruction	**Personal Relationship**
Autobiography	Understanding one's own learning and teaching approaches.	Understanding one's own communication style, how it can impact different styles.
Feedback	Collecting feedback on one's teaching from students.	Collecting feedback from significant others and family members.
Collegial Discussion	Receiving insight into one's own practice through discussion with a trusted colleague.	Receiving insight into one's communication style through discussion with a friend.
Research	Conducting research and reading literature on learning and teaching methods.	Conducting research and reading literature on communication in relationships.

Source(s): Information adapted from Brookfield 1995, 29–39.

In the second model, Fook and Gardener created a series of steps and questions to support nurses and social workers who interact daily with individuals who may not be privileged or may have difficult personal lives. Fook and Gardener developed various questions in their model to guide a critical reflection under four categories: reflective practice questions, reflexive questions, postmodern/deconstructive, and critical questions. Each section is comprised of two stages of questions. The first stage aims to identify and analyze the incident, and the second stage moves towards re-constructing a new approach to speech and behavior for future interactions. In the critical questions category, the first stage contains questions about underlying assumptions or beliefs. For example, "what assumptions are implicit in my account and where do they come from?" (Fook and Gardener 2007, 76). In the second stage, the questions shift towards planning and reflecting on how to change or consider future interactions. For example, "what might I do as an individual that will contribute to broader-level collective changes (with immediate colleagues or in my workplace)" (Fook and Gardener 2007, 76). These questions are a part of a larger process that involves training in an introductory session, followed by reflection, and, finally, discussion to move towards addressing changes in thinking or behavior (Fook and Gardener 2007, 52). This involves a social aspect and encourages group discussion to help facilitate the reflection as well as help provide insight into one's own reflective process. Fook and Gardener emphasize the importance of engaging in a safe and non-judgmental environment to help support and facilitate a positive experience and result. This kind of critical reflection can be used in one's personal experiences. Many of the questions are written broadly and can be adjusted to suit a different incident or experience. However, Fook and Gardener's model involves a social aspect, which may prove more challenging in the personal life if there is little trust or fewer links to trusted friends or family who have the training to facilitate a discussion as well as the resources to support the discussion.

In the third model, the Ideology Critique, four steps are outlined:

- Identifying the experience and dominant view, belief or attitude;
- Analyzing the experience to identify contradictions or omissions;
- Explaining how and why the dominant view, belief or attitude affects different people or groups;
- Creating a new structure that meets the needs of those involved and different groups or people (Tripp 2012, 59).

The Ideology Critique gives more flexibility in the type of questions that one would ask during a reflection. It also focuses on identifying dominant views and their impact on particular individuals or groups. The unearthing of a dominant view or ideology helps to unpack how our own personal beliefs are shaped by our unique life and experiences. This ensures that we approach a critical reflection with empathy and consider various perspectives and experiences. This model pointedly directs the reflection towards identifying different perspectives and building more self-awareness.

These three models, Brookfield's Four Lenses, Fook and Gardener's Critical Reflection Model, and Tripp's Ideology Critique, can be used to help guide the critical reflection to ensure that issues around power and assumptions are addressed during this process. While the models provide a guide, there are various strategies for facilitating the reflection on paper or in zine form such as life stories, metaphor/analogies exercises, and concept mapping. The models can provide some guidance on what to discuss, however, the strategies help engage the creator in the reflection.

Personal stories can help others connect with different perspectives. They are particularly effective through the zine medium which encourages one to write or draw their life story as a narrative. In education, storytelling is considered valuable "in enabling [the] reconstruction to go forward in a more reflective way.... The personal story is a powerful means of becoming aware of the taken-for-granted arrangements and constraints of one's own culture" (Elbaz-Luwisch 2001, 84). Brookfield's *Four Lenses* can help the creator unpack the past through an autobiography in the form of a zine; a zine exchange with students and colleagues can help one understand different life stories from various backgrounds. Simply create a zine with your life story or some aspect of your life you would like to share and exchange that zine with a student, colleague, or friend to learn more about other perspectives. The exchange of one's story through writing or images can help reduce any pressure to speak to express oneself in a group. A zine exchange can also create a sense of community with those involved in the activity. "[Zines] are predominantly circulated via subcultural networks and represent a convenient way to exchange information within these contexts" (Kempson 2015, 1081). Sharing one's autobiography through zines opens up opportunities to educate people on issues of diversity and encourage them to better understand unique environments and situations. In the case of the professional life, a teaching librarian can better understand the struggles a student or other professors' experience that create barriers to their success. In addition, one can better understand how other people's social context affect their lives.

When you are exploring new ideas, metaphors and analogies can be helpful in simplifying or connecting different or new ideas. Metaphors can be described as "[comparing] without doing so explicitly. It appears to be the very essence of a metaphor that the grounds of the comparison are hidden" (Duit 1991, 650). For example, some librarians may feel that "Information literacy (IL) one-shots are the opening act to a headliner." This statement refers to quick 10–15 minute database instruction requested by faculty before or after a lecture. Metaphors are typically described as tools for learning and exploring new ideas (Duit, 1991; Jensen 2006; Wormeli, 2009). Utilization of metaphors is also described as an important process in learning, helping simplify complex ideas or difficult topics (Jensen 2006). In the context of zines and critical reflection, metaphors can help the creator visualize their reflection and remove any rigid structures that may prevent creative thinking or deep thought. See below for an example of a critical reflection using Fook and Gardener's Critical Reflection Model.

Here is an example:
Information literacy (IL) one-shots are the opening act to a headliner

Question: What assumptions exist and where do they come from?
- Assumption: IL one-shots are non-collaborative
- Source: May be rooted in previous experiences with a few faculty
- Assumption: IL one-shot is typically structured to be shorter than a lecture
- Source: Structure observed with a few librarians
- Assumption: Sage on the stage approach for lectures and for IL instruction
- Source: Personal student experience with postsecondary education

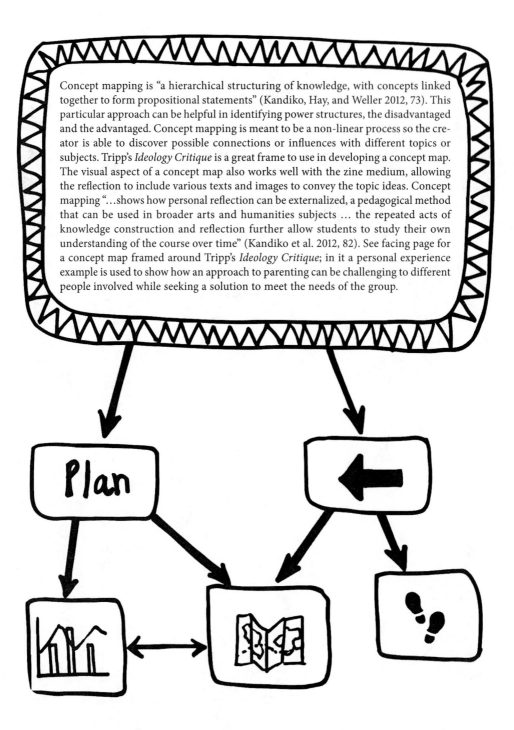

Concept mapping is "a hierarchical structuring of knowledge, with concepts linked together to form propositional statements" (Kandiko, Hay, and Weller 2012, 73). This particular approach can be helpful in identifying power structures, the disadvantaged and the advantaged. Concept mapping is meant to be a non-linear process so the creator is able to discover possible connections or influences with different topics or subjects. Tripp's *Ideology Critique* is a great frame to use in developing a concept map. The visual aspect of a concept map also works well with the zine medium, allowing the reflection to include various texts and images to convey the topic ideas. Concept mapping "...shows how personal reflection can be externalized, a pedagogical method that can be used in broader arts and humanities subjects ... the repeated acts of knowledge construction and reflection further allow students to study their own understanding of the course over time" (Kandiko et al. 2012, 82). See facing page for a concept map framed around Tripp's *Ideology Critique*; in it a personal experience example is used to show how an approach to parenting can be challenging to different people involved while seeking a solution to meet the needs of the group.

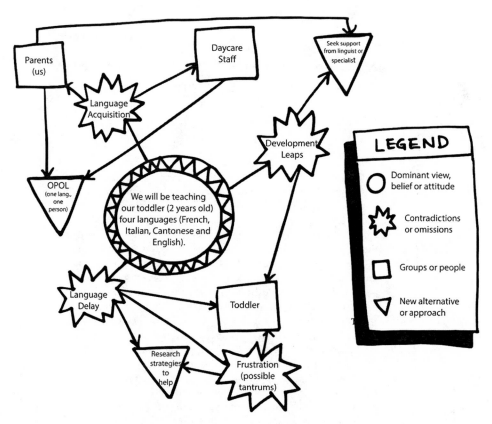

Concept map for personal development related to parenting.

·C·O·N·C·L·U·S·I·O·N·

These are just a few critical reflection frames and strategies that can be used to engage in critical reflection and zine-making. While these methods are effective, it is worth exploring other ways of critically reflecting on one's professional and personal experience. The zine medium helps facilitate the reflection by allowing one to develop the creative direction either through images or text. Moreover, these texts or images do not have to be structured and do not follow a rigid formula. This gives one freedom to explore ideas through the creation of the zine; it also allows to create a record to observe development or shifts in attitude or perspective.

Critical reflection is an integral part of the service-related work in librarianship as well as our day-to-day interactions. It informs and reminds us of the various lives and backgrounds that affect different people and ensures that we respond empathetically and sensitively to others' needs. It is important to note that critical reflection does take some time to master; simply put: practice, practice, and practice! Critical reflection should be integrated into our daily work, particularly for librarians who interact with patrons.

REFERENCE LIST

Bassot, Barbara. 2016. *The Reflective Practice Guide: An Interdisciplinary Approach to Critical Reflection*. New York: Routledge.

Brookfield, Stephen D. 1995. *Becoming a Critically Reflective Teacher*. San Francisco: Jossey-Bass.

Desyallas, Moshoula Capous and Allison Sinclair. 2014. "Zine-making as a pedagogical tool for transformative learning in social work education." *Social Work Education* 33, no. 3: 296–316.

Duit, Renders. 1991. "On the Role of Analogies and Metaphors in Learning Science." *Science Education* 75, no. 6: 649–672.

Elbaz-Luwisch, Freema. 2001. "Personal Story as Passport: Storytelling in Border Pedagogy." *Teaching Education* 12, no. 1: 81–101.

Fook, Jan and Fiona Gardener. 2007. *Practising Critical Reflection: A Resource Handbook*. Berkshire, England: Open University Press.

Fook, Jan, Val Collington, Fiona Ross, Gillian Ruch and Linden West. 2016. "The Promise and Problem of Critical Reflection." In *Researching Critical Reflection: Multidisciplinary Perspectives*, edited by Jan Fook, Val Collington, Fiona. Ross, Gillian Ruch, and Linden West, 1–7. New York: Routledge.

Freedman, Jenna. 2011. "Pinko vs. Punk: A Generational Comparison of Alternative Press Publications and Zines." In *The Generation X Librarian: Essays on Leadership, Technology, Pop Culture, Social Responsibility and Professional Identity*, edited by Martin K. Wallace, Rebecda Tolley-Stokes, and Erik Sean Estep, 147–160. Jefferson, NC: McFarland

Jensen, Devon. 2006. "Metaphors as a Bridge to Understanding Educational and Social Contexts." *International Journal of Qualitative Methods* 5, no. 1: 36–54.

Kandiko, Camille, David Hay, and Saranne Weller. 2012. "Concept Mapping in the Humanities to Facilitate Reflection: Externalizing the Relationship between Public and Personal Learning." *Arts and Humanities in Higher Education* 12, no. 1: 70–87.

Kempson, Michelle. 2015. "'I Sometimes Wonder Whether I'm an Outsider': Negotiating Belonging in Zine Subculture." *Sociology* 49, no. 6: 1081–1095.

Mezirow, Jack. 1990. "How Critical Reflection Triggers Transformative Learning." In *Fostering Critical Reflection in Adulthood: A Guide to Transformative and Emancipatory Learning*, edited by Jack Mezirow and Associates, 1–20. San Francisco: Jossey-Bass.

Saleebey, Dennis and Scanlon, Edward. 2005. "Is a Critical Pedagogy for the Profession of Social Work Possible?" *Journal of Teaching in Social Work* 25, no. 3: 1–18.

Tripp, David. 2012. *Critical Incidents in Teaching: Developing Professional Judgement*. New York: Routledge.

RESOURCES

Block, Francesca Lia and Carlip, Hillary. 1998. *Zine Scene.* Los Angeles: Girl Press.

Brent, Bill and Biel, Joe. 2008. *Make a Zine! When Words and Graphics Collide.* Bloomington: Microcosm Publishing.

McElroy, Kelly. 2011. "Teaching Info. Literacy with ZINES." Last modified on July 21, 2011.

Todd, Mark and Watson, Esther Peal. 2006. *Whatcha Mean, What's a Zine? The Art of Making Zines and Minicomics.* Boston: Graphia.

Wrekk, Alex. 2005. *Stolen Sharpie Revolution: A DIY Zine Resource.* Portland: Microcosm Publishing.

It's in the Cards

Using Tarot Reading
to Access Professional Creativity

LAURA WIMBERLEY

Introduction

An invigorating career in libraries requires creativity at both the large and small scale. In the big picture, we need creative thinking to envision opportunities to bridge across different types of libraries; to integrate knowledge from other professions to librarianship; to find ways to serve communities where libraries are unrecognized. Librarians also need to creatively solve little problems every day—to make an unexpected connection to recommend a surprising, but appreciated, resource to a patron; to find appealing slogans to market our services; to improvise solutions on a shoestring budget.

For example, imagine you maintain Twitter and other social media accounts for your library. You want to post daily, highlighting a wide range of library holdings and resources, but you have trouble generating enough fresh content—you're so familiar with the collection that it can be hard to remember what might surprise or intrigue patrons. How can you quickly tap into a random, creative jolt of energy?

Having expert knowledge means having a reliable toolbox of solutions that have worked before, which can discourage librarians from taking a gamble (Stokes 2014). But if we constrain our choices, preventing ourselves from falling back on old patterns, we can find new sources of knowledge or techniques to apply, resulting in creative outcomes (Stokes 2014).

One unconventional yet potentially fruitful source of these creative constraints is tarot cards. While they have been long associated in the popular imagination with palmistry, crystal gazing, and other forms of divination, tarot cards can be simpler than that. Tarot cards are a pool of symbols that can prompt our intuition to bring previously unconscious connections to the surface. A reader interacts with tarot cards by posing a question, and then using the semiotically rich imagery on the tarot cards to craft a narrative that answers the question. In telling ourselves a story, we discover something we knew all along.

Furthermore, telling a story lets us see our professional development, the arc of our careers, as an inspiring path. We can tap into the archetypal hero's journey through tarot cards. Seeing the trajectory of a library career through beautiful, personally resonant artwork is inspiring. It gives us a vision for how we can shape knowledge and our communities.

There are also creative advantages simply to trying anything new. Approaching a tradition heavily laden with occult symbolism is a good reminder that library patrons are often equally mystified by call numbers and subject headings. Inhabiting a beginner's mind in one area can help us see our regular work with fresh eyes.

Of course, tarot reading is no substitute for evidence-based decision making. Assessment and creativity are interdependent: creative ideas need to be assessed, and the feedback from assessment needs to be creatively implemented. Where tarot reading can help is brainstorming, or, to put it more formally, hypothesis generation. Tarot cards can suggest lines of inquiry to pursue, paths to explore, or factors that have been overlooked.

Moreover, tarot cards are compact, portable, inexpensive, and, with practice, can be useful in as little as fifteen minutes.

What Are Tarot Cards?

Tarot decks have been in circulation for centuries. Decks of playing cards in four suits, similar to modern decks used for games like poker and blackjack, were available across Europe by the mid-fourteenth century (Farley 2009, 9). In the early fifteenth century in the courts of Milan and Ferrara, the nobility began to play with decks that added trump cards depicting deities and virtues (Farley 2009). The symbolism and structure of these decks coalesced into a standard, and then the game fell out of favor, only to be rediscovered as an occult practice in France in the early nineteenth century (Farley 2009).

Contemporary tarot decks derive from this nineteenth century reinvention of the fifteenth century game. They have two types of cards, the major arcana and the minor arcana. The major arcana evolved from the trump cards, and depict archetypes, typically 22 in number. Most decks begin with the Fool, numbered 0, and proceed through a Hero's Journey to The World (or The Universe) numbered 21.

The minor arcana are composed of four suits. Each suit is numbered Ace through 10, plus the court cards of Page, Knight, Queen, and King.

- The suit of Swords is associated with the intellect, reason, judgment, logic, and wisdom. This suit is clearly relevant to reference, research, and classification.
- The suit of Cups is associated with the heart and emotions. In libraries, this especially relates to reader's advisory, managing personnel conflicts and issues, and handling problem patrons or assisting patrons in crisis.
- The suit of Wands is associated with creativity and the force of will. In libraries, will expresses through the creation and implementation of policies—everything from codes of conduct to cataloging standards.
- The suit of Pentacles is associated with the material world, physical possessions and health, and husbandry. In libraries, this suit speaks to acquisitions, weeding, grant and donation seeking, and the library building itself.

Each card is illustrated with a different set of symbols that evoke different aspects of the suit or archetype. Although the illustrations vary widely by deck, some elements are common to each card across decks. For example, the Magician, number 1 in the major arcana, is often depicted as a human figure inscribed with the infinity symbol, looking down or away from the viewer, at a table or altar scattered with ritual objects, with one hand raised and one hand lowered. Any one of these elements or choices made by the artist can spark an idea or connection in the reader.

While the reader's intuition is the entire purpose of the exercise, sometimes the imagery of the cards can feel remote, inapplicable, or daunting. To elucidate the meaning of the cards, readers can draw on many different sources. Most decks of tarot cards, as discussed below, come with books to aid in their interpretation, and there are thousands of other books and websites that discuss tarot symbolism more generally. A particularly useful interpretive guide for professional creativity is *The Creative Tarot: A Modern Guide to an Inspired Life* by Jessa Crispin (2016).

How to Read Tarot Cards

Tarot card readings begin with a question, an open-ended challenge facing the reader. Here are some good examples of library-relevant questions to ask of tarot cards:

- What should be the theme of next year's conference?
- A colleague and I are in a bitter dispute about a seemingly trivial matter. What's the underlying issue?
- What type of book selection would spark the best discussion at next month's book club?
- How can I motivate my colleagues to take assessment projects seriously?
- What direction should my research agenda take?
- How can I best respond to a specific frequent problem patron?
- What is the ideal vision for our library space after renovations?
- How can I inspire the staff I supervise?
- Which books or other resources should I highlight in our next display?

The simplest way to read a tarot card is to think of a question, shuffle the deck, draw a single card, and contemplate how the imagery and meaning of that card responds to the question. The example from the beginning of this essay, of a librarian creating daily social media posts, is a good time to draw a single card. You could draw one card, choose a word or concept that captures the essence of that card, and use that to suggest an interesting resource to highlight in the daily post. For example, the Four of Swords points to quiet mental focus—it might be a good time to remind patrons if they can book individual study rooms or carrels. If the Seven of Cups comes up, which is associated with illusions and lazy thinking, post a guide to spotting fake news.

The question of the theme of next year's conference is another example of a question suitable for a single card draw. Suppose you draw the Empress as inspiration for a conference theme, a card with associations of both luxury and nurturance—that might suggest focus on the library as a welcoming "third place" (Dickson and Shanks 2017). Pulling the card Judgment points directly to assessment. A draw of the Eight of Pentacles, which represents craftsmanship, could inspire a conference on implementing makerspaces.

And if, after some reflection, that single card isn't helpful? Just draw another.

Reading tarot for questions like these, and like the above examples of a specific problem patron or reading choice for a book club, taps into rich symbolism and recurring themes to meet concerns that can be quite small and mundane. By linking everyday issues with mythic imagery, we can see the importance of our labors, and be inspired. Remembering the connection between our daily tasks and our vision for our life's work helps us with everything from writing a compelling cover letter to making wise choices about priorities.

More complex questions, questions that prompt the reader to reflect on underlying causes, or on trade-offs, or different aspects of a situation, call for spreads of tarot cards. There are thousands of spreads of tarot cards, some traditional, others improvised by readers as questions occur to them.

The simplest multi-card spread is three cards: one for the past, one for the present, and one for the future. For example, an academic librarian who has just wrapped up a book project might be casting about for the next step in their research agenda. Imagine drawing a three-card spread for inspiration: the Ten of Pentacles for the past, the Ten of Cups for the present, and the Seven of Swords for the future. The Ten of Pentacles is a card of affluence and tradition: a hope that the completed book will receive royalties and citations, and a reminder that it is time to mentor another researcher. The Ten of Cups signifies happiness in the home: a suggestion to take a pause for personal time before diving into the next project. The Seven of Swords implies dishonor or deception, so perhaps a study on plagiarism prevention should be next.

If a reader wants to consider two different options—for example, a graduate student debating an internship in a public library's youth services versus a school library internship—then the reader can simply lay out a pair of past, present, and future spreads, one for each scenario.

Another option for a multi-card spread is the A-to-B tarot spread, which lays out the cards to help the reader see a path to a goal (Maiden 2015, 38). This starts a bit differently, with the reader deliberately choosing a card that represents a goal. For example, an academic librarian seeking tenure might choose the Hierophant, a card representing systematized knowledge and hierarchy, or a librarian seeking to improve collegiality and cooperation might choose the Three of Pentacles, which suggests teamwork and competence.

To read the cards, lay the chosen goal card at the far right, then shuffle and draw four more cards laid left to right. In order, the spread will read:

2: Present situation	3: Challenge blocking the goal	4: Skill or resource to get to the goal	5: Advice overall	1: Goal

The reader creatively interprets the symbols on the five cards in a way that links them together into a coherent narrative that is also congruent with the reader's understanding of the facts on the ground. Telling a story that fits all of these constraints usually requires shifting some pre-conceived notions or linking ideas in new ways, generating new possible insights, considerations, or strategies—in a word, creativity. But because the process involves pre-printed cards laid out in a recommended spread from a random draw, it works for a reader who thinks they're not the "creative type." Someone who would be stymied by a blank page and a mandate to write a short work of fiction can still make a meaningful narrative from the raw materials of the cards as applied to the events in their own life.

Recommended Tarot Decks

While there are a few standardized structures to the major and minor arcana, there are infinitely many different ways to illustrate the cards and represent the symbolism.

Many decks even rename the suits or individual cards—for example, changing the Kings, Queens, and Knights to gender-neutral terms, or renaming the Hierophant to represent a different religious tradition. Archetypes are inherently multifaceted, and readers should choose a deck that appeals to them on a personal level. The imagery must resonate with the reader in order for the reader to use it to make connections.

That said, not every tarot deck is appropriate for every purpose. Some tarot decks are too playful (like the Happy Tarot, which has an aesthetic similar to Candyland) or too focused on a specific theme (like the Lover's Path Tarot, for questions of romance) to spark useful ideas for library work.

What follows is a list of decks to consider for creative librarianship. All of the new, original tarot decks below come with guidebooks to interpretation of the cards and their symbolism.

The Rider-Waite-Smith Tarot—This is the best known tarot deck, originally created in England in 1909 (Farley 2009, 145). Books and other tarot resources often assume the Rider-Waite-Smith deck as a baseline. The imagery is clearly influenced by the Pre-Raphaelites, but simplified. The representations of people are strictly gender normative and all white. This deck is now in the public domain, so it is widely re-printed and available.

The Raven's Prophecy Tarot—Written and illustrated by bestselling young adult author Maggie Steifvater, this tarot was specifically created for those new to tarot reading, and for a balance of logic and reason with creative inspiration. It follows the structure of the Rider-Waite-Smith tarot, with the only change being Coins for Pentacles. The deck's illustrations draw on Welsh mythology, with images of fire, roses, and ravens; people are represented mostly by iridescent hands. A good balance of the abstract and accessible. Available via Amazon.

The Urban Tarot—This is a vividly colorful, contemporary deck, an homage to New York City, inclusive of a wide variety of ethnic and gender presentations. The illustrations are more specific and literal than on many other decks, which can make the deck easier to read for beginners but more limiting in its interpretations. Some of the imagery is quite grim: the Tower, a card that traditionally represents catastrophe, is depicted here as the Twin Towers falling on September 11. Other cards are joyful: Strength, which is usually shown as a lion, is represented here as Fortitude, the beloved lion sculpture from the New York Public Library. Ideal for creative work in challenging yet vibrant urban libraries. Available as an app for Android and iOS, and as a deck from U.S. Games.

The Wild Unknown Tarot—This deck is mostly black ink sketches with some watercolor highlights. The illustrations are dream-like, symbolic, and pared down, depicting animals, plants, and artifacts, but no people at all. This is, essentially, the opposite of the Urban Tarot—rural, more challenging to interpret, but with a wider scope for imagination. A good choice for abstract, conceptual thinkers. Available from the Wild Unknown website.

The Numinous Tarot—This deck, like the Urban Tarot, is full of bright colors, detailed imagery, and diverse people. The richness of the illustrations gives the reader lots of hooks for interpreting the cards. The court cards are replaced with the gender-neutral Dreamer (Page), Explorer (Knight), Creator (Queen), and Mystic (King). The deck also replaces the suit of Pentacles with Tomes, and most of the scenes depicted on the Tomes cards are in libraries. Available on Kickstarter.

Librarians who are uncomfortable with the occult connotations of tarot cards, or who prefer text over images, can have a similar interaction with the Oblique Strategies deck created by musicians Brian Eno and Peter Schmidt (Greenwalt 2014). These cards suggest abstract options like, "Balance the consistency principle with the inconsistency principle," or "Revaluation (a warm feeling)."

Conclusion

Tarot cards prompt readers to tell themselves a story about the issue they are facing, using the symbolism of the cards and the realities already known to the reader. The constraints imposed by the structure of the spread of cards and the imagery of the cards themselves serve to break the reader out of a rut, and to prompt even the most literal-minded to think creatively. The detailed, archetypal illustrations help to connect even small, workaday concerns to the inspiration of the hero's journey.

While creativity cannot be rushed, it can be prompted. Reading tarot is a way to take a brief break from screens, patrons, and co-workers for quiet introspection, which gives the mental space necessary for creative sparks to catch. The cards themselves, and the rich imagery and symbolic associations accrued over centuries, provide the tinder for the flame. That creative fire, when fed by knowledge gained from rigorous analysis, warms our communities and brings the light of knowledge to the world.

REFERENCES

Crispin, Jessa. 2016. *The Creative Tarot: A Modern Guide to an Inspired Life*. New York: Simon & Schuster.
Dickson, Steve, and Shanks, Edward. 2017. "The Word: A Library for the 21st Century, Delivering Social, Cultural and Economic Objectives." Presentation at the International Federation of Library Associations and Institutions World Library and Information Conference, Wrocław, Poland, August 19–25, 2017. http://library.ifla.org/1667/1/243-dickson-en.pdf.
Farley, Helen. 2009. *Cultural History of Tarot: From Entertainment to Esotericism*. London: I.B. Tauris. PDF e-book.
Greenwalt, R. Toby. 2014. "It's All Around You." *Public Libraries* 53 (1): 24–25. http://libproxy.csun.edu/login?url=http://search.ebscohost.com/login.aspx?direct=true&db=eft&AN=94589409&site=ehost-live.
Maiden, Beth. 2015. *Little Red Tarot Spreads: 21 Original Tarot Spreads*. Machynlleth, UK: Little Red Tarot. PDF e-book.
Stokes, Patricia D. 2014. "Thinking Inside the Tool Box: Creativity, Constraints, and the Colossal Portraits of Chuck Close." *Journal of Creative Behavior* 48 (4): 276–289. http://libproxy.csun.edu/login?url=http://search.ebscohost.com/login.aspx?direct=true&db=ehh&AN=99596500&site=ehost-live.

PART II

Out of Comfort Zone

What Is Your Quest?

Learning Through Role-Playing Games

Michael P. Buono

Role-playing games, from rule-heavy games like *Dungeons & Dragons (D&D)* to rule-light games like *Dread*, can help public service staff develop the necessary soft skills for customer service, leadership, and outreach that are vital in an increasingly competitive marketplace. The potential benefits of role-play, gaming, and simulation are clear in academic research. However, the use of role-play in order to develop these skills requires intention, an open mind, and commitment to the idea. It also requires an understanding of why it works, what it is, and how to play.

I have been enjoying role-playing games for 22 years. Through such play, I have forged lasting friendships. I have met new people, one of whom convinced me to finally become a librarian. I have written tens of thousands of words of prose, most of which I hope are never read by other souls. With a help of gaming, I have worked through my personal views on complicated topics. Role-playing has helped me develop my active listening, communication, and problem solving skills, my understanding of body language, my ability to reason with someone else through a problem, and my ability to anticipate the needs of others. Most importantly, it has helped me develop empathy for other people. Empathy is key to everything we do. It is the foundation of customer service, user experience and customer experience.

Learning Soft Skills

The skills I have listed are considered soft skills, the buzzword for skills that are difficult to assess in a traditional manner but that are vital to the success of people in life. Over the years, there have been attempts to define them in scholarly circles, government, and in popular business books. In recent years, they have received renewed attention, and there is a perceived lack of soft skills among professionals in every field. The gap appears to be wider among young professionals. In the *Soft Skills Gap*, Tulgan notes that over 20 years of research data indicates a decline in soft skills, and that the youngest workers show evidence of a severe inability in one or more soft skills. He categorizes soft skills into three areas: Professionalism, Critical Thinking, and Fellowship. He then further breaks down each of those categories into specific "basic" skills. Tulgan blames the decline in soft skills among young professionals on the prevalence of technology in their lives, helicopter parenting, and a breakdown of older community structures (Tulgan 2015).

From Tulgan's examples using the Marine Corps and Disney, we can arrive at two truths. One, soft skills can be learned. People are born with different gifts. Some people might be born with a natural inclination for soft skills, but most soft skills can be developed by anyone. Second, that the most expedient and effective way to develop soft skills is through immersion, culture, and practice (Tulgan 2015).

In management and customer service training, one of the most widely and accepted training practices for soft skills is the use of role-play. In corporate settings, individuals often take on a persona, and they are asked to act as that persona for the sake of instruction. This activity usually involves one or more other individuals who are participating in the training, the audience and the trainer. There are times when trainers ask participants to use their own persona or the persona of someone they know for the sake of illustration. The crafted situations may be very simple, with only a couple of lines of setup, or very elaborate, and may require immersion on the part of the participants (van Ments 1983; Cherrington and van Ments 1994).

I think people universally loathe the highly artificial corporate training use of role-play, but there is another way to role-play in the work place. Companies have begun to use *Dungeons and Dragons*, or another role-playing game, as a team-building exercise. Employees of Code & Theory in New York note that their *Dungeons & Dragons* game "has fostered creativity, friendship and collaboration" (Leporati, 2018). Game to Grow is a 501(c)3 nonprofit that champions the use of gaming in therapy and education. They use role-playing games to teach people soft skills, and they craft specific scenes to help their charges build specific skills such as communication or confront specific difficulties such as bullying (Gametogrow, 2018).

What Are Role Playing Games?

Learning through simulation is not only common but ancient. Simulation and gaming have been used to learn skills for thousands of years. The game of *Go* was created in approximately 3000 BCE in China and was used to teach strategic thinking, a soft skill valued by civil and military leaders. War games such as *Kriegspiel* had hundreds of rules, thousands of pieces, and were used in actual military training (van Ments 1983; Fine 1983). These were followed by games based on historical battles that civilians took up as a form of entertainment. Modern games such as *Chainmail*, *Warhammer* and *X-Wing* arose from people wanting to create war simulations around the speculative fiction they were interested in. These games all required players to take the role of generals facing opponents on a battle field.

One of these was the precursor to *Dungeons & Dragons*. Partially developed by the creator of *D&D*, *Chainmail* drew inspiration from Tolkien and Conan. *Chainmail* focused on large armies, but in *D&D* each player took on a character. They moved through a dungeon attempting to survive its traps and monsters to seek treasure. Players called the dungeon masters "run" the game. They controlled the monsters, determined locations of the traps, and constructed a simple story around the dungeon (Fine 1983).

Over time, the game evolved as players and dungeon masters wanted more. They began to craft elaborate stories around their characters, the dungeon, and their battles. The creators of the game responded by providing them with more material, including original fictional worlds. People wanted to add meaning to their adventures and to contextualize the gaming experience within the persona of their character. The dungeon masters strove to add meaning to their roles, and they began writing detailed scenarios with puzzles, riddles, and tense social encounters. *D&D* has inspired hundreds of other role-playing games, each with their own rules, settings, and learning curves (Fine 1983).

If you can define a soft skill you wish to learn, then I think there is a game that will help you learn it. I am going to break soft skills into three broad categories: strategic thinking, emotional and social intelligence, and self-awareness.

Strategic Thinking

Strategic thinking is a category of skills that focuses on preparation, planning, and execution. Creative problem-solving, resource management, and situational awareness are all skills that fall under this category. Strategic thinking is at the core of war gaming, and that is why it was used to train military leaders. It is also the core of any role-playing game that has a lot of rules focused on combat, like *D&D*.

Everyone in *D&D* plays a character. Each character class has a variety of abilities that make it unique, and playing any class requires resource management. Every character has hit points (a numerical value representing a character's health) and the potential to use certain abilities a limited number of times in a given time period. People often use up their abilities against one enemy, only to find themselves needing that same ability again or more so against another adversary.

Combat in *D&D* can be played out on a grid of one-inch squares, sort of like a chess board that the dungeon master can shape into different environments such as a cave. Players get a set number of actions with each turn. How they can use those actions is based on how they created their character. The very act of character creation is a strategic thinking exercise. Players try to balance who they want the character they play to be versus what choices will give them the maximum advantage in combat situations.

The combats that take place in *D&D* often involve many characters and monsters. Each can take several actions per round. Player teamwork is often vital to the survival of their characters. This requires an awareness of what the other players and the dungeon master -controlled enemies are doing. It also requires careful observation of the dungeon master's description of the environment. All of these factors are involved in combat. This constitutes simplified situational awareness, made more realistic because groups often force players to make decisions if they are taking too long.

While I have used *D&D* as an example, these skills are employed in many other games, including most games involving combat, and other games that are more focused on the social aspect of gaming.

Emotional and Social Intelligence

Emotional and social intelligence is a category of skills that focuses on our ability to understand our own emotional state and our interactions with others. It includes skills such as empathy, etiquette, active listening, de-escalation, and patience.

Engaging in a role-playing game is an inherently social act. The majority of the story is told through description delivered verbally with some visual aids. A game of

Dungeons & Dragons usually has between three and six players, including the dungeon master. Even in the most simplistic adventures, the players act in keeping with their characters and have social interactions. The more involved in the role they become, the more social and emotional intelligence players must exercise. Most gaming groups get very involved in their characters, and they create complex stories and worlds for their characters to move through. Often this generates in-character conversations that have real emotional weight and tension (Fine 1983; Buono 2012a, 2012b).

To separate the feelings the player has as being part of a "role" versus the player-to-player relationship takes emotional intelligence. The more dissimilarities exist between the character and the player, the more skill is required to effectively portray the character. For example, as a librarian, I have a great deal of knowledge about research and research methods. I am also very talkative. Playing a character opposite my personality, say a strong silent type with little interest in knowledge acquisition, is a challenge. It requires me to imagine the kind of person I want to play, and to empathize with that character. If I play a caricature, such as a "jock" or "bruiser," then my interest would be lessened. Fleshing out a role alien to oneself requires empathy for other people. It requires looking past people's most basic attributes and thinking about what motivates them.

When role-playing, it is easy for people to make common social mistakes, such as dominating a conversation, interrupting others, and failing to fully listen. However, if any gaming group is to survive, the players must work through these bad mistakes. They learn to exercise patience and to use active listening skills to keep role-play going. They learn to read the body language of other players to know when they are about to do something in game, or when they are unhappy with the strategy that you are taking.

The style of game most beneficial to improving social and emotional intelligence forces a player to speak and act as the chosen character as much as possible. It can be a more traditional tabletop game with heavy social elements like *World of Darkness*, or it could be one of the systems with simpler rules like *Fate*. The best games for encouraging social and emotional intelligence are live action role play games, or LARP. LARP is a fully immersive, improvisational acting experience where players take on the role of their characters for whole weekends. They dress like them and they talk like them. LARPers are really committed. They often craft their own costumes and storylines, and work on the game even when they are not playing. Some schools and enrichment programs have begun to use LARPs to teach financial literacy, responsibility, and personal fitness (Buono 2013).

There are games that bridge the gap between traditional tabletop role-playing games and live action role-play. These games involve small number of rule sets. They generally focus on interpersonal roles. One time I played a game where the players acted as rulers of countries in a 24-hour period. Each group took on the role of a president and their cabinet. As a political leader, each player had their own goals they needed to complete to win. We had to navigate an international crisis, but we still had to try to meet our own goals. The game *Urban Shadows* has a fairly simple system, and its system is built around politics in an urban fantasy setting reminiscent of *True Blood* or *Dresden Files*.

Self-Awareness

Self-awareness is the ability to acknowledge our own flaws, failures, feelings, and successes. To be self-aware is to recognize when your emotions are getting the better of you, when your body is overtaxed by what you are trying to accomplish, or when you need to find flaws in your own work. Self-awareness is a necessary skill to learn in order to achieve success in life and in role-playing games.

Using games to acquire self-awareness skills requires players to pause and reflect on their actions. In many of the *White Wolf* titles, an end of session discussion about the game, plot, and character actions is part of the characters' advancement. It compels players to participate, and it leads to a heightened understanding of the characters. The exercise is simple: at the end of session the players take turns sharing what they learned about the characters, the story, or the world. In Boy Scouts, we did a similar activity called *Roses and Thorns*. We would each share something we did or did not enjoy that day. The period of reflection at the end of the experience helped us internalize lessons, and the conversation forced us to verbalize the most influential moments of that experience out loud. In formal execution of role play in adult education, this stage of the process is called "debriefing." By reviewing and verbalizing what they learn, it cements the lessons in the players mind (van Ments 1983).

Playing vs. DMing

There are two ways to engage in a role-playing game. The first is to be the player, a single person playing a single character. The second is to become the Dungeon Master (DM). I have mostly discussed the first role, because for every four players, only one gets to be a DM. Also, the DM role does not exist in every game. Some games do not have a player "in charge" of the world but are fully cooperative.

The DM role provides someone with the most potential growth. When running a game, the DMs are not taking on the role of one character. They are taking on the role of every character in the world that does not belong to a player. These are called Non-Player Characters or NPCs. This means that a DM can conceivably move through multiple roles and personality types in a single session. Additionally, DMs design the challenges the players face, including combats. Most people playing will control a single character in a game session, and they will only be responsible for managing the resources of a single character. A DM could have 10–20 different characters in combat and will have to manage all the resources at his or her disposal.

The trade-off is that the DM role requires the most work. Most players can show up on game night and just play. DMs usually need to prepare beforehand. They need to develop the NPC, stories, the world they inhabit, and they need to do so while taking their players into consideration. There is probably no greater challenge in gaming than running a game for a group of people and actively trying to adjust the game to meet individuals' expectations and interest.

Gaming with Skill Development in Mind

To acquire soft skills purposefully and intentionally through any method requires a level of self-awareness, forethought, and commitment if you are a player; you may wish to craft a specific character to help gain a specific skill. In short, before the game even begins, you need to decide what your personal learning goal or quest is. Using the basic role I described earlier, to play a quiet bruiser, I would have to practice keeping my mouth shut in social situations. I would need to exercise patience and restraint. I would need to set a boundary for myself in order to define the character. In this case, I would play this character to practice not interrupting others and listening with intention.

People who struggle in social situations, and specifically with detecting lies, might play fast-talking rogues who lie as easy as they breathe, but also know when they are being lied to. This can help them learn to bluff, a useful skill when someone is complaining about something absurd. It can help them learn to fill silence, or it could help them learn the art of sale.

This can be difficult, as it requires the player to be willing to invest fully in playing the character, and it leaves little room for falling back on dice. To fall back on a roll would be to sabotage their own progress as soft skills are only gained through actual practice. For full immersion, it would be best if the people you play with have similar goals.

If everyone playing intends to use a game as a fun learning experience, then much more can be accomplished. Characters can be crafted with similar goals, but conflicting personalities. A DM can create stories that feature hard decisions or that really challenge players to operate outside their comfort zone. A DM could run a single-session game to practice a specific skill, such as bluffing, or a whole adventure, for example, a political coup focused on bringing all soft skills into play.

How to Get Started

In the last ten years, hundreds of smaller games have appeared online, some use social mechanics and some with soft skills as their focus. *Dungeons & Dragons* can be difficult for some new players due to the large number of books, and the more complicated rule set. Combat in *D&D* is still very similar to a war game, and that is the main focus of the rule set. Many of these new games focus strongly on improvisation or social interactions. The rules are written to make those actions feel as intense as combat in *D&D*.

To learn social and emotional intelligence as well as self-awareness, I would recommend starting with the game *Dread* by the publisher The Impossible Dream. *Dread* is a survival horror game that avoids dice use, instead using a Jenga tower as its main mechanic. If the tower falls, something bad happens to your character. *Dread*, which focuses on single session stories, may have the player characters playing against one another at some point. Even if there is no traitor, the horror that is generated from the simple mechanics combined with the story style leads to a more intense focus on role play. You know that moment when you are yelling at a character in a movie "Don't go through that door," because you become so invested in their survival? Imagine yelling that at your friend, and then watching as they pull blocks out of a Jenga tower to decide their fate.

If you do want to get started with *Dungeons & Dragons*, I recommend starting with a basic adventure. Play a game where you slay a dragon, save a royal heir, or defend the town against the zombie horde. You can always build out from there. You could also purchase *The Curse of Strahd* or another module (a module is a book that contains characters, adventures, story, and world building for a DM to use instead of creating their own from scratch).

Conclusion

To learn soft skills using role-playing games, players need to immerse themselves in the role, the world, and the game. Now is one of the best times to get into the hobby. In the last few years, tabletop role-playing games have become their own entertainment medium. New media properties like *Critical Role, Harmon Quest* and *Geek and Sundry* have raised the profile of the games. Wizards of the Coast, the publisher of *D&D,* is taking action to attract and retain female gamers and game design talent. The publisher is now pivoting to increase its new media presence. It is now possible for players with different levels of comfort and experience to find a game best suited to the types of skills they wish to strengthen. People also have the opportunity to witness how games are played without having access to a gaming store or group.

The landscape of the role-playing game industry and the culture of the players is in a period of transition, and it can be overwhelming. To help you get started, I've prepared a resource list, available at michaelpbuono.com/quest. However, even without these resources you can get started. First, you need to find a group of people interested in playing. Second, you need to choose what you want to become better at. Third, you need to craft a character that will force you to practice those skills. If you do that, then you can use role-playing games to improve your soft skills whether the game is organized for that purpose or not.

REFERENCES

Buono, Michael. 2012a. "Getting the Most Out of RPGS in Your Library Pt. 1." *YALSA* Blog. http://yalsa.ala.org/blog/2012/09/24/getting-the-most-out-of-rpgs-in-your-library-pt-1/.
_____. 2012b. "Getting the Most of RPGS in Your Library Pt. 3: Tabletop RPG Programming." *YALSA* Blog. http://yalsa.ala.org/blog/2012/12/31/getting-the-most-of-rpgs-in-your-library-pt-3-tabletop-rpg-programming/.
_____. 2013. "Getting the Most of RPGS in Your Library Pt. 4: Into the World of LARP." *YALSA* Blog. 2013. http://yalsa.ala.org/blog/2013/03/20/intotheworldofLARP/.
Cherrington, Ruth, and Ments, Morry Van. 1994. "'God, What Am I Doing Here?'" *Adults Learning* 5 (7): 175–77.
Cherrington, Ruth, and Ments, Morry Van. 1994. "Pinning Down Experiential Learning." *Studies in the Education of Adults* 26 (1): 15.
Cherrington, Ruth, and Ments, Morry Van. 1994. "Who's Calling the Shots?" *Adults Learning* 5 (5): 128.
Fine, Gary Alan. 1983. *Shared Fantasy*. Chicago: University of Chicago Press.
Gametogrow. 2018. "What We Do | Game to Grow." *Gametogrow*. 2018. http://gametogrow.org/what-we-do/.
Leporati, Gregory. 2018. "Build Morale by Slaying Monsters After Work." *Engadget*. 2018. https://www.engadget.com/2018/06/08/dungeons-and-dragons-corporate-team-building-timm-woods/.
Ments, Morry Van. 1983. *The Effective Use of Role-Play*: A Handbook for Teachers and Trainers. Worcester: Billing & Sons Limited.
Tulgan, Bruce. 2015. *Bridging the Soft Skills Gap*. Hoboken: Wiley & Sons, Inc.

Growth Lessons Learned from a One-Year Fellowship in a Nontraditional Library Environment

DANA E. THIMONS

In December 2015, I packed up all of my belongings, purchased a winter coat, and drove with my two greyhounds from Fort Lauderdale, Florida, to Alexandria, Virginia. I took a "temporary leave of absence" to embark upon a one-year journey as the Sewell Memorial Fund Learning Partnership Fellow at the American Association of Colleges of Pharmacy (AACP). In this case study, I share some of the growth lessons I learned from my experience leaving an academic health sciences library to complete fellowship in a non-traditional library role. These lessons include the importance applying for opportunities, staying positive, adapting to change, asking for help, and transferring one's skills.

About the Fellowship

The Grace and Harold Sewell Memorial Fund's mission is "to increase librarians' identification with medical, pharmaceutical, and health care professionals." To help achieve this mission, the Sewell Fund provides a stipend and a learning partnership program. The stipend program provides funding for librarians to attend the national professional meetings of their clients, such as AACP and the American Public Health Association (Grace and Harold Sewell Memorial Fund 2014a). Without this funding, it might not be financially feasible for librarians to participate in these meetings—especially if librarians are mandated to use their professional development funds to attend library conferences. The learning partnership program was designed to immerse librarians into a host organization for up to a year. The host organization can be a private sector company, nonprofit organization, or public agency and must be involved in health sciences services, research, or product development (Grace and Harold Sewell Memorial Fund 2014b). Examples of past learning host organizations include the Public Health Foundation, Rural Wisconsin Health Cooperative, and San Antonio Metropolitan Health District (Grace and Harold Sewell Memorial Fund 2014c).

AACP is a national organization that represents pharmacy education in the United States (American Association of Colleges of Pharmacy n.d.[a]). The association is comprised of institutional and individual members. The institutional members are the 142 schools of pharmacy accredited by the Accreditation Council for Pharmacy Education. The individual members include administrators, faculty, and staff (American Association of Colleges of Pharmacy n.d.[b]).

It Never Hurts to Apply

In 2013, I started working in the Health Professions Division Library at Nova Southeastern University (NSU) as a reference librarian and library liaison to the Colleges of Pharmacy and Dental Medicine. In order to learn more about pharmacy education, I applied for and received a Sewell Memorial Fund stipend to attend AACP's 2014 Annual Meeting in Grapevine, Texas. It was at this meeting that Lucinda Maine, AACP's Executive Director, announced the Sewell Memorial Fund Learning Partnership fellowship opportunity to the Library and Information Science Section. When I heard Dr. Maine describing the fellowship, I did not consider applying. The fellow was expected to create a knowledge management framework for AACP. According to the American Productivity & Quality Center (APQC), knowledge management (KM) is "a collection of systematic approaches to help information and knowledge flow to and between the right people at the right time so they can act more efficiently and effectively to create value for the organization," (APQC n.d.). Because I was not familiar with KM at that time, I did not think I had the expertise to build a knowledge management framework.

Additionally, I did not give much thought to applying for the fellowship because I had not been at NSU for very long. I loved living in South Florida, and I loved my job. I had recently enrolled in NSU's health law master's degree program to take advantage of the employee discounted tuition rate. Leaving Florida or my job was the last thing on my mind.

The director of the Health Professions Division Library at NSU, Kaye Robertson, is the type of supervisor that I wish led every library. She always wants the best for her team and is supportive of their growth endeavors. Kaye frequently encouraged me to apply for grants and awards, saying, "It never hurts to apply. At the very least, you get your name out there." Just as she had with many other opportunities, Kaye encouraged me to apply for the fellowship.

I took Kaye's advice and applied. I started the application process by researching KM so I had an understanding of the concept when I filled out my application. I searched Google and numerous library databases. I also borrowed several books about KM from the library.

I would not have a life-changing event to write about if I had not applied for this fellowship. If the fellowship had been awarded to someone else, I would not have lost anything by applying. In fact, I still would have benefited from the application process because I learned about KM. A final part of the application process was a Skype interview with several AACP executives. The interview experience was another valuable thing I would have gained even if I was not selected as the fellow. Now before automatically assuming that something is not possible, I remember Kaye's words and apply. This has resulted in many other unexpected positive experiences, including writing my first book chapter.

Focus on the Positive When Others Are Talking About the Negative

I was surprised when I received the news that I had been selected as the learning partnership fellow. This was not part of my five-year plan, but I recognized it as a rare and valuable opportunity for growth. Unfortunately, there were people who focused on the negative aspects of the fellowship. A few librarians commented on a library listserv regarding the cost of living in Alexandria and the fellowship, saying that only millionaires could afford to live there. The comments worried me. However, AACP owned a condominium not far from its office. The fellowship included housing and utilities. My two large dogs were even able to live in AACP's condominium with me. The condominium was close to the office, so I was able to walk to work.

Friends and coworkers teased me about moving to a cold climate and joked that I would forget about them. I know that no one meant to be malicious, but the jokes only added to my doubts about making such a huge change. I was happy in Florida and did not know many people who lived in Virginia. I could have easily been discouraged and decided to stay where I was comfortable. Instead, I chose not to let the comments or my doubts keep me from moving forward. Things that are worth doing are typically not easy, and there will always be people who point out the negative. Library school was not easy. If I had a dollar for every comment I heard about the bleak future of the library profession due to ebooks and the Internet, I could retire today. Not everyone is going to fully support or understand every decision you make in order to grow or succeed professionally. Embarking upon the fellowship helped me realize and come to accept this fact.

Another concern I had about accepting the fellowship was that I would be leaving a job I recently started. I worried that I might not succeed. I also worried that pursuing the fellowship made me a selfish person because I was adding to my coworkers' workload while they searched for my temporary replacement. A few weeks before I left NSU, one of the pharmacy faculty members offered congratulations. He reminded me, "Your only loyalty is to yourself and your family." He was not encouraging me to be a job hopper, but rather to make decisions based upon what was best for my family and me. He was telling me not feel bad about moving to grow professionally. This advice helped to ease the guilt of leaving. I consider it as some of the best advice I have received. I stopped apologizing for leaving and started focusing on why this was a good move for me. I allowed myself to feel excited and proud.

Change Is Necessary for Growth

I have never grown as a person without first encountering change. Sometimes adapting to change can mean adapting to a new supervisor or new work environment. Other times, it can mean moving to a different town, state, or country. For me, it was getting out of my comfort zone and moving to a city that I had never visited prior to the move.

I am not advocating for every librarian to move across the country in order to grow. Moving is not for the faint of heart. Nor is it always best decision for every person. Moving can be difficult on a librarian's salary, especially if the librarian is paying off student loans. The decision for an individual to move is not the same as the decision for an entire family to move. For those who are considering a big move, I have found that creativity and planning can make moving not only possible—but also fun.

Planning for the Move

Use Your Research Skills. I started to research the city of Alexandria while I was applying for the fellowship. I searched the city's website to learn about utilities, taxes, vehicle registration, local government, parks, and of course, libraries. I used cost of living calculators, such as http://money.cnn.com/calculator/pf/cost-of-living/index.html, to get a better understanding of how far my salary would stretch. I also looked at sites such as Reddit.com and City-Data.com to read about what living is like in the area. I spoke with my car insurance company to determine how my rates would change. Additionally, universities and other employers sometimes provide moving guides with useful information on their websites.

Plan Your Moving Budget. I used an Excel spreadsheet to map out my moving budget. I estimated the cost of gas using Google maps. I included food and hotels in my budget. Other items to consider might be the cost of breaking a lease, security deposit for a new lease, and fees to turn on utilities.

Look for Creative Ways to Save. Instead of hiring movers, I used U-Pack and packed the moving truck myself. Prior to the move, I tried to sell or donate items that I never use to cut down on what I had to bring. I was moving into a fully furnished condominium, so I sent the moving truck with all of my belongings to my hometown of Pittsburgh. I had already planned to visit my family for the holidays and would be driving back to Virginia. I was fortunate to be able to save on storage costs by storing my furniture with family. Additionally, they helped me to unpack the moving truck.

Keep Your Receipts. Many employers will reimburse the cost of a move. Unfortunately, moving reimbursement was not included with the fellowship. I kept receipts and was able to deduct the move from my income taxes.

Apps to Organize Your Life. I recently discovered Moved and Sortly. Moved is a free app that helps you coordinate your move. Sortly helps you catalog and label your moving boxes so you know what is in each box. I do not plan to move again any time soon. Nevertheless, the next time I move, I will try to be more organized by using apps.

Get Your Friends and Family Involved. As I already mentioned, my family was a huge help with loading and unloading the moving truck and storing my belongings. During the move to Virginia, I drove a little out of my way to meet up with a friend from high school who lives in Atlanta. She also had planned to go home to Pittsburgh for the winter break. She agreed to come along on the journey to Virginia and joined me on the drive. It was nice to have another driver and to catch up with an old friend.

Settling In

Be a Tourist in Your New Town. I like to learn about the history of places where I am living. That is why I read a few books about Alexandria and visited local museums. I also used travel guides and websites to help find interesting and exciting places to visit.

Prepare for Guests. Plan for friends and family to visit. I had a number of friends and family who stayed with me. I also met up with several friends while they were visiting D.C. for work-related reasons.

Use Your Hobbies and Interests to Make New Friends . Since I am a single woman, coordinating a move for one person was simple. However, moving alone meant that I did not have the built-in network that moving with a partner or children provides. I found that Meetup.com, recreational sports leagues, and alumni and professional associations are good ways to meet new people.

Let Your Coworkers Guide You. Get to know your new coworkers. They are a good resource to learn everything from the best lunch spots near work to the best local stores. In addition to their local knowledge, you could form some amazing new friendships.

Ask for Help

People who know me well know that I hate to ask for help. It is a combination of pride and not wanting to inconvenience others. I will roam around alone for hours before I ask for directions simply because I do not want to appear incompetent. Sometimes I do not ask for help because I want to avoid rejection.

From working in an association to living in Virginia, many aspects of the fellowship were new to me. I had to learn to overcome my fear and pride and ask for help. Otherwise, I would have failed miserably.

The first step toward getting over my fear of asking for help was asking for letters of recommendation. The application only required a letter of support from my supervisor, but I thought it would be helpful to have additional letters from pharmacy faculty members. I asked two faculty members for letters. One faculty member was excited to help me and wrote a glowing recommendation. The other faculty member was not as willing to help. I survived the rejection. I was off to a good start.

One of the questions I asked during the Skype interview was if my dogs could live in the condominium with me. Greyhounds are large dogs, and many condominiums have weight restrictions. If I had assumed that my dogs were not allowed to live with me in the condominium, I would have been stuck paying for alternative housing. If that was not affordable, I may not have been able to do the fellowship. I was surprised and thrilled to learn that I could bring my dogs. I avoided a lot of stress by getting that question out of the way.

Starting any new job can be intimidating. When I started the fellowship, I set up appointments to meet with AACP staff. I did this so I could meet everyone and learn about his or her roles. I had to come out of my shell to set up these appointments. People were happy to talk about their work, as well as what they expected of me.

Throughout the fellowship there were many times that I asked others for help. I met a library professor at a book club who was a knowledge management expert. I asked him to meet with me to discuss my knowledge management framework. We met over lunch at his university. I learned new things from him, and I was able to tour another library. Lucinda Maine suggested that I reach out to three librarians who worked at other pharmacy associations. All of the librarians were excited to give me a tour of their association and tell me about their work. People were always willing and excited to help, but they only knew that I needed help because I asked.

Your Skills Are Transferrable

It is important to remember that you have plenty of skills, and your skills are transferable. Many people have trouble making the connection of how their skills are transferable in order to advance their career. I struggled with this connection when I was applying for the fellowship and even during my first few weeks there. Throughout the fellowship, I used the skills that I gained as a communications writer and at various libraries to be successful in my new role. Additionally, I applied what I learned during the fellowship to help land my current role as a tenure-track faculty librarian.

Marketing and Communication. Whether working in a public, academic, or special library, librarians frequently have to market their services. I was the only librarian at AACP, so I looked for creative ways to inform others about my field and market my services. For example, I celebrated National Medical Librarians month at AACP by setting up a table with snacks and a list of ways medical librarians help people.

Finding Information. As librarians, we are skilled researchers. I also marketed my skills by frequently reminding everyone at AACP that I could help them find information. In particular, I could help them with literature reviews. My coworkers learned that if they were stuck finding articles about a topic, they could ask me for help.

Reference Interviews. When conducting a reference interview, we try to determine what information the patron wants to find. I used the reference interview listening and questioning skills to determine the information needs of AACP members during my fellowship.

Organizing. Librarians frequently wear many hats. In order to balance so many different tasks, we develop some amazing organizational skills. I do not think I have ever met a disorganized librarian! Organizational skills are easy to transfer to different jobs and different fields.

Tech Ninjas. The days of the card catalog are long gone. Most librarians have to be tech-savvy in order to do their jobs. The web skills that I picked up while on the usability committee at NSU came in handy when I was on the website revision working group at AACP.

Other Skills You Have Honed. There are many skills that we pick up along the way that people may not realize we have. For example, I frequently helped students with citation management software at NSU. I jumped at the chance to solve a citation management issue that someone was facing at AACP. The person did not think to ask me for help with the issue because she was not aware that I had that expertise. Sometimes it just takes a little bit of creativity to see how those skills can be applied in new or different ways.

Choose Your Own Adventure

The fellowship provided me with immeasurable professional and personal growth. It enabled me to tour several health sciences libraries and colleges of pharmacy, as well as network with librarians, academic and research faculty, and deans. Through various conversations with AACP staff and members, as well as attendance at AACP conferences, I gained an in-depth understanding of admissions and accreditation processes in higher education. I also learned more about a variety of teaching modalities, including active learning and the flipped classroom. One of the primary goals of the fellowship was to build partnerships with AACP's staff, leaders, member institutions, and affiliate partners. This goal, and AACP's office location in the D.C. metro area, facilitated my interaction with numerous library, education, and healthcare associations.

Sometimes these opportunities present themselves and we have to be flexible. Over the course of the fellowship, I worked with AACP staff and members to create a knowledge management framework for the association. I lived right over the river from our nation's capital and made many new friends.

At the conclusion of the fellowship, I made another difficult decision and did not return to NSU. AACP offered me a full-time position to continue my work on knowledge management. I struggled with the decision and sought advice from several more experienced professionals. I wanted to return to NSU, Florida, and academic libraries. However, I also enjoyed the travel opportunities presented by the new position and wanted to wrap up a few projects. One year did not feel like enough time to accomplish my goals. I accepted the offer. Eventually I did return to academic libraries in a tenure-track faculty position at UNLV. The lessons listed above applied to that move, too.

Of course, not every reader is going to follow my career path. However, the lessons I learned are applicable to a variety of library staff in their creative quest for professional and personal growth and development. We work in an interesting field with endless possibilities. As technology evolves, we have the opportunity to evolve and redefine our roles. Enjoy the journey!

REFERENCES

American Association of Colleges of Pharmacy. n.d. (a). "About Us." Accessed January 5, 2018. https://www.aacp.org/about-aacp.
American Association of Colleges of Pharmacy. n.d. (b). "Who We Are." Accessed January 5, 2018. https://www.aacp.org/article/who-we-are.
APQC. n.d. "What Is Knowledge Management?" Accessed January 5, 2018. https://www.apqc.org/what-knowledge-management.
Grace and Harold Sewell Memorial Fund. 2014a. "Home." Accessed January 5, 2018. http://www.sewellfund.org/.
Grace and Harold Sewell Memorial Fund. 2014b. "Learning Partnerships." Accessed January 5, 2018. http://www.sewellfund.org/learning-partnerships.html.
Grace and Harold Sewell Memorial Fund. 2014c. "Past Learning Partnerships." Accessed January 5, 2018. http://www.sewellfund.org/past-learning-partnerships.htm.

Applying Improvisation in Libraries and Librarianship

Anthony Stamatoplos

When you were growing up, did you envision the professional life you have today? I certainly did not. Given where I started, I am a far cry from what and where I ever imagined I would be. I was a kid who saw limited possibilities for my future. My journey to a creative life entailed discovering new things about the world and myself, and a transformation to a successful information professional and educator who uses previously untapped creativity in work and life. Improvisation has been one of the greatest discoveries of my life. Performing and applying it has had positive effects on my life, relationships, and work. Applying improvisation intentionally in my work has enriched it in many ways.

Who Do I Think I Am?

Do you remember why you became a librarian? My reasons boil down to a desire to help people, the enjoyment of research, and a love of information—being an "information geek." Most librarians I know share my motivations. Why we chose this profession says a lot about how we see ourselves. How we define our work and ourselves is at the core of our professional identity, and determines what being a librarian means to us. My professional identity has evolved in ways that make me a more creative and successful librarian and educator.

I am both a librarian and an improviser. I perform in improvisational theater, and for several years, have also applied improvisation principles and other creative techniques regularly in my work. Some people are surprised when I talk about librarians as improvisers, seeing that as a contradiction. But I observe librarians improvising frequently, without calling it that or understanding it is improvisation. I believe improvisation can be a natural and valuable tool for creativity and successful practice in our and other professions.

Mindset

For many years, I accepted that I was just "wired" a certain way, to be what I was, and that was that. I grew up with what psychologist Carol Dweck calls a "fixed mindset."

50

Our mindset shapes our attitudes and behavior, often without us even being aware of it. It can have a powerful influence on our lives. A fixed mindset is a belief that one's personality, abilities, and other traits are fixed and unchangeable. You are what you are. The converse is what Dweck calls a "growth" mindset. This is the belief that one is capable of learning and growing, and is accompanied by a desire to learn and change. With a growth mindset, one is empowered and free to discover. As my mindset evolved, so did my sense of identity, including my professional identity. For me, this was precipitated by several choices and life changes, and by encouragement from others.

After earning two degrees in anthropology and working for a time in the human services field, I made a decision to enter the information profession. That decision led to my moving across the country for library school and resulted in a career in academic librarianship. I had begun to teach part-time in a graduate program. I was a long way from where I started and expected to be. By learning to trust myself, and taking risks and gaining new experiences, I became more creative and growth-minded. This transformation from a fixed to a growth mindset was perhaps the most significant contribution to unlocking and freeing my creativity, both personally and professionally.

Professional Identity

Librarians share a professional identity that reflects how we understand our purpose, and determines how we see our work and role. For librarians, this has revolved around information. We are experts in using various resources to help people address information problems. We know information systems, strategies, and resources, and we teach people to use them. In fact, many librarians define themselves professionally in terms of those skills and tools.

There can be a danger in seeing our relevance and value only in terms of job functions, skills, and tools. Our non-technical skills, what some refer to as "soft skills" or "people skills," are also important. They enhance our job skills and contribute to our effectiveness. I believe we need the dimension of creativity in our professional identity, and that perspectives and skills of improvisation can enhance our practice and contribute to our success.

We are in the midst of constant societal and technological changes that affect how people perceive of librarians and the work we do. Today, we seek new ways to remain relevant and demonstrate value to the communities we serve. The creative dimensions of our work often go unrecognized or are unappreciated. The application of improvisation can provide fresh approaches and practical skills to implement in our work.

How We See Our Work and Profession Is Important

A "lens" is a common metaphor for how we perceive things. We all see and interpret the world through a particular lens. Librarianship was defined for me as being "about information." We librarians see our professional world through an information lens, which influences how we think and what we do. This also influences how we interpret user needs and information problems. In our world, there are people who need information, and we use our skills and expertise to assist them in solving information problems and helping educate them. We learn to see reference interactions, instructional activities, and other situations through a lens of information and tools. I adopted this perspective as I learned my job and began to make my way in my career. There are other lenses, of course, such as those of other disciplines and professions, and those unique to us as individuals. Because of my background, I found myself looking through multiple lenses, such as those related to my education, research, and work experiences.

My early career was a time of tremendous personal growth for me, which extended into my professional life. I began experimenting with different ways of doing things. I found myself trying different techniques and approaches in reference and instruction. I was beginning to realize in real terms that library science is more of an art than a science, and that it requires creativity in its practice. As my experience and confidence grew, so did my creativity.

Coincidently, during this same time, I was also developing a creative aspect in my life outside of work. One of the most impactful experiences of my life occurred when I auditioned for an improv comedy troupe. People who had known me a few years before would have seen that as completely out of character for me. This was both a result and a test of my evolving growth mindset. My significant other, a seasoned actor, was a member of a local improv comedy troupe. When the troupe held auditions for new performers, she encouraged me to audition. Having no experience in theater or any public performance, I was hesitant and the thought of it caused anxiety in me. I had not thought of myself as "the kind of person" who would do such a thing. It simply "wasn't me." I was not keen on trying new experiences that were so far out of my comfort zone. With encouragement and help from others, however, I auditioned, joined the group, and began training and performing with them.

Some time after that, I realized I had begun to improvise in my work and was finding it useful in many circumstances. I gradually applied improvisation principles and techniques intentionally to teaching, reference, research, and other aspects of work. I soon discovered that professionals were doing similar things in business, education, and other fields. And, somewhat to my surprise, I realized that many of my librarian colleagues also used principles of improvisation in their more creative practice, but did not realize it.

What Is Improvisation and How Does It Work?

Psychologists and other scholars who study creativity explain that it involves not only thinking differently and generating new ideas, but also connecting and combining existing things or ideas in new ways, to make something new and of value. Improvisation is a form of creativity that is surprisingly common, though it can go unrecognized. It is prevalent in high performing and innovative businesses and organizations. It can be a useful and practical model for creativity in general.

A useful way to understand improvisation is to see it in action in improvisational theater, such as an improv comedy show. Rather than working from a script, improv actors use a process in which they "write" and perform scenes spontaneously and collaboratively on stage. They make it up as they go along. Perhaps the most widely known example of improv comedy is the TV show, "Whose Line Is It Anyway?" Based on suggestions, the actors create humorous sketches and songs to entertain the audience. By considering what makes this work, one can get a basic understanding of improvisation in general, and begin to see applications of the skills in work environments.

Improvisers will tell you that they follow certain basic rules on stage. Different actors, teachers, and books may explain these a little differently. When I teach improv, I usually teach "principles" rather than rules. Here are those principles, which, with a little imagination, can be applied off-stage in work settings:

- "Yes, and…." This idea expresses the most basic principle of improv, *agreement*. That is, as actors offer ideas, the other actors embrace them wholeheartedly and add to them. Metaphorically, they say, "yes, and…." With this process, they begin to build a scene.
- Awareness. Actors must always *listen* and pay attention to everything that is happening in a scene. They must be in tune with one another and everything else. This includes what they say, facial expressions, body language, tone of voice, and so on.
- Be "in-the-moment." This is about staying in the present. Improvisers must focus on what is happening "right now," and respond to that. There is no script or planning.
- There are no mistakes. A common saying among improvisers is: "There are no mistakes, only gifts." Something that is unintended or accidental is not treated as a mistake. It simply becomes more material with which to create.
- Make connections. Actors play off of associations and patterns, continually connecting and reincorporating.
- Commit. Actors must commit to one another, to ideas and premises, and the scene.

You might already recognize these principles as potentially useful in work. There has been a lot of attention to what many people call, "soft skills," the non-technical but vital people skills we use in our work. They include skills such as communication, self-confidence, teamwork, flexibility, and problem solving. Improvisation embodies and uses many of these skills and can be an integral part of our skill set. I know that I use these principles unconsciously and consciously every day in both my personal and work life. Consider the basic "Yes, and…" principle. This does not mean that you literally agree with everything a person says or does during a reference interaction, an instruction session, or a meeting with colleagues. It does mean that you accept ideas and validate them as a starting point for conversation and collaboration. This promotes positive and productive dialogue, group dynamics, and cooperation. Similarly, "no mistakes" in a work context does not mean that everything is right and nothing is wrong. It means that you can take things that are imperfect or seeming failures, and turn them into something positive. And of course, paying attention and responding to what is happening is always a benefit in one's work.

Structure in Creativity and Improvisation

People commonly believe that improvising is simply making stuff up as you go along, but it's not that simple. Besides the principles, a key aspect of successful improvisation is that it always occurs within a structure. This provides a framework and is why it is so valuable. Wherever it takes place, improvisation is grounded in some established practice. Jazz musicians, for example, improvise regularly, but do so using recognizable instruments and musical structures. Likewise, though there is no script in improvisational theater, the actors still use theatrical structures such as acting techniques, dialog, characters, and relationships.

Improvisation allows for flexibility and creativity within the structures of one's work, while keeping to an overall purpose. When improvising in work, it must respect the context, make sense, and have value. That might mean solving a problem or using new ways to accomplish tasks and address an organization's mission. Something may be unfamiliar and seem "brand-new" or "revolutionary" on the surface, but on closer inspection, one can see that it is grounded in existing practice, addresses a need, and provides a solution to a problem in a domain.

Applying Improvisation to Work

I have discovered that effective librarians improvise to some extent in their work. This can be seen in both reference and instruction. Within the structure of the reference encounter, librarians' interactions with users epitomize certain aspects of improvisation as they apply their knowledge, skills, and available resources. Effective reference interactions are marked by not only good interviewing skills, but by adaptability and creativity of the facilitator. During reference interactions, librarians essentially facilitate a dialogue with the user. They listen actively and engage users. Regardless of how inarticulate a user's questions or comments might be, or how seemingly flawed their thinking, the librarian refrains from arguing or correcting them harshly. Instead, they work with what the user offers while guiding the conversation toward a productive direction and outcome. There is give-and-take as they work together as a team. They perceive and assess users' needs, calling on various resources to respond to them. Librarians must be flexible and able to adapt processes and strategies to different situations and users as is appropriate.

In my early career, instruction consisted of matching perceived student needs with appropriate reference resources and searching skills. We taught those sources and techniques, usually as guest instructors in a class session. There also were preplanned lessons and activities we were expected to follow, much like "scripts." This did not allow for much flexibility when things didn't go as planned or students did not respond as expected. I began to take some risks and discovered ways to be flexible and respond to unforeseen needs and teachable moments, and use a variety of examples to help students understand better. I also discovered that experienced teachers improvise in the classroom. No matter how prepared they are for a lesson, they are also prepared and willing to be flexible and respond to students' questions and unforeseen needs. The key to this is to see students as partners in their education, and improvise "with them," rather than perform for them. They feel more engaged and are more likely to connect and learn.

Lessons from Improvisation at Work

Since I have been applying improvisation and working with a more creative mindset, I have made some discoveries and faced certain challenges that are worth sharing.

- *Improvisation is not always necessary or productive.* After I began to improvise and study the scholarship of improvisation, I saw potential applications everywhere. For a time, there wasn't a major aspect of my work where I could not see ways to improvise in some way. I was tempted to improvise in almost everything, when possible. I learned that, while improvisation often supplements or complements structured and routine practice, it is not the answer to everything.
- *One should not expect others to be receptive and readily embrace the creative process.* Some are less amenable to or practiced in creativity, and may not accept or adopt something new right away. People sometimes need some preparation and explanation to understand it. It is sometimes necessary to lay some groundwork.
- *Improvisation is collaborative.* It is important to bear in mind that improvisation is not really a sole endeavor and does not work as well without the participation and buy-in of others it affects. It is always best when it involves a group of people working together. This is part of what "makes it work" and makes it beneficial.
- *Improvisation practices can be used to explore and experiment with new ideas and new ways of doing things.* One of the biggest benefits is that these discoveries can be structured more and incorporated into the work routine.
- *Improvisation is most effective in an environment that encourages, or at least accepts experimentation.* It is even better if it nurtures and rewards it. This isn't "all or nothing," though, and should be seen as relative or on a continuum. Such an environment can feed into or become a part of a "creative culture" or "culture of innovation."
- *Improvisation is not always successful.* While the process itself may work, it does not guarantee an improvement or better solution to a problem. It is not "magic" in that way. It is about experimenting and trying to innovate. Sometimes experiments fail to produce useful or desired results, but they are still worth the effort.

Challenges in Improvising at Work

Improvisation is a form of creativity that is surprisingly common, though it can go unrecognized. It is prevalent in high performing and innovative businesses and organizations. It can be a useful and practical model for creativity in general. Certain popular stereotypes about improvisation can hinder its acceptance and use. Assumptions and misconceptions about lack of structure or disconnect from established practice can lead to prejudice about or outright dismissal of the idea of improvisation in work. In this light, it is helpful to look at some examples of what improvisation is and is not.

What improvisation is:

- A natural human activity
- A collaborative process
- A way to explore new ideas
- A way to achieve goals in new ways
- Focused on identifying and addressing needs, and solving problems

- Interactive and responsive to needs
- Grounded in existing practice
- Use of intuition, based on knowledge and experience
- Growth focused
- The recombination of familiar things in new ways
- A set of practical skills for work

What improvisation is not:

- Something one resorts to because a plan has failed
- Something people do when they don't know the "correct" way
- Making up stuff without a purpose of direction
- Doing just anything "off the top of one's head"
- About joking or being humorous
- Acting without preparation
- Haphazard, random, or disorderly
- Something only certain, special or gifted people can do

It is not uncommon, particularly among those in positions of authority or leadership, to be suspicious of or feel threatened by new ideas and practices. This is often because of misunderstanding or lack of understanding. After I had improvised in my teaching for several years, I discovered that such assumptions and conceptions had created an inaccurate perception of what I was doing and why. One perception was that improvising meant I was unprepared, and just "winging it" in my instruction. Another assumption was that I was using improv to entertain students, rather than teach them, or as part of my teaching. On a few occasions, I invited some of those people to observe and participate in classes where I used improvisation in teaching. They were surprised when they realized how prepared I was and how the lessons flowed well, and that students and their instructors responded positively. Each time, they went away with a better understanding of improvisation and how I used it.

I have found that, if people are generally open-minded or open to new ideas and innovation, there is an opportunity to explain and persuade them, if you have the proper attitude. They also may have good questions or suggestions that you can incorporate. Sometimes, however, they may perceive a threat from new or creative ideas and practices, or resist getting out of their comfort-zone.

Your License to Be Creative

A problem I sometimes encounter is the question of who gives me "permission" to be creative or improvise. Ultimately, the answer to this question should be—me. But it is not always that simple and there can be risks. Ultimately, your "license" or decisions about improvisation in work must be negotiated—usually with those around you and those to whom you answer. You can often lay some groundwork for this, such as experimenting on your own and doing some creative discovery before "unveiling" it. In this way, you might "prototype" ideas or practices, and are prepared to discuss, advocate, and perhaps explain in more familiar or understandable terms.

Creative thinking and practice at work includes a responsibility to help colleagues be more creative and work together creatively. One should bring others along on the journey, help empower them, include them, and benefit from their collaboration. We can "push the envelope" and use creativity as an integral part of our work without confusing or upsetting our colleagues. It helps to be in the company of others with a similar mindset. A creative culture can encourage participation and contributions from everyone and foster more innovative practices.

Conclusions

My journey has been one from a limited view of my capabilities and future, to one of endless possibilities and growth. Changing my thinking led me to a life of continual discovery, growth, and creativity. My discovery and involvement in improvisational theater stimulated and fostered my creativity, giving me a model and valuable skills to apply to my work and our profession.

Improvisation embodies a set of skills and tools that can have a significant effect on the creativity and success of librarians. To reach its true value in our profession, improvisation should be recognized and nurtured in our staff and various aspects of our work. When it is understood for its potential, we can train and practice these skills, and experiment with their application. Like any creative process, improvisation draws from the collective knowledge, experiences, and any other points of reference available to an individual or group. Within work structures, we should recognize and use these multiple references, as they make up a storehouse of material, enabling creative thinking and action. The more sources and frames of reference one has and is willing to draw from, the more material they have available to mine and combine to create new things. An improvisational perspective can help us avoid a "mechanical" approach to our work.

Improvisation can help librarians discover new ways to combine and incorporate traditional things in new and surprising ways, with a new purpose, or in other circumstances. This is a key benefit of improvisation in work, finding new ways and nuances that can be kept and reused. Useful discoveries can become the "new norm" for a person or organization. This exemplifies improvisation and is the essence of creativity and innovation.

A growth mindset is connected to creativity, so it is important to nurture it and an environment that encourages, promotes, and rewards creativity and innovation. Everyone can be creative and everyone is capable of improvisation. Incorporating creativity in work entails making choices, such as choosing to be open to experimentation and discovery. Then one can recognize and apply the principles of improvisation in work. A first step could be simply recognizing creativity and improvisation in what you already do in your work. Then you can look for ways to be more intentional and experiment in those and other areas. You also can look for opportunities to train formally in applied improvisation. Many improv theaters offer such training, and will tailor it to the needs and goals of a particular group or organization. Nurturing improvisation can be a valuable part of professional development, both for your organization and you. I know it was for me.

Let Your Voice Be Heard

Libraries as Publishers

Kathleen Christy

Everyone has stories. Every region, neighborhood, and family, has anecdotes, tales or even sagas that are unique to them. Whether sad, funny, or factual, these are bits of history that make up our lives. Blount County Public Library in Maryville, Tennessee, is nestled in the foothills of the Great Smoky Mountains. Part of our county even falls into the Great Smoky Mountains National Park. Our region is steeped in history and the uniqueness which comes from being part of Southern Appalachia. As with any region, we have our own culture and history, which we want to preserve through storytelling and present for everyone to enjoy. Our library conducted a program that can be used to record the local history of any region.

Our library published an anthology of 12 creative nonfiction stories giving voice to people in our region. Through library programming twelve amateur writers from the community learned about copyright, grammar, historical research, writing, and other relevant subjects from published authors, university journalism professors, and other experts. After fourteen months, the Blount County Public Library, with the assistance of the Friends of the Library, published our first anthology: *Foothills Voices: Echoes of Southern Appalachia*, which has won honors from *Storytelling World Magazine*. The stories in this anthology cover a wide range of subjects, for example, a new bride's move from Rhode Island to a coal camp in Kentucky, ancestors who impacted the Revolutionary War, Decoration Day, Native Americans, civil rights pioneers, feuding mountaineers, and a murder.

How It Started

The library director, K.C. Williams, and Nancy McEntee, local author, were discussing creativity, family stories, and preservation. During this conversation, they came up with an idea for the library to host a program for amateur writers who may be interested in preserving local history. The library had the venue, vision, skilled staff, contacts, and funding. The idea would fit under the umbrella of one of our programs, the Southern Appalachian Lecture Series. This popular program provides speakers on topics such as the Cherokee culture, early European settlers, native plants, invasive species, and folklore, all subjects relevant to the Southern Appalachian region. Preserving people's stories for the future was a natural continuation of the existing series. These stories could include family histories, memories of neighbors, or anecdotes from the author's childhood. The unifying link would be Southern Appalachia. The writer would not have to be a native as long as the story had taken place in this region.

A project of this magnitude doesn't just happen. It took extensive planning, hard work with skilled teachers, and the support of many people. Two reference librarians on staff, Brennan LeQuire and Jennifer Spirko, were recruited to plan and implement the program. In addition, McEntee offered valuable assistance. With determining requirements, mechanics, speakers, and teaching, this was a difficult task. Since Spirko has worked as a freshman composition instructor at both the University of Tennessee and Pellissippi State Community College, she has both knowledge and skill in teaching. LeQuire has a passion for genealogy and local history. She showed writers how to ferret out less obvious information. McEntee is also a historian, a former college professor, Marine, and private pilot. She helped organize the project and offered outstanding advice.

Before we started recruiting authors, we designed a logo. We planned to use it on our anthology and also as an identifier for all aspects of the program, from searching for applicants to classroom folders to marketing. Branding was important because it allowed us to present the series as a stand-alone project, while maintaining it within the larger Southern Appalachian Studies scope, which has four components. Linda Marcus, the facilitator of the Southern Appalachian Lecture Series, is an accomplished and creative quilter who has crafted a different quilted center for all Southern Appalachian Series logos. The Foothills Voices logo reflects our mountains and has words faintly written across the sky. Each logo has a coordinating band of color encircling the quilted piece, and uses the same typeface to link the different logos together.

Initial Plans

There were so many questions at the beginning. How long should the book be? What would be the optimal number of authors to include? What writing skills level should they have? What is the best way to publish the completed anthology? Whom should we invite to be the speakers? So many questions, that it almost felt like we were trying to determine how to eat an elephant: in little bites.

One of the first "little bites" was for LeQuire, Spirko and McEntee to establish some basic criteria. According to these criteria, writers had to meet the following requirements:

- be novice or amateur writers
- have a basic grasp of English and a basic level of literacy
- have a working knowledge of computers, specifically internet searching and MS Word

To ensure that the applicants met our requirements, they had to complete a competitive application process:

1. Apply through the library website to ensure that they were computer literate.
2. Submit on paper a prose writing sample of 250 or fewer words to ensure

that the applicants could write complete sentences and coherent thoughts (See Lessons Learned).

    3. To prevent bias, samples were submitted without names.

LeQuire, Spirko, and McEntee read, conferred, discussed, and agreed on accepting 12 applicants. Once accepted for the class, authors were given a few guidelines on choosing a topic. The topic chosen had to be factual, based on a little-known person, object, or place in Appalachia and have both a local and personal connection. These stories were supposed to describe previously unknown parts of people's lives. In addition, the research could be done locally. A.J. Coulter, one of the authors, explains how he wed creative writing to a nonfiction narrative: "While the dialogue provided cannot be proven and should not be taken as historical fact, historical documents support the scenarios these individuals had to navigate in order to survive" (Coulter 2017, 15).

Finances

We relied on our Friends group to underwrite the entire project. All finances would be run through them; in addition, any profit would be theirs. The initial program proposal requested $3,600 from the Friends. That included miscellaneous speaker fees, supplies, program director stipend, expected publishing costs, and buying anthologies to resell. Debited against that were the expected revenues of student registration fees and the proceeds from the sales of the anthology, projected at $2,200. Denise Robertson, President of the Friends of the Library Board, reports that the Friends group has "recouped [its] expenses. Sales continue to trickle in" (personal communication).

Topics, Syllabus and Speakers

Each class utilized both research and writing components. Syllabus topics included:

- *Records at Risk.* Understand the importance of research to accurately preserve history. Understand the use of primary vs. secondary resources. Using an old photograph, write a one-page story to share in class.
- *Family Records.* Tour library reference and genealogy areas, showing census records. Choose topic. Write a "crossroad experience" and share it in class. Interview a class member and write two paragraphs about this interview.
- *Interviewing and Finding Lost Citizens.* Learn how to interview. Study the introduction to military records. Find a soldier's record online and write a letter to the government requesting a pension. Learn how to use facts or emotions.
- *Secrets, Misdeeds, and the Mundane.* Learn to use pedigree charts. Think about your learning goals and objectives. What do you want to learn and how do you use the information you find? Understand the importance of correct grammar and spelling. Determine where would you like to start your story. Complete the outline for the story.
- *Online and Offline Ideas.* Pros and cons of using the internet, FamilySearch, RootsWeb, vital records, Social Security Index, death certificates. Go to a

cemetery, find and photograph a tombstone. Research this person. Write an obituary.

- *Technology as Your Friend.* Using online resources, access Cyndi's List, university libraries, National Archives, probate records.
- *God and History.* Practice researching religious records. Find a record. Pretend you're a rabbi or priest and write a letter from their position. Practice writing in first or second voice.
- *Self-Publishing and Related Matters.* Understand different types of publishing. Conduct online search for publishers. Learn and practice editing and proofreading.

Speakers

During the course, experts motivated, taught, advised, and showed different ways of communicating stories in entertaining and approachable ways.

- The kickoff speaker was Bill Landry, a long-time host of a popular area TV show, *The Heartland Series.* Landry talked about his work and his writing process as he preserved the stories of everyday people in his show.
- Jack Neely has been a writer and editor in Knoxville, Tennessee, for more than twenty years. He successfully captured the flavor of a story's setting in his writings.
- Pamela Schoenewaldt is a national author who uses accurate historic details in her novels. She shared with the class how to weave true historic specifics into a seamless narrative.
- Kate Clabough, local author, shared experiences as a freelance researcher and writer.
- David Duggan, lawyer and historian, clarified copyright issues and shared the advice on the use of photographs. As a bonus to our project, David also serves as a Chair of the library's Board of Trustees.
- Ed Caudill, Jim Stovall and Chris Wohlwend, three University of Tennessee professors, read anthology contributors' drafts and offered a great deal of practical suggestions.

Since the goal of this project was to produce a published anthology, it was essential to include structured writing time during each class. In addition to presenting the speakers, every lesson and exercise included time for writing.

Preparing for Publication

After eleven months of classes, speakers, research, and writing, there were still two steps necessary to prepare the anthology for publication: editing and formatting.

Editing

The lack of uniformity became apparent during the editing stage. We learned that anthologies are hard to publish because of variations in styles. Editing the finished products for publication took at least 100 hours. "It's like birthing a baby," an exhausted editor explained. Questions arose over Oxford (serial) commas. Araby Greene, a Friends volunteer and formatter, explains Oxford commas "are seen by some folks as hopelessly old-fashioned, and by others as God's gift to disambiguity" (personal communication). Proofreaders made over one thousand corrections, almost entirely removing the Oxford commas, "with one memorable exception in the sentence: 'Annie plowed, hoed, pulled fodder, cut wheat, took care of the stock, washed, ironed, cooked, and raised the kids' (Seals 2017, 199). If she had 'cooked and raised the kids' she might not have made it into the anthology" (Araby Greene, personal communication).

Formatting

There are two basic ways to format. In one, the author or editors submit a text file to the publisher who then does the final formatting. In the other, the author or editors prepare the manuscript for publication, including formatting, chapter headings, illustrations and indexing. If the publisher formats the publication it will be more expensive. We chose to format *Foothills Voices* ourselves.

The formatting and design process includes setting up the layout to correspond with the publisher's standards. This can include steps such as ensuring the photographs are high quality, inserting additional material such as an index, choosing the correct typeface and font size, the book shape and size, margins, page numbering, paper and binding, headers, footers, chapter titles, block style or indented style for paragraphs, line spacing, paragraph alignment, and organization of content. It also includes designing the front and back covers. We used a photograph taken of the mountains and the *Foothills Voices* logo.

It is important to make decisions about the physical size of book and typography before the formatting is done. To an inexperienced person "while changing the dimensions and font size sounds trivial, it causes awkward page-breaks as content and images flow into new positions relative to surrounding content" (Araby Greene, personal communication).

All the *Foothills Voices* photos required straightening, cropping, resizing, adjustments, or restoration. We learned that photographs and other images should be scanned at 300 dots per inch (dpi). Photocopiers should not be used because the quality would not normally be at the proper resolution. Even though it might slightly degrade quality, we sometimes had to use Adobe Photoshop to edit these images which were at a lower resolution.

Valerie Hendrix, the indexer, states that while it is important for any document of genealogical value to have an index, it is not an easy process. She created an index of approximately 700 entries. "Our group submitted a list of terms, but then when I got them I found that some people left out many characters and places that I felt should be included. So, I ended up marking the entries by hand" (Valerie Hendrix, personal communication).

The following tasks should be considered when planning the editing and formatting process.

Editing checklist
- Decide on bibliographic style
- Complete editing

- Fact check
- Proof and re-proof

Formatting checklist

- All images should be available and of the best quality possible
- Decide ambiance
- Decide book's dimensions
- Decide paper quality and size
- Design front and back covers
- Proof and re-proof

Non-Traditional Publishing

Non-traditional publishing served our needs the best. At the time of this writing, three of the several well-regarded companies are Createspace by Amazon, BookLocker, and Tate Publishing. We self-published *Foothills Voices* with CreateSpace, a print-on-demand (POD) platform with online tools to help.

In POD the book is printed after the customers buy them. The author's portion of the proceeds is then deducted when purchased. Financially, this is less risky to the authors. Other self-publishing companies require the author to order and pay for books up front.

Some things to be aware of include the cost of the books being ordered, which can be determined by the choice of color or black and white photos. Hardback and paperback creates another difference in prices. The addition of an e-book format might add cost as well. A hosting fee is also required by most publishers to store your files. Regardless of the list price, which was determined by the library, the publishing company automatically gets a percentage of each book sold. Many companies handle the ISBN, but include it in the cost. Marketing the final project became the responsibility of all authors, editors, and volunteers.

Celebration

After a massive amount of work, *Foothills Voices* was submitted. When the boxes of books arrived from the publisher, we were euphoric to see how beautiful they looked: *Foothills Voices* was launched. It was time to celebrate with a launch party. We shared the joy with a room full of families, friends, Friends of the Library, Board members, a newspaper reporter, and library staff. Several writers talked about their stories, the process, and what the project meant to them. The authors then signed the books. It was a satisfying culmination for not only the authors, but also LeQuire, Spirko, McEntee, and staff.

Challenges and Lessons Learned

The *Foothills Voices* collaborative team and all the supporters worked hard to ensure a successful project. However, with a project of this scope, unexpected problems and errors can occur, and we are learning how to improve as we move forward.

Our problems ranged from issues with computer skills to image problems to making changes midstream. Not every writer was able to complete their chapter on time. Even though most of the students were familiar with MS Word, some writers struggled with technology issues which we didn't realize until the point when writers had to use their computers to format and export the files. "We thought we had forewarned our potential writers because the application stated they must be 'familiar' with certain kinds of software. The application was online, but we accepted paper copies of their writing samples. To correct that, the application for the new class states that they must be 'proficient' in technology. All stages of the new application process will be done online, including the writing submission" (Brennan LeQuire, personal communication).

One of the time-consuming edits occurred because some of the authors pressed the enter key at the end of each line making it a separate paragraph, using the word processor like a typewriter carriage return. "It took hours to remove unnecessary paragraph marks, extra spaces, and spaces used in place of tabs" (Valerie Hendrix, personal communication). She advises that someone should be available to clean up the documents of those with limited word processing skills.

One of the library's goals for this project was to nurture a healthy community of writers who connected as a group. The group met once a month, but editors found that this did not facilitate the relationships. "Instead of that," says LeQuire, "the next year we are going to try to get the writers to bond sooner in the project. So this year we will meet more often at the beginning (twice a month for several months). We're expecting that will help the writers bond" (personal communication). In addition, the library will focus more on the topic, research, writing the draft and editing. One change that Hendrix suggests would be for authors to narrow their research to a single event or person. Her story was about an ancestor's experience in the Mexican War but got bogged down because her focus was too broad (personal communication).

Conclusion

We have successfully completed our first class and published our first anthology. *Foothills Voices* has begun preserving previously unheard stories. Amateur writers researched and wrote engaging works based on the Southern Appalachian area and history. The community has responded positively. People continue to borrow the book from the collection, and sales continue to slowly come in. The library still intends to have classes and publish an anthology every two years. Twenty people have been accepted for the next class. We now have a library writer-in-residence who will add his expertise to the program.

While still quite ambitious, the *Foothills Voices* program remains critically important. "We need to preserve our regional and cultural 'flavors' and speech before it disappears, and encouraging people to write about their unique history or the history of a community is a wonderful way to unite families and neighbors" (Valerie Hendrix, personal communication).

REFERENCES

Coulter, A.J. 2017. "Alexander's Long Road." In *Foothills Voices: Echoes of Southern Appalachia,* edited by Brennan LeQuire, Nancy McEntee, and Jennifer W. Spirko, 15–37. Maryville, TN: Blount County Friends of the Library.

Seals, Linda. 2017. "Legacies of Hope: Three Centuries of African-Americans in Blount County, Tennessee." In *Foothills Voices: Echoes of Southern Appalachia,* edited by Brennan LeQuire, Nancy McEntee, and Jennifer W. Spirko, 189–209. Maryville, TN: Blount County Friends of the Library.

PART III

Exercising
Imagination Muscles

The Art of Pseudo-Archives and Its Role in Advocacy

ANASTASIA S. VARNALIS-WEIGLE

Archives and Artists

"Sometimes you have to create your own history" (Jackson and Moore 1998, 499). Cheryl Dunye made the statement in the final credits of her film, *The Watermelon Woman,* released in 1996. Dunye, professor in the School of Cinema at San Francisco State University, was seeking information on Black women and lesbians in early films but found very little as many of these actresses did not receive film credits. Dunye decided to create a pseudo-character, an African-American actress known only as "the watermelon woman," in a fictional film titled *Plantation Memories* (Kallgren 2018). The film represented a forgotten and disremembered Black lesbian cinematic figure (Richardson 2011, 100). It was the first feature-length narrative film "by an out black lesbian about black lesbians" (Richardson 2011, 101). Dunye's film was presented in a documentary style format using 16mm, 8mm, and video footage. Audiences believed the characters represented in *The Watermelon Woman* were about real people. Dunye, along with photographer Zoe Leonard, created the Fae Richards Photo Archive, a photographic narrative of the fictional character (Archives n.d.). Dunye interweaved this character alongside historical figures creating a believable story. Even pseudo-archives can teach us something about our past.

As a source of inspiration, museum objects offer the artist new ideas—something to chew on, think about—to create new works of art. There is an intersection between archives and art creation. British artist Tacita Dean used a single archival document to create a historical narrative blurring the line between truth and fiction (Magee and Waters 2011, 273). In Dean's book *Teignmouth Electron,* she retells the story of Donald Crowhurst's ill-fated voyage during a 1968 solo around-the-world yacht race. Dean incorporates essays, travelogues, 16mm footage, and photographs taken by Crowhurst, but also adds her own "oblique" approach to the events by incorporating herself in the story building a parallel narrative (Gleadell 2001).

Herbert Distel's *Museums of Drawers,* 1970–77, used a tall box once containing reels of sewing silk from a haberdasher's shop. It totals 500 small compartments, each containing an original piece of artwork from various artists from the 1960s and 1970s (Bedford 2012, 193). George Marciunas *Flux Cabinet,* 1975–77, is a 20-drawer cabinet filled with objects anthologizing 16 years of the Fluxus movement (McShine 1999, 83). Barbara Bloom's *The Reign of Narcissism*, 1988–89, is a personal exhibition impersonating as a compilation of artifacts for a catalogue raisonné (Tallman 2011). Distel, Marciunas, and Bloom create art that projects a museum-like quality with its own backstory. My art studio looks like an archive and my tools, materials, and objects are the physical evidence to the process of my creations.

Ransom Riggs, an American writer and filmmaker is best known for his use of "orphaned" photographs in his books, *Miss Peregrine's Home for Peculiar Children* (Riggs 2011) and *Talking Pictures: Images and Messages Rescued from the Past* (Riggs 2012). The latter book reveals his fascination with antique found photographs and the stories behind the images. The inscriptions on the backside of the photographs give us a brief glimpse to a past long gone. It is the random bits and pieces of history in which art and archives collide.

I have been involved in archives and special collections for almost 30 years in the museum and library setting, with my earliest recollection in 1989 when I was assigned the task of transcribing 18th-century maritime journals at St. John Fisher College, Lavery Library in East Rochester, New York. This was the first time in my career that I worked with special collections. I never thought working as an archivist would influence my artwork.

My undergraduate degree is in natural science illustration. I had considered a career as a medical illustrator. But the information science world was of interest to me, so instead of pursuing an MFA, I sought out an MSLIS with a concentration in archives management. After 20 years, I will be defending my dissertation in library and information science in the spring of 2019. My dissertation defense focuses on the materials experience of studio artists. I have found a way to combine information science and my love of the visual arts.

My artwork started to reflect my profession as an archivist in 2001 when I abandoned my love for scientific illustration for something more personal. The very nature of archival materials influenced this major change in my art medium. It was a natural progression for me as an artist. As archivists, we have the privilege of documenting the memories of people. We read diaries and letters. We look at photographs and try to interpret not only their physical attributes but the subject matter in context. These "stories" give us a glimpse into the extraordinary lives of people—happiness, sadness, sacrifice, suffering, love, and death.

I am always interested in finding the story within the story in the archives, so I absorbed every facet of the documents I processed, from subject content to style of penmanship. The 18th and 19th century letters I read revealed backstories about the creators' lives. One such story came from the collection I was processing in 2012 as project archivist for the Maine Maritime Museum in Bath. The letters were written by a captain during a transatlantic voyage to deliver goods and cargo to various ports in Europe. The captain's handwriting was exquisite and the letters spanned an entire year. The letters were written to the owner of the vessel living in Bath, Maine, and pertained to the Captain's trials and tribulations dealing with difficult crewmen, cargo delays, and personal illness. During this one-year period, I observed the Captain's handwriting slowly dwindle down to a weak and shaky form of script. I was witnessing the decline of the Captain's spirit and health by the very nature of his handwriting. The last letter was from the Captain's wife to the ship owner acknowledging receipt of her husband's last pay and thanking the ship owner's kindness towards her after the passing of her husband who died at sea. These letters, this story, became real to me. The sacrifices made by the Captain to ensure the safe passage of his crew and the cargo cost him his life. These are the hidden stories found in archives that I shared with donors, students, and patrons.

The work of an archivist connects our modern world to the lives of people long gone in the most profound way. That is the role of our work as archivists. The historical and intrinsic value of archival documents helped illustrate certain events that transpired in our past. My profession as an archivist forever changed my work as an illustrator and brought me into the world of assemblage art. I never looked back.

Assemblage Art Used in Academic Instruction

I started to collect materials such as objects, photographs, letters, books, diaries, and anything else that "spoke" to me. I never purchased objects or documents half-heartedly. My selection process was intuitive. I would walk by many items and touch them until something caught my attention. I only focused on objects and documents that were from the mid-century era or older. The materials felt no different from the materials I processed in the archives. The only difference was that those materials were orphaned—detached from their original owners. My role as the artist was to give the materials a new life and purpose.

The idea of using my assemblage work to advocate for archives came to me during an exhibition of my works. A patron commented that one of my pieces evoked a powerful memory of loss. It was a very emotional experience for her. I always shared with observers that materials I used in my art works were orphaned and the stories I created were fictional. Their true voices were long gone. It is at this point that I would stress the importance of good stewardship of our cultural institutions (museums, libraries, historical societies) and the value of preserving and protecting our own personal papers. If I can promote good stewardship in the gallery through my pseudo-collections, then why not use my pseudo-collections to stimulate and teach archival practices to students?

As assistant professor in library and information science at the University of Maine in Augusta, I teach introduction to archives management. I have been teaching this course since January 2000. I believe this was one of the first online courses in archives management taught at the academic level in the United States. The challenge was determining how to teach theory through practice online. If students were to learn how to collect, preserve, and make available historical documents or records, they would need access to real physical collections. The lesson plans I designed took advantage of the digital environment, which included discussion board use, live chat, and viewing both online collections and video tutorials. Yet, I found students struggling with the theory of collection arrangement. In particular, students had difficulty understanding the rules of original order when sorting collections into groups, sub-groups, series, and sub-series. All my students were required to visit an archive and look at collections. However, there were times in the course program when I had students who lived in rural areas where cultural centers were too far away to visit. For these students, I created small pseudo-collections, virtual and real, consisting of letters, photographs, and other types of documents. I would gather "orphaned materials" from various second-hand shops and flea markets and piece together a fictional collection of a person or organization.

When building a pseudo-collection, I want to also create the illusion of wear and tear. I applied various mix-method techniques to age documents. I used tea or coffee to tone papers followed by an application of beeswax, dirt, dust, and shellac. I also aged plastics, metals, and wood by using inks, paints, sandpaper, stains, and various waxes.

Pseudo-Collections

Building a pseudo-collection required some thought and logic. Objects, papers, and other artifacts have to connect together in a meaningful way. For me, I looked for that one item or document I found interesting. It is a creative process. It requires imagination because you have to create a believable story. If you incorporate real events with your imaginary characters, it adds a sense of validity to the collection. The Anne Lidstone Papers was an example of this process.

The Anne Lidstone Papers

I created a pseudo-collection for an archives course in 2015. I found a vintage photograph at a second-hand shop dated 1966 depicting three women posing in front of a camera. The inscription on the back of the photo read, "D.A.R. ladies L to R: Mary Jones, Anne Lidstone, Mabel Bell." The inscription drove my narrative. I chose Anne Lidstone as the creator of the collection and wrote a fictional biography along with its provenance. Anne Lidstone's biography was supported by the artifacts I created. Below is an excerpt of the biographical note.

> Anne Lidstone was born in Houlton, Maine in 1896 and spent her childhood years at 45 Cleveland Street in Presque Isle, Maine. She is the daughter of Frank and Jane Moore Lidstone. Anne attended local schools and graduated from Presque Isle High School in 1913. From there she attended Gorham Teachers College and earned her teaching degree in 1917. She taught in Mt. Vernon, Maine as an elementary school teacher. In 1934, Anne had to quit teaching when she contracted tuberculosis. She never returned to teaching, but throughout the years she remained in contact with some of her students. Anne's parents owned a small dairy farm in Presque Isle, and when Anne moved back home to recover, she helped her parents run the farm. Anne was a member of the Rebecca Emery Chapter of the Daughters of the American Revolution (D.A.R.) and the American Red Cross.

The collection contained school photographs, documents revealing "Lidstone's" ancestry in the American Revolutionary War, letters from past students, early school papers, and two elementary primer books. Initially, the pseudo-collection was digitized and saved as a .pdf file before being linked to the students' virtual learning environment. Assignments were created to support the pseudo-collection such as collection survey, series order, and finding aids. Some students still had difficulty understanding series order. This is when the pseudo-collection was packaged and sent to the student in its physical form. This was advantageous because students were able to comprehend the theory of arrangement faster when handling physical items as opposed to the digital collection.

Pseudo-Artifacts

Adding three-dimensional objects to my pseudo-collections provided an opportunity to teach material handling and preservation. Although they were created for teaching,

I found creating small collections of artifacts most enjoyable because it felt more like art than work. Some of these collections would end up in art shows.

Artifacts as Teaching Tools for Preservation and Handling

Included in pseudo-collections were small boxes containing artifacts. Purchasing antique pencil and cigar boxes made of cedar were ideal. If necessary, I would build and distress boxes for specific collections. Boxes were imagined as if owned by a child or adult, which meant determining what would be placed on the box exterior because, it too, was an artifact. Who remembers saving a rubber ball and jacks, charms, and bubble gum cards in a pencil box? The box was filled with various materials representing a specific theme along with supporting documents created by a fictional character. This gave the user the impression that the box belonged to someone at one time; that it had a history of its own.

I created a biological specimen collection using an old microscope slide box. There I placed various biological specimens (bones, shells, leaves, etc.)—all tagged and identified with their scientific names. The box came with supporting documents and historical notes to back up the fictional account of a retired biology professor. Again, the premise was to teach students about the varied organic materials found in archives and how they should be handled, identified, and processed. This type of pseudo-collection also taught students how to write descriptive notes and put together finding aids. I still use boxed pseudo-collections from time to time to help students learn to analyze artifacts. I believe the inability to touch objects may be one of the cognitive barriers for online learning. Allowing students to engage with physical collections during instruction enhanced learning in the online environment.

Pseudo-Collections Used in Research Studies

I was involved in a small pilot study to identify various attributes of user experience in the archives (Weigle 2013). I wanted participants to have access to a variety of documents and artifacts, not just paper-bases documents. The institution at which the study was performed had very few three-dimensional artifacts in their archives. To resolve this, I included a small pseudo-collection created for the study alongside the institution's African-American collection of mid-nineteenth century circulars, correspondences, and artifacts. The pseudo-collection, housed in a small archival box with supporting documents contained late 19th and early 20th century medical artifacts. By including the pseudo-collection in the study, I was able to observe and compare the user's engagement with two- and three-dimensional artifacts.

Pseudo-Collections as Art and Advocacy

Creating pseudo-collections for instruction influenced my personal work as an artist. As previously stated, found objects and ephemera was and still is the predominate medium used in my works. It is these creations that fill my studio space and local galleries in my community. Pseudo-collections, as forms of art, can be a gateway to advocating for museums, libraries, and historical societies.

Pseudo-Archives as Exhibition Work:
The Birth of Dr. Cycloid

In 2010, I started working on a project to create a fictitious character of stature that "fell from grace." I wanted to combine my love of archives with my natural science illustration skills. My fictional character would be weaved into the real world of medicine. This was supposed to be a traveling exhibition that contained documents, photographs, and artifacts. The subject matter would be early practices in neuro-psychology, medical devices, quackery science, and early carnival shows—a great combination that allowed me to gather and create a variety of materials. The premise of the project was to create an interesting collection that could capture the imagination of my audience. Presenting the collection as real meant that my research had to seamlessly blend with factual events.

The pseudo-collection, called *Dr. Cycloid's Traveling Laboratory,* tells the story of a 19th century doctor. The fictional character's "true" name is Dr. Phyneas Aloyisius Kykloeidis. Dr. Cycloid is a derivation of the name Kykloeidis. The project included antique photographs (orphaned photographs) representing members of the "Kykloeidis" family, fabricated medical diplomas, a family genealogy, and various medical artifacts that I either purchased at antique shops or I designed and built. The collection had an aged or distressed appearance. A great deal of research went into the project and I continue to do research to fill in gaps to blend this fictional character with true historical events in early neuro-science and turn-of-the-century medical quackery.

The biography of Dr. Phyneas Aloyisius Kykloeidis (b.1860-d.1958) was supported with documents I created to give the collection a form of authenticity. In the biographical notes I weaved in real people in the medical profession during Kykloeidis existence. For example, Kykloeidis attended the University of Leipzig where he befriended Emil Kraepelin, who studied mental disorders under the tutelage of Dr. Paul Flechsig. In 1888, Kykloeidis received a Ph.D. from University of Paris in Neuro-Pathological studies and taught at London University and Pennsylvania Hospital. These were all real people, real locations, and degrees of study. All had to be supported by documents I created in order to make the collection feel true. The name Dr. Cycloid came about after unfortunate medical accidents, which caused the death of two patients during Kykloeidis' unconventional practices. These events forced the doctor to resign from his post in London in 1903 after the first accident and from the Pennsylvania Hospital in 1925 after the second accident. He disappeared for a number of years and later reappeared at a carnival side show as Dr. Cycloid.

Dr. Cycloid's Traveling Laboratory will be unveiled later this year (2018) at the 19th Century Curran Homestead Village and Museum in Newfield, Maine. The presentation will include a lecture on early practices in neuro-science, psychiatric care, and medical quackery, which will be illustrated by the pseudo-collection and its supporting documents. The presentation will be used to introduce the museum's collections of medical devices.

Summary

Creativity is a large part of my professional career as an archivist. I process collections as if they are my works of art—it is evident in the way I build enclosures for books or pamphlets or the way I use a metal-edge ruler to write, script, or print my notes on collection folders so they are straight and even. When I work in my studio creating assemblage works, I treat them both as an archivist and as an artist would. So intertwined are these actions that I cannot tell when I am an archivist or an artist; I am both at the same time.

REFERENCES

Archives and Creative Practice. n.d. "Zoe Leonard & Cheryl Dunye." Accessed August 15, 2018. http://www.archivesandcreativepractice.com/zoe-leonard-cheryl-dunye/.

Bedford, Jennifer Wulffson. 2012. "Thomas Kramer (ed.), Herbert Distel, The Museum of Drawers 1970–1977, Five Hundred Works of Modern Art; Herbert Distel, Das Schubladenmuseum 1970–1977." *The Sculpture Journal* 21, no. 2: 193–194.

Gleadell, Colin. 2001. "Making It by Faking It." *The Telegraph,* February 1, 2001. https://www.telegraph.co.uk/culture/4721385/Making-it-by-faking-it.html.

Jackson, Phyllis J., and Moore, Darrell. 1998. "Fictional Seductions." *GLQ: A Journal of Lesbian and Gay Studies* 4, no. 3: 499–508.

Kallgren, Kyle. n.d. "The Watermelon Woman—Who Are We Forgetting?" YouTube video, 43:54. Accessed March 31, 2018. https://www.youtube.com/watch?v=FFdsT5roD4Y&t=26s.

Magee, Karl, and Waters, Susannah. 2011. "Archives, Artists and Designers." *Journal of the Society of Archivists* 32, no. 2: 273–285.

McShine, Kynaston. 1999. *The Museum as Muse: Artists Reflect.* New York: The Museum of Modern Art.

Richardson, Matt. 2011. "Our Stories Have Never Been Told: Preliminary Thoughts on Black Lesbian Cultural Production as Historiography in The Watermelon Woman." *Black Camera: An International Film Journal (The New Series)* 2, no. 2: 100–113.

Riggs, Ransom. 2011. *Miss Peregrine's Home for Peculiar Children.* Vol. 1. Philadelphia: Quirk Books.

Riggs, Ransom. 2012. *Talking Pictures.* New York: HarperCollins.

Tallman, Susan. 2011. "Artists Project: Barbara Bloom." *Frieze.* April 1, 2011. https://frieze.com/article/artist-project-barbara-bloom.

Weigle, Anastasia. 2013. User Engagement with Physical Objects: An Investigation on the Multidimensional Experience of Archival Users. Unpublished manuscript. Boston: Simmons College.

Reinvention Through Necessity

*One Librarian's Evolution from One-Shots
to For-Credit Teaching*

MARY TODD CHESNUT

In 2013, I was in my sixth year as Coordinator of Information Literacy at Northern Kentucky University (NKU), managing the library instruction program and teaching library one-shots. Additionally, I was teaching two courses for NKU's online library informatics (LI) bachelor program (LIN 175: Information Literacy and LIN 414: Advanced Information Literacy) for supplemental pay. When a twelve-month Lead Faculty position was created for the LI program, I knew it was the job for me. I was selected for this position in June of 2013, beginning an exciting new phase of my career. While there were some challenges associated with the transition, I ultimately found myself re-energized with creative new job responsibilities and a number of transformative professional development opportunities.

A Unique Bachelor's Program

In the fall of 2009, NKU launched a unique online bachelor's program in library informatics (LI). The program is unique because it is one of only a handful of library science bachelor's degrees in the country, is a solely online program, and is taught primarily by library faculty from NKU's Steely Library. When the program began, five Steely Library faculty members and one adjunct (non–NKU) instructor taught the core classes. This program began as a "bachelor completer" program in conjunction with an established library associate degree (with the Bluegrass Community and Technical College in Lexington, Kentucky) but later evolved into more of a standalone bachelor's program.

Two substantial IMLS (Institute of Museum and Library Services) Grants (Bridging the Gap: Supplying the Next Generation of Librarians to the Underserved Counties of Rural Kentucky, in 2009 and another focusing on West Virginia in 2011) provided scholarships and helped to significantly grow the library informatics program. As NKU's LI bachelor's degree expanded, so did the need for additional instructors. Currently, there are ten instructors from the Steely Library faculty, and two non–NKU adjuncts. Since 2009, over three hundred students have taken LI classes and fifty-six students have graduated from the program.

A Newly Created Position

The LI Lead Faculty position was created as a full-time faculty position, charged primarily with teaching multiple classes (up to twenty-four hours a year) for the bachelor's degree, driving curriculum efforts for the program, and providing pedagogical and assessment leadership for the LI faculty. It is the only library faculty position dedicated solely to teaching. However, a number of library faculty members continue to teach courses for supplemental pay for the LI program or other academic disciplines on campus (English, History, and Communication) in addition to their normal job responsibilities.

To transition from Instruction Coordinator to my new role, I initially divided my old duties with my new duties for several months, until an Interim Coordinator of Instruction was named. Fortunately, the transition occurred at a slower time in the academic year, making the dual positions possible. I was hired in mid–June, and one of my first duties was to prepare an online course to be taught in August. Juggling the new duties alongside my Coordinator position certainly required multitasking and creativity, but I was excited for the challenge.

It is difficult to foresee all parameters of a newly created position, and unexpected issues must be addressed. In four years in the position, my job description has been adjusted seven times to account for such changes. As is true with many new positions, it took some experimentation and growing pains to align all aspects of the job. It was necessary to determine matters such as the optimal division of teaching hours with administrative duties; the most appropriate job title to reflect my job responsibilities; and the extent of my involvement in projects within the library education department. After several years of trial and error positioning, an equitable balance was achieved.

One of These Is Not Like the Others

I am the sole full-time teaching faculty in the mix of nineteen library faculty. In my new role, I no longer work at the reference desk, conduct library instruction sessions, serve as a liaison to academic departments or as an embedded librarian, nor work with collection development. While my office is in the library and I attend library faculty meetings, and serve on some library committees, I am not involved in any traditional functions of the library. This was initially quite an adjustment for me. The magnitude of my uniqueness became apparent as I perused a schedule for an upcoming library conference, soon after I changed positions. I quickly realized that none of the topics in the conference was relevant to my new position. I found the same to be true for library literature and the library listserv that I followed. All of the areas of librarianship that I had grown into and felt comfortable with were gone, and I was in a completely new world. Soon afterward, I had a mini identity crisis, feeling that for all practical purposes, I was no longer a librarian. This realization, while initially staggering, actually helped me to carve my own niche. By repurposing skills from my eleven-year career as a librarian and exploring new areas of professional development, I was able to reinvent myself as a teaching-faculty librarian.

Personal Growth Opportunities

In her editorial piece in School Library Monthly, Deborah Levitov speaks of an inspiring conference session that encouraged participants to wear red shoes, their euphemism for embracing change and widening horizons in order to experience new opportunities (Levitov 2015). My job change gave me the perfect chance to don my red slippers and delve into the world of online learning. I began seeking out professional development that focused on subjects that would enhance my teaching such as:

- Providing audio feedback
- How to be "up close and personal" in online courses
- Best Practices in Online Learning
- "Service-Learning Essentials"
- Working with Muslim Students
- ADA Reasonable Accommodations
- Best Practices for First Generation College Students
- Encouraging Active Learning at a Distance

I began subscribing to non-library listservs such as The EDUCAUSE Blended and Online Learning Constituent Group Listserv and The Distance Education Online Symposium to garner new ideas about online teaching. I also looked at my library listserv with a new lens. While I had previously subscribed to the American Library Association's Information Literacy Instruction Discussion List as a resource for library instruction, I realized that it could also be tremendously helpful in generating teaching ideas relevant to my for-credit teaching. I also found *Library Link of the Day* emails to be great starting points for class discussion boards.

Additionally, I began to rely less on the literature in traditional library journals, seeking instead those that focus on online learning. The job change also altered my scholarship focus. I began shifting my scholarship interests to issues that relate to teaching strategies and distance education. I have presented at regional teaching conferences and written journals articles and a book chapter related to my teaching role. I also was published in a peer-reviewed online pedagogical repository where I shared a teaching technique.

Pioneering

I had previous experience teaching online classes for the bachelor's program prior to my new role by teaching my two LI classes a total of five times. My online teaching efforts had already proven successful a year prior to my job transition, when I was awarded NKU's *Online Faculty Member of the Year Award* for 2012. While I was always motivated to experiment with new technologies and pedagogies, my new position pushed me even further. It became my personal mission to learn about and test as many online teaching strategies, tools, and pedagogies as possible so that I could share them with other LI instructors. As a result, I was the first of the LI faculty to incorporate service learning into an online class, to provide audio and video feedback to the students, and one of the first NKU instructors to pilot a new learning management system, Canvas.

This pioneering spirit also led me to pursue certifications from Quality Matters, a national leader in providing and assessing quality and consistency in online classes. I successfully completed the *Applying the QM Rubric* and *Peer Reviewer Course*, and became certified as a Quality Matters' Peer Reviewer. This professional development opportunity expanded my knowledge of online course design and led to a number of improvements in my online courses. Among these changes were improved navigation; clearer directions; increased alignment between student learning outcomes and individual assignments; and other cosmetic changes, in an attempt to improve usability. The Quality Matters training also prepared me well to assist colleagues with course design.

As I took advantage of professional opportunities at my institution and beyond, I felt rejuvenated in my teaching and eager to learn more strategies to enhance students' experiences in my courses. One ever-present goal was my desire to bring community to my online classes, to mimic face-to-face (f2f) courses as much as possible. I employed creativity and innovation as I designed my online classes, and it fueled me with new energy professionally. A sampling of comments from my course evaluations seem to indicate that I achieved some success through my dedication to these principles, as evidenced below:

- She made it like a classroom setting and that helped me ease into the subject. Each week was informative and clear. The Tegrity videos were a big help to me.
- Greatest online class I've taken. For me seeing her each week was as close as being in a classroom as I could imagine.
- Led an extremely well organized class that had a wonderful flow. I was very appreciative of how everything was clearly defined and how accessible she made herself.
- You can tell she really loves teaching online and the subject matter. She cares about us students and it really shows. I'm taking another of her classes in the spring and I am excited
- I've taken many online classes to fill up my academic schedule and this is probably the best-structured one. All the material is in the open and clear as to what I need to do for the week.
- As a professor I think that you do a really great job communicating with your students, even with this being an online course which can often times make it harder to communicate with students.
- I think she is a very effective instructor. Everything is laid out, clear, concise.

Repurposing Foundational Library Skills

In addition to obtaining new abilities and tools to boost my teaching, I also realized that I could employ skills gleaned from my traditional library experience to enhance my online teaching. For example, I used some of the strategies from traditional one-shot sessions in my online teaching:

- breaking up the material into manageable chunks
- using short videos to teach concepts
- offering small assignments where students could apply concepts
- creating activities to make learning fun
- providing choice in assignments

- creating opportunities for active learning
- polling students to determine what was not clear

From my experience on the reference desk and with chat reference, I was able to repurpose the reference interview and other strategies when communicating with students via email. At times, email communication can be unwieldy, requiring many emails before an issue is resolved. I found it helpful to offer a phone call or skype session at those times when email did not seem adequate; applying strategies, I had learned during chat reference.

I also was able to repurpose practices learned while being an embedded librarian, into my online classes. As an embedded librarian, I was placed in literally hundreds of different online courses across the disciplines, over the years. I was afforded a bird's eye view into a number of courses I would not have ordinarily encountered, and able to witness some best practices in action. In my embedded librarian role, I found that I personally felt more engaged by certain elements that I observed in the courses:

- offering glimpses into the instructor's personality/life via weekly announcements
- providing instructor introduction with a photo and small bio
- utilizing pictures or color to make the course visually appealing
- designing a well-organized course with easy navigation
- creating assignments with clear instructions
- providing small touches in the courses that distinguished them from other courses
- communicating frequently via announcements

When I began teaching in the online environment, I was able to emulate some of the best practices I had vicariously admired in my embedded librarian role.

Confessions from an Uncharted Position

As with any career, there are both benefits and obstacles. While the benefits have always outweighed the negatives, I did encounter challenges with the new position. One obstacle relates to timing. As the only full-time teaching faculty in the library, I am on a different timetable than my other library colleagues. This has resulted in several stressful deadlines for me. It is common to have major report deadlines or larger planning meetings scheduled during library downtimes. The end of the semester, when services have begun to diminish considerably, is particularly popular for these occurrences. While this is a more manageable time for many, it is one of my busiest times, as I finish grading or prepare classes for the upcoming semester. Several times, I have had to request an extension or remind others that I am overloaded. My work cycles are certainly not synchronized with my library faculty colleagues.'

Additional issue associated with timing involved my responsibility to assist my LI colleagues with class development. Since I teach frequently, I am very comfortable with the learning management system and various aspects of teaching online. Colleagues that teach less frequently often turn to me for assistance. In my first year as Lead Faculty member, I allotted time to prepare my courses several weeks prior to the semester, only to learn that my colleagues had the same idea, and needed my help. After my course preparation plans were derailed several times, I sought a new approach. I learned to schedule my own planning a few weeks in advance. I also designated office hours to work with colleagues, so I could work them around my class planning. While the office hour solution seemed promising, it did not come to fruition. Instead, impromptu drop-ins from colleagues ultimately overruled. As I adjusted to the realities of timing related to course preparation, I was able to develop a rhythm that was win-win for all involved. Providentially, when reorganization occurred in my area, these responsibilities were removed from my job description, eliminating these challenges.

One concern posed by my job change was a financial one. While the position change was a lateral move, I had not fully considered the salary differences that would result from the loss of supplemental pay for my two courses. After the sting from the first few paychecks, I learned to accept the financial disparities, since I was employed in my "dream job." Ultimately, job satisfaction is a huge motivator for happiness, and the ability to be creative and explore new paths has kept me satisfied, despite a slightly smaller paycheck.

One important matter I encountered was related to workload. At times, the new nature of the position made it difficult to predict how much work would be too much in any given semester. At one point, a colleague moved to another area in the library, and some of her duties were meshed with mine. At another time, the administrative tape to get a non–NKU adjunct prepared to teach took much more time than expected. At times, I found myself taking a lot of work home to stay afloat. Fortunately, I have a kind and flexible supervisor who has always been willing to make adjustments, to make things flow smoothly. Flexibility is a trait that has been crucial when dealing with the nuances of a new position.

Reaping the Benefits of Expansion

One pivotal program advancement with great impact on my position was the addition of the Information Literacy class, LIN 175, into the General Education curriculum as a pilot course from 2013–2016 and then as an official Gen Ed course in 2016. Since the course fulfills the Individual and Society Gen Ed requirement, the demand for the course monumentally increased. This necessitated multiple sections and additional instructors to teach it. It also opened new teaching avenues for our program. In addition to our online modules, we now offer LIN 175 in a f2f environment as well. These changes afforded me more opportunity for creativity and growth, both in coordination and teaching. In addition to my other responsibilities, I lead development for the four LIN 175 instructors. In this role, I convene meetings for the group, oversee a repository of resources to teach the course, and provide orientation to new LIN 175 instructors.

These changes to LIN 175 also afforded me growth opportunities for teaching. We now offer the course in a number of different formats:

- Online, eight & 16 weeks
- f2f, eight & 16 weeks
- Hybrid (one day f2f, the rest online) at a remote campus
- f2f to two campuses simultaneously, utilizing iTV video conferencing technology
- Accelerated online, seven weeks

Last fall, I pioneered the iTV experience. I had 20 students in my f2f classroom and two students via iTV technology. This was a time of both growth and challenges. After three years of teaching solely online, I was back in the classroom, which took some adjustment. In addition, while it is common to alter an f2f into an online one, it is less common to go in the other direction. Fortunately, a colleague had recently transformed her LIN 175 section from online to f2f, so I was able to share some of her resources, but there was still a bit of a learning curve for me. Perhaps the biggest obstacle/learning experience resulted from limitations associated with the iTV equipment. There were early problems in maintaining a connection with the two students at the remote location. The Information Technology (IT) Department soon discovered that bandwidth was the culprit. Apparently, my class met at the busiest bandwidth time of the day, 12:15 pm–1:30 p.m. so IT increased the bandwidth. Additionally, I had planned several innovative ideas for class that did not work successfully, because of the technology. I had designed an interactive jeopardy-like game to encourage active learning and allow the students to compete with each other, and quiz practice exercises that involved the Kahoot app. Both options failed miserably due to a considerable time delay for the remote campus. I also had created several group activities that would pair the remote students with the other students, and again the technology threw me a curveball. I was able to remedy this by having the students communicate via FaceTime on their cellphones in a remote corner of my classroom. I soon learned that innovative practices involving technology would likely always require a back-up plan. I added alternative plans to my arsenal of teaching tricks and was able to survive the semester. As a result, I gained a renewed appreciation for "regular" f2f classes. This class did provide me growth through the weekly technology challenges, and I believe ultimately strengthened my teaching skills.

This past summer, a colleague and I accepted another teaching opportunity related to the LIN 175 class. We were part of a summer bridge program for high school graduates called Summer Spark, which involved us co-teaching the class in a five-week f2f format, two hours a day for five days a week, to eighteen pre-freshmen. I was presented with the chance to grow professionally as I worked with high school students, converted the course to a five-week format that met every day, and as I co-taught the course for the very first time. All were valuable learning experiences that I will likely repurpose someday in another leg of my teaching journey.

Currently, I have yet another pioneering opportunity associated with LIN 175. Our campus is partnering with an outside vendor to provide accelerated online learning experiences, and I am designing LIN 175 to fit their seven-week model, and preparing to teach the course for the first time in this format. It is another chance to grow and learn as an instructor and I am approaching the experience with hopeful trepidation. There will undoubtedly be more chances for personal growth as I continue on this accelerated learning adventure!

Conclusions

In a recent article in the *Journal of Career Development*, the authors explain, "we consider a career-defining moment as a point that substantially alters an individual's career trajectory. The change in career trajectory can mean an accelerated or decelerated trajectory along the current career path or it can lead to a career pivot, taking the individual in a different career path" (Ensher, Nielson, and Kading 2017). My lateral move in 2013 led to my career-defining moment, whereby I departed traditional librarianship to explore the world as a full-time library science instructor. When I left my position as a Coordinator of Instruction to embark upon my "dream job," I could not imagine how many opportunities for personal growth and creativity that I would experience. My new role continues to invigorate me and consistently offers chances to grow as both a person and a faculty member. While my position is widely different from other positions in my library, I have found my niche and continue to seek out ways that I can expand my horizons.

I have matured as a teacher as I have learned new pedagogies, tools, and strategies for reaching my students. I have served as a leader for my colleagues as I have explored new teaching possibilities. Experimenting with alternative teaching formats has afforded me a number of valuable learning experiences that I will likely repurpose in the future. I have also learned much through trial and error as my position has grown and evolved. Changing positions was the impetus that I needed to remove me from my comfort zone and renew my innovative spirit. I am excited for new lessons that await me in this position and am ready to embrace them with arms, eyes, and mind wide open!

REFERENCES

Ensher, Ellen Ann, Nielson, Troy R., and Kading, Wesley. 2017. "Causes of Career-Defining Moments." *Journal of Career Development* (Sage Publications) 44, no. 2: 110. Complementary Index, EBSCOhost (accessed December 7, 2017).

Levitov, Deborah. 2015. "Wearing Red Shoes." *School Library Monthly*, April. Library Literature & Information Science Full Text (H.W. Wilson), EBSCOhost (accessed December 7, 2017).

Sherman, Robert, and Sherman, Richard. *The Wonderful Thing About Tiggers*. The Walt Disney Company, 1968.

The Library as Laboratory

Using Makerspaces to Cultivate Organizational and Personal Creativity

Courtney McAllister *and* Christine R. Elliott

Higher education is ripe with opportunities for students of all disciplines, backgrounds, and ages to develop a plethora of skills. Within the classroom, unique pedagogies, lesson plans, and activities are used to inspire critical thinking and problem solving. These same activities can also be used to cultivate creativity and innovation beyond traditional learning environments. Due to their interdisciplinary essence and underlying commitment to student success, academic libraries are uniquely positioned to encourage creative engagement throughout the campus community. At The Citadel, The Military College of South Carolina, the personnel at Daniel Library have established a culture of creativity and personal development that has positively enhanced professional services and personal endeavors.

In 2017, Daniel Library launched The Citadel Makerspace, which has provided a wellspring of inspiration for the surrounding community and demonstrated the intrinsic value of creative thinking and unconventional problem solving. Specifically relating to library culture and personnel, this essay explores and reflects on how the incorporation of the Makerspace has enhanced creativity's perceived value and led to increased opportunities to incorporate creative practice and experimentation into both professional and personal growth. The authors reflect on how exposure to these new makerspace and circulating technology innovations has made them more adaptive information professionals and expanded their personal creative interests.

Creativity in Academic Libraries

In order to remain relevant in society, academic libraries have embraced accessibility, community, and lifelong learning. New technologies and the evolution of patron needs in the 21st century have continuously prompted change in the library's self-perception and its goals to maintain supportive services. As society's interests expand to use innovative technologies and applications such as 3D printing, augmented reality, virtual reality, and beyond, libraries have strategically incorporated these interests into existing and evolving library functions. Academic libraries are particularly motivated to adopt new technologies and applications to meet the needs and interests of their patrons to perpetuate lifelong learning and ensure that graduates have the skills and experiences they need to succeed. Many existing publications state that creativity is necessary for academic libraries to participate in collaborative initiatives across campus, to integrate new technologies into existing workflows, to establish accessibility to new technologies for the community, and to integrate new pedagogies into ongoing information literacy instruction (Conner and Plocharczyk 2017; Evener 2015; Shapiro 2016; Wong 2015). In essence, creativity is already a core element of academic libraries and their missions and goals on campus, though it may not be explicitly stressed or purposefully cultivated. Successfully attaining these goals ultimately instills a culture of creativity that permeates the library as a whole, and transforms the individuals who make the library prosperous.

Libraries have already established a strong precedent of creating spaces for library staff to exercise their creative muscles. Glogoff (1994) describes a staff creativity lab (SCL) at the University of Arizona Library where personnel were encouraged to play and experiment with new technologies that affected their area of work. The SCL served as an example of a supportive program that enabled individuals to develop presentation skills and strengthen interpersonal networks within the library. In more contemporary literature, Shapiro (2016) presents the academic library as a central hub for campus creativity, discovery, and collaboration. Due to shifting internal identities and external perceptions of libraries, it is vital to demonstrate their versatility beyond traditional roles, such as serving as a repository for books and physical documents. Libraries serving an academic institution should be visibly encouraging "the creative process by becoming intellectual incubators that nurture new ideas, multidisciplinary collaboration, discovery, and entrepreneurial spirit" (Shapiro 2016, 25). As libraries continue to evolve in the academic environment, trends seem to dictate that they will continue to play a role in stimulating creativity campus-wide.

The Citadel's Culture

The academic environment at The Citadel presents unique challenges and opportunities for incorporating innovation and creative practice into professional and personal development. The college, which is located in Charleston, South Carolina, was founded in 1842 as an academy that combined military training with the educational development of young men. Since the 1800s, the Corps of Cadets has resided in barracks, rather than dorms, worn military-inspired uniforms, and participated in rituals steeped in military tradition, such as parades, salutes, and courtesies. The Citadel has since expanded and diversified its student body and course offerings. It is now a state-funded liberal arts college where graduate students and undergraduates in civilian attire are intermingled with Cadets in both online and brick-and-mortar learning environments. The gender dynamics have also changed, as the Corps has been co-ed since 1996. Despite these developments, The Citadel still struggles to find an optimal balance between military discipline, Southern tradition, and academic curiosity.

As a result of The Citadel's past and present sense of identity, there is a strong emphasis on hierarchy and status. Within the Corps, freshman students (better known as "knobs") are deprived of certain privileges that upper-class students enjoy. Knobs must walk in certain areas on campus, must use the rear entrance for many buildings, and have other restrictions imposed on them until they are fully initiated into the Corps during Recognition Day.

Social stratification also structures faculty life. Citadel professors wear military uniforms and are assigned military ranks to parallel their academic titles. Assistant professors are typically captains, associate professors are majors, and full professors are lieutenant colonels. These military designations are visibly represented on faculty uniforms, and lower ranking faculty are expected to salute their superiors when they encounter one another on campus.

These hierarchies can complicate collaborative endeavors and pose significant obstacles for cross-pollination and innovation. This dynamic can also perpetuate highly formal interactions between faculty and students, particularly the Corps, which can impede the open exchange and cultivation of ideas. Military discipline and social expectations influence The Citadel's values, which emphasize precision, practicality, and success. As Hill (2015) observes, "military norms tend to be task-oriented and convergent (focused on narrowing options and meeting mission requirements) as opposed to idea-oriented and divergent (focused on developing good ideas and expanding the range of ideas under consideration" (88). In this cultural environment, experimentation and risk-taking are not rewarded or encouraged to the extent one might see on a more mainstream liberal arts college campus.

The Makerspace at The Citadel

Considering The Citadel's emphasis on hierarchies, traditions, and structure, an interdisciplinary, innovation-focused, and unpredictable endeavor like the creation of a makerspace represented a significant paradigm shift. The concept of a makerspace and its role as a space dedicated to cross-pollination, experimentation, and collaborative projects that cut across distinctions between faculty and students was not in alignment with The Citadel's larger institutional culture. Although the Engineering department had previously invested in a fabrication lab, with 3D printers, laser-cutters, and other industrial materials for their students, this space was highly structured around following set operations, rather than experimenting with possibilities. Access was also limited to students and faculty working on approved academic projects. Similar spaces were formed in other departments: the Innovation Lab in Business, the Multimedia Studio in Fine Arts, and a planned creative space in a new building housing the School of Business. In other words, prior to the introduction of The Citadel Makerspace, there was no centralized access to makerspace technologies for the academic community as a whole. There certainly wasn't a creativity lab marketed campus-wide towards faculty and staff who wished to try these new technologies for personal, open-ended exploration.

In 2017, the Daniel Library began to formulate a plan to rectify this deficiency by converting one of its instruction labs into a makerspace, which would feature sophisticated emerging technologies like 3D scanners and printers alongside more familiar equipment like a sewing machine and vinyl cutter. The vision for the Makerspace was to provide access to vital tools and technologies to the entire campus and to concretize the library's commitment to intellectual growth in all its forms, from traditional scholarship to practice-based and experiential learning. In order to accomplish this vision, access to technologies and a centralized creative space had to be accompanied by cultural changes that would enhance the perceived value and positive connotations of creativity and innovative practices.

The Citadel is an academic institution that takes pride in tradition, and while this fosters cohesion for cadets, faculty, and military veterans, it can also serve as an obstacle for new initiatives and pedagogies. Rather than being deterred, Daniel Library established The Citadel Makerspace with the support of the college's Provost's Office. Evener (2015) recapitulates that a library that applies principles of innovation that promote "autonomy, flow, the growth mind-set, experimentation … discovery skills, and implementation" within and beyond the institution "engages employees, cultivates creativity" and ultimately enables them to serve patrons more effectively (297). In line with ongoing plans to establish interdisciplinary programs and spaces, the Makerspace is a library-supported initiative that meets the ongoing and future needs of our evolving campus and enables us to incorporate the principles Evener outlined.

The effects of creating an open-for-all makerspace were immediately evidenced as professors and students from all departments and academic programs began using the Makerspace for projects and personal endeavors. For many, this was an opportunity for first-time exposure to makerspaces, which enabled faculty, staff, and students to learn more about what a makerspace is and how these technologies could be incorporated into their research and personal interests. Professors have started to use 3D printing to fabricate ancient coins, model experimental mouthguard pieces, utilize virtual reality to tour museums beyond U.S. borders, duplicate found fossils using 3D scanning, and revitalize syllabi using Blippar software (web-based augmented reality software). Instructors and staff dipped their toes into personal 3D printing projects, such as building small figurines, phone cases, and business card holders.

In addition to these positive campus-wide effects, changes were also echoing throughout the Daniel Library. Employees from all service points became engaged in a new initiative vastly different from their daily routines and responsibilities. With support of the Library Director, everyone was invited to experiment with innovative technologies and applications. Library personnel were encouraged to become self-taught users as they explored 3D printing, GoPro cameras, interactive presentation software, and more. Once they became comfortable with these technologies, they created internal workshops, where their peers could also learn how to use the resources available to students, faculty, and staff. In response to a library-wide survey, 67 percent of respondents felt that their interactions with the Makerspace and circulating technologies had enhanced their general creativity. Internal trainings continue to provide staff with opportunities to showcase their developing expertise and establish a sense of ownership and buy-in regarding makerspace technologies and services.

Professional Development and Creativity

In the full year since the establishment of the Makerspace, various internal training sessions were scheduled and executed to expose all personnel to designing software, creative presentation concepts, and basic usage of all makerspace and circulating technologies. Internally, faculty and staff have embraced creative design practices to influence internal signage, digital graphics, reports, and printed materials. In 2017, Daniel Library changed how it used the design platform Canva to encourage internal collaboration among library personnel and student workers. It became a central design tool to aid in professional and personal creativity. Canva enables users to easily create infographics, reports, unique presentation templates and slides, social media graphics, and more in a collaborative, online environment.

In an introductory training session, a library-wide login was shared and basic instruction was given to all personnel. While specific design theories were not mentioned during the training, since the initial adoption of Canva, the creative outputs of staff and faculty have surged. A standard signage template was created for all temporary and permanent signs, instructional libguides showed an increase in graphical sophistication, and internal presentations have become much more interactive and professional.

While it has not been explicitly stated, innovation and experimentation have been encouraged in all staff instruction sessions. When librarians and staff attend external conferences and meetings, they create presentations for the rest of the library staff to inform them of what they have learned, and provide creative suggestions on how these new concepts could be integrated into library services. Previously established annual reports have been redesigned using new software to appeal visually to library visitors, stakeholders, and the academic community served by Daniel Library. Library events have been better marketed through the creative use of social media and cleverly designed invitations. Our library has incorporated a positive attitude towards innovation and experimentation within our working culture, and while initially new ideas may not be successful, all library personnel have taken this as an opportunity to refine new ideas and adopt a broader definition of success within their service areas.

Personal Development and Creativity

Creative practice clearly enhances both the experience and outcomes of professional development. However, the benefits are not limited to professional applications. On the contrary, an organizational culture that values creativity and the exploration of new ideas can nurture personal creativity and skill development. As the Daniel Library has systematically integrated creative practice into its values and operations, personnel have begun applying the concepts of hands-on learning and innovation in their personal lives.

The introduction of emerging technologies and open discussions about the importance of creativity have catalyzed holistic changes that permeate professional and personal spheres. Since the Makerspace was established, Daniel Library personnel have exhibited a variety of creative skills and self-expression strategies, such as incorporating technologies and DIY techniques into personal projects. One staff member has been inspired by easy access to a sewing machine. Instead of disposing of her bag after its strap broke, she reconfigured the remaining fabric panels to create a "new" bag. In a similar vein, graduate student employees have been eager to learn how to hem their trousers and complete basic repairs like fixing seams.

Library staff have also engaged with makerspace equipment and the creative process to explore new talents and hobbies. The easy access to Google Cardboard and GoPro equipment have inspired more personal experimentation with virtual reality and video recording/editing. A librarian with a baking hobby has experimented with 3D-printed cookie cutters to elevate her confectionary creations. With great online resources like

Thingiverse, Pinshape, and Tinkercad, baking enthusiasts can easily download .stl files of creative cookie cutter shapes and stamps for personal use and for individual customization. Now, instead of using store-bought baking tools, she is able to print out unique shapes that cater to her creative needs. For example, as a fan of Lewis Carroll and *Alice's Adventures in Wonderland*, she has been able to bake butter cookies shaped as the Mad Hatter's hat, the Cheshire Cat, and other character shapes. It is now easier than ever for her to create themed treats for personal and library events. We are hopeful that the self-reliance and cultivation of DIY thinking will become even more pronounced as the Makerspace and its offerings are further integrated into the library's mainstream operations.

Conclusion

Although The Citadel's Makerspace is still relatively new as both a concept and physical space, its introduction and impact on the library has prompted ripple effects that designate creative work as important, desirable, and legitimate. Library personnel are expanding the relevance of their facility with the use of emerging technologies, and acquiring new practical and conceptual skills that will empower them to better adapt to the rapidly changing environment in both academia and libraries.

In addition to facilitating technical skill development, the Makerspace has revitalized staff attitudes towards problem solving, creative practice, and innovation. Learning how to refine ideas and constructively respond to mistakes or unexpected results is a fundamental part of maker culture. As Papavlasopoulou, Giannakos, and Jaccheri (2017) note, making involves a "problem-solving process through discovery," instead of the passive acceptance of inherited ideas or solutions (58). Within the library, the cultural support of creativity has engendered more resilience, long-term thinking, and a willingness to try something that isn't a guaranteed success. This has shifted the library's internal definitions of success and failure away from the rigid delineations inherited from the college's military identity and towards ongoing learning and persistence.

Perhaps most importantly, The Citadel Makerspace has put a spotlight on the academic, professional, and personal benefits of creativity. Rather than being seen as a novelty or indulgent hobby, creative skills are now perceived as directly tied to the library's mission, vision, and strategic plan. This connection between creativity and ongoing learning has encouraged library staff and faculty to rediscover makerspace technologies within the realm of their personal interests. Now, graphic design software adopted for library marketing is further used to create graphic designs for personal blogs and portfolios. Examples like this, and the others mentioned in this essay, are well within the reach of all libraries that want to encourage discovery and innovation in their organizations. As a result, the entire library culture is more open to a variety of problem-solving strategies, and is better equipped to meet its users' perpetually evolving needs and expectations.

The Daniel Library has been fortunate to have a Makerspace to catalyze its cultural and organizational changes. However, even institutions without this salient push toward innovation can nurture creativity on professional and personal levels. Instruction and signage can be two aspects of traditional library operations that can be elevated with creative practice. Experimental, interactive presentation styles can be used to positively impact students, faculty, and library personnel. Information literacy sessions can showcase interactive technologies and more dynamic, versatile communication methods. Internal trainings can also serve as platforms to inspire creative expression.

Embracing more contemporary or engaging signage, especially if its creation is decentralized through a tool like Canva, can infuse the library with a more creative inclination and collaborative mentality. While there is no formula for cultivating creativity in one's organization, the visibility of these particular endeavors can improve overall outcomes and serve a secondary purpose of signifying the inherent value of creativity and innovation within the library's culture.

At the Daniel Library, this shift has fostered more personal commitment to, and identification with, one's daily work. Because creativity revolves around an individual's insights and ideas, its mainstream appreciation can help offset some of the ennui or disengagement that often stifles employee morale. Rather than feeling like cogs in an indifferent machine, library personnel understand that their contributions matter and their ideas are worth cultivating. This dynamic supports holistic growth in professional and personal spheres, which benefits the library's end users and organizational culture.

REFERENCES

Conner, Matthew, and Plocharczyk, Leah. 2017. "Creative Use of Library Skills in Campus Collaboration." *Collaborative Librarianship* 9 (1), 39–46. https://digitalcommons.du.edu/collaborativelibrarianship/vol9/iss1/7.

Evener, Julie. 2015. "Innovation in the Library: How to Engage Employees, Cultivate Creativity, and Create Buy-In for New Ideas." *College & Undergraduate Libraries* 22, 296–311. doi: 10.1080/10691316.2015.1060142.

Glogoff, Stuart. 1994. "The Staff Creativity Lab: Promoting Creativity in the Automated Library." *The Journal of Academic Librarianship* 20 (1), 19–21. doi: 10.1016/0099-1333(94)90130-9.

Hill, Andrew. 2015. "Military Innovation and Military Culture." *Parameters* 45 (1), 85–98.

Papavlasopoulou, Sofia, Giannakos, Michail, and Jaccheri, Letizia. 2017. "Empirical Studies on the Maker Movement, a Promising Approach to Learning: A Literature Review." *Entertainment Computing* 18, 57–78. https://doi.org/10.1016/j.entcom.2016.09.002.

Shapiro, Steven D. 2016. "Engaging a Wider Community: The Academic Library as a Center for Creativity, Discovery, and Collaboration." *New Review of Academic Librarianship* 22 (1), 24–42. doi: 10.1080/13614533.2015.1087412.

Wong, Shun Han R. 2015. "Where Creativity Meets Technology: A Library-Led, Multi-Disciplinary Online Showcase for Artworks, Creative Writings, and Movies Displayed with 3D and HTML5 Technology." *New Review of Academic Librarianship* 12, 206–215. doi: 10.1080/13614533.2015.1031257.

Firing Up Personal Growth with the Spark of Creativity

How to Start a Creativity Group for Library Staff

LESLIE A. WAGNER

Creativity. Some call it talent. Others call it artistry. But the ability to create isn't relegated to an elite group of individuals. We all have a creative spark within us. Perhaps we're too shy or too modest to attempt something creative. We're afraid we'll fail. Maybe we don't believe in ourselves or we tell ourselves we have no talent. Or perhaps it's just that no one ever taught us the basic skills needed to be creative with certain materials or media. Having failed to learn to knit or crochet when I was only twelve years old, a mere ten years later, I had a second chance to try my hand at crochet during my lunch break with some crafty coworkers. Their encouragement and guidance helped me become proficient at crochet, and that experience served as my inspiration to implement creativity sessions at the University of Texas at Arlington Libraries.

Inspiration is one thing. Implementation is another. How do we encourage ourselves as well as others to take on the challenge of trying new things, learning new processes, and thinking out of the box? How do we get the light bulbs in our heads to burn brightly with fresh new ideas? How do we encourage our colleagues to step out of their comfort zones and dare them to try something new and creative? Those were the questions we asked going forward. But first we took a look back at our work environment.

While many of us certainly enjoy our work and we are good at what we do, there are times when we are working through our lunch hour and the workload spills into our personal lives. Top that with family commitments, and there's no time left for personal creativity. When can we possibly squeeze in time for creativity? That's when I recalled my first encounter with creativity at work, challenged with learning a new handcraft, and actually completing several projects in the span of my daily lunch hour. This is how we can put the creative spark back into our lives and our workplace.

Hand in hand with creativity, we realize, too, that job satisfaction goes beyond a basic sense of accomplishment in our work. Library administrators want to find ways to infuse staff members with fun and enthusiasm, allowing staff to step away from the desk free of the guilt of not being on the job. Even greater satisfaction derives from meeting new challenges, sharing ideas with coworkers, and learning new things. And the good news is that creative activity doesn't have to be work-related, even in the workplace, to bring back enthusiasm to our jobs.

By starting a creativity group that meets at work but is not work-oriented, we allow our staff members to break away from the job and do something fun. By having weekly creativity sessions, we allow participating staff to embrace their creativity, from learning new skills to building on those skills to create new and different projects. And because we are learning things that have no bearing on our job performance, stress just melts away. Creativity is fun. So how did we do it?

For our library, we focused on how to start a creativity group in arts and crafts. The Crafty Creativity Circle has been ongoing for nearly eighteen months as of this writing. Like-minded individuals come together for hour-long sessions twice a week. Thus far, sessions have consisted of a variety of yarning projects and sewing, concentrating on knitting, crochet and, more recently, loom weaving.

Steps to Take to Implement a Library Creativity Group

- Discuss ideas with administrators or chain of command. Query them about available budget funds, if any, for such a project/activity. Discern staff policy about time spent in a session (policy allows our staff to be paid while working on a charitable community project).
- Conduct a survey and review the responses.
- Select crafting activities based on survey results.
- Choose a location conducive to working on projects.
- Select a day and time to meet regularly.
- Plan activities for the first few meetings.
- Consider acquisition methods for tools and supplies.

Meeting with Administration

With our library administration, we already knew we had a go-ahead for the group. We never asked for funding but rather started out with several skeins of donated yarn and a few inexpensive knitting needles and crochet hooks. We also didn't bug our administration about where we could meet, what the content might be, and whether we would take on any community projects. We didn't need to bog down our administrators or ourselves with that level of detail. For that matter, a program for staff that has no cost to the library budget won't get chopped when it's time to cut costs.

Conducting a Survey

To determine the interest in our library, we began with a brief online survey asking the following questions:

1. Would you be interested in participating in an arts and crafts group during the workday? Options for responses were: yes, no, maybe, not interested.
2. What crafting skills do you currently have? A checkbox list of commonly popular crafts was listed: knitting, crochet, sewing, embroidery, cross-stitch,

weaving, beading, woodworking, and other (we included a comment box for staff to add items not listed).

3. What crafting skills would you like to learn? The checkbox list for current skills was repeated.

4. What days and times would work best for you to meet as a group? Respondents were asked to select from a range of weekdays and times.

5. What is your skill level (none, beginner, intermediate, advanced, expert) and in which crafts? A comment box was provided to give their response.

6. Would you like to work on making items for charitable community projects? Again, we provided the options to answer: yes, no, maybe, not interested.

The survey with the link was sent out to all staff via email. About a week or so after the initial email, a reminder was sent out with the survey link. It was noted that we received more responses to this survey—about 20 percent—than to most in-house staff surveys.

Select Activities

The survey revealed that the most popular interests were knitting, crochet, and sewing, so we planned on beginning with those activities. As anticipated, we had individual staff members who were skilled in one or two listed crafts, others who wanted to learn new crafting skills, and some who just needed a little refresher. Less popular activities from the list weren't ignored, but rather kept in mind for future sessions.

Select a Day, a Time and a Place

Based on the responses, we mulled over what would be the best day and time, as the survey answers didn't provide much guidance on what would work for the majority of respondents. Even the two of us who spearheaded this effort couldn't find a mutual time to meet, so we finally decided to just do it, choosing the upcoming "I Love Yarn Day," October 15, 2016, for our first session, setting the schedule for the Crafty Creativity Circle to meet every Friday from 1:00 p.m. to 2:00 p.m. Rather than muddle the issue of where to meet in the library from week to week and having to reserve space in advance, we chose the always available staff lounge. Furnished with tables, chairs and cabinetry, it never needs to be set up for our sessions, and it provides plenty of workspace and storage for our materials, tools, and books.

Our first meeting brought a mix of skill levels, from beginners to avid knitters and crocheters with decades of experience. With plenty of yarn, crochet hooks, and knitting needles, we were able to show work on personal projects and provide instruction to novice handcrafters in basic crochet and knitting skills. Even when we are not assisting beginners, we find ourselves providing each other helpful suggestions or demonstrating an advanced technique in sewing, knitting, and crochet. The one thing a YouTube video cannot do is show you what you are doing wrong as you follow along. Your fellow coworker, on the other hand, is right there with you, ready to help if needed.

Frequently, our crafty colleagues use session time to further progress on their own special project. However, on days when they forget their projects, they still join in on the fun, learn to make something new, or help us along with our community projects.

Planning and Advertising Your Session Activities

Of course, you won't have much luck if you simply set a time and place but don't tell anyone about the activities offered during an upcoming session. Obviously, we had to spread the word to our library staff about our Crafty Creativity Circle meetings. We especially wanted our coworkers to know that we were providing personal instruction in our sessions. Here is how to consistently update staff on what is planned for any particular session or special event:

- Send email blasts to all staff for special events, such as no-sew projects, special projects (e.g., Hurricane Harvey relief efforts), introduction of a new craft, special times, or extended hours.
- Send email reminders for regular attendees and interested staff about session activities with photographs of the project.
- Send calendar invites which staff can add to their Outlook calendar.
- Share articles and photographs on the group's past and upcoming activities for the staff newsletter.
- Submit posts to staff-oriented website pages or staff-only social media.
- Maintain the session schedule on the staff calendar.
- Tie arts and crafts activities to other staff events.

On this last note, we held a county-fair-style arts and crafts competition in conjunction with our fall festival staff potluck. Staff members were asked to vote on their favorites. For our first competition, we invited crafters throughout the library, whether they had attended our craft sessions or not, to enter items that they had made themselves. It turns out that most of the crafters that entered the competition were not regular participants in the craft circle. Furthermore, the crafts they brought to the competition were different from those introduced in our sessions. The biggest benefit here, in my mind, was finding potential presenters for future craft sessions.

Funding Resources for Your Creativity Group

Depending on the activities planned for a creativity group, and on whether the group will be working on community projects, there are ways to start without spending money. For our library, the group's enthusiastic promoters donated items from their private yarn stashes (a bountiful yarn supply accumulated by avid yarners) and either purchased new or donated their duplicate tools to encourage participation. Once individuals have successfully learned the basics and are confident enough to continue in their newfound handcraft, they usually purchase their own yarn and tools. Experienced handcrafters will bring their own tools and supplies for their own projects, and they often will purchase yarn so they can work on a charitable project at home as well as at work.

Other considerations for funding are whether there is a budget for certain activities. When we worked on knotted fleece blankets for Hurricane Harvey relief, UTA Libraries made budget funds available for the purchase of materials as part of a campus-wide campaign, UTA Cares. This particular project was also opened up to students as part of the library's FabLab program. Fleece, flannel, and batting were also purchased with special Library funds when we worked on pet blankets and pillows for the Arlington Animal Shelter. It's possible to get a deep discount for your organization and savings on sales tax if your organization is tax-exempt when working on charitable community projects. Even if the materials are purchased by individual staff members, it's helpful to note that those expenses may be tax-deductible on their individual income tax returns.

At our library, the two of us who spawned the creativity group are particularly passionate about its success, so we've donated many skeins of yarn from our personal yarn stashes. Although I initially brought my personal knitting needles and crochet hooks, I got so tired of lugging them back and forth that I finally purchased small sets in a range of sizes to use for our projects. To stretch our dollars, we saved on these purchases by using 50 percent discount coupons offered by our local craft stores. We used the same strategy when we added a set of knitting looms to our supplies when several attendees expressed interest in learning to loom-knit.

Continue to Grow the Program by Keeping It Interesting

We have found that our participants like to mix it up, so when we work on a special project for several weeks, we add opportunities to do something else during that same time.

- Do make-and-take projects that can be done in one session.
- Add another time during the week to concentrate on beginner skills.
- Build on previous sessions with new techniques and methods.
- Introduce new crafts.
- Offer occasional no-skills-needed crafting opportunities.
- Allow time to practice new stiches or patterns over several sessions
- Introduce outside experts or knowledgeable coworkers to lead special sessions.
- Sponsor projects benefiting community charities.

Make-and-Take Projects

Do little projects that can be completed on the spot as well as multiple session projects. For example, create a theme for your quick make-and-take projects. February calls for small make-and-take hearts. Try four-leaf green clovers in March around St. Patrick's Day. Create five-pointed stars for the Fourth of July. And because it's a library, any time works for a make-and-take bookworm bookmark session, but it's also great for National Library Week. Even finger puppets are very popular for staff members with children or grandkids. And for our desks at work, we've also made quick and easy beverage coasters.

Add a Weekly Session for Beginners Only

We often have days when nothing is planned because we are all working on items to fulfill our community projects or practicing basic skills with a little coaching from our experienced members. It is in these sessions that we can adjust for individual learning curves and give attention to each beginner as they strive to become successful in their newly learned craft. Teaching every participant who wants to learn basic skills for sewing, knitting, or crochet takes patience and keen observation to assist the novice with the details of manipulating the tools and holding the yarn. While the skills are easy to learn for some, if these small details are not explained, success is harder to achieve. Giving the one-on-one attention that our beginner's sessions provide ensures a greater chance of success. While tutorials are available on YouTube and through a variety of websites for free or for a charge, they don't provide the personal attention needed to figure out what the beginner may be missing. The personal level of attention provided in our sessions carries over to the job as well, where we practice the same patience and assistance in training and problem solving.

Introduce New Crafts

We recently introduced loom weaving to our sessions for the first time. We made certain to feature it in our staff newsletter, held a special two-hour session that allowed more people to attend, and brought plenty of looms and yarn with which to learn and practice. No one in the group knew how to weave anything more complex than the woven potholders we made as kids. We had purchased a number of simple looms over the previous year, mainly to reduce the impact of purchasing several looms all at once. While some of us had the general idea of how to proceed, others actually read the directions that came with the loom. All in all, we had a great time learning to weave on our little looms together, making mistakes along the way, but nevertheless meeting a challenge, leaving the thought of work outside of our space, and focusing on the simple task at hand.

Offer No-Skills-Needed Crafts

Our previous two-hour session was a drop-in opportunity for all staff to create a scarf that required no special skills. Participants simply selected from a wide array of yarns (at least 60 skeins to select from) in a variety of colors, textures, and sheens from which they cut several eight-foot lengths to combine into their own unique combinations to create a knotted fiber scarf. They simply tied three to five knots along the entire eight-foot length of blended fibers and they were done. It was an easy make-and-take project that they could take home for themselves or donate to the area women's shelters.

Allow Practice Time for New Skills and Techniques

Plan not to plan every minute of every session. While some of your crafters will pick up a new pattern and run with it, others will need a couple of sessions to grasp a new stitch or technique. Give them time to practice what they've learned and they'll appreciate your patience at helping them succeed. Some participants will want to take their projects home to work on them further, while others will only have time to devote to a project during group sessions. We find that most of our beginners appreciate the one-on-one instruction they receive until they are ready to break out on their own.

Bring In an Expert

One of our coworkers loves to sew. Because she is a whiz with a sewing machine and actually has several machines, she brought one in to the staff lounge during the month we sponsored the Arlington Animal Shelter to demonstrate how to make a pet pillow/bed. It was a quick and easy project, but many in our group had never used a sewing machine before. She gave clear directions and let each of them run the machine. Because our sewing whiz is also an avid quilter, we invited her in for another session on basic quilting methods. One of our regulars was so enthused by the quilting demonstration that she, too, has taken up quilting and has already made three quilts over the past few months. Now, that's personal growth!

Sponsoring Community Projects

Options for selecting charitable groups to support include:

- Choosing one or two charities to support per year.
- Choosing one community charity per month based on needs, opportunities, or themes (National Pet Month, National Heart Month, etc.)

Provide feedback to administration on the success of your community projects. (How many items were created and donated by the group for a particular project and for what charity?)

Assessing the Success of Your Craft Sessions

- What are your participation numbers?
- What were your most popular activities vs. what were some of the less popular activities?
- Were there conflicting staff activities that affected attendance?
- Was there sufficient preparation for special sessions?
- Conduct another online survey of all library staff, starting with whether an individual coworker attended, and ask for suggestions for improving the session content and scheduling.
- Add or adjust meeting days and times to provide more staff the opportunity to attend.

Why Do It? The Ulterior Motive Behind the Creativity Group

Our creativity group and its projects serve a number of purposes that sync with our library's goals, chiefly the efforts to innovate, experiment, and collaborate, and additionally, to provide an outreach to the community we serve. What has made the creativity group successful is the willingness of our participants to learn, share, and collaborate on the many projects that we have developed in the past year and a half. We have had a variety of community projects but session attendees felt free to participate in a charitable project or to work on personal projects. Whether attendees wish merely to learn a skill to use as they wish, or to build on that skill, is up to each individual. As they become more proficient in the skills learned in these sessions, we hope they will join us in making items for projects that are part of our campus community commitment program, UTA Cares. A list of some of the charitable projects that our library staff members have worked on as well as potential projects is provided at the end of this essay.

Benefits to Personal Growth

Understanding that a particular craft will not be of interest to every member of your staff is an important consideration. Starting with the more common or popular crafts was easy, and many of our staff, male as well as female, have participated in our learning sessions. Once the essential skills are learned for a particular craft and participants have developed a certain level of proficiency, they are often ready to take on a new craft, or will move onto more complex projects as they develop confidence in their abilities.

For workaholics, it forces them to break away from their job and gain a spot of refreshing stress relief, making it easier to go back to the job. For some, it is a welcome break to forget about the daily workload and focus on a singular activity. Just doing something different and fun, learning a new skill, a new stitch, or making something in a short span of time, gives you a sense of accomplishment. Meeting that little challenge enables you to return to whatever job challenge necessitated a break in the first place and may even help us solve the challenging problem that had us perplexed.

Our attendees often comment on how much fun they are having when we are working together on a community project, or how focusing on the task of creating one stitch after another allows them to push away thoughts about their job for that brief respite. Just taking a break from the comparative monotony of the computer screen and picking out a yarn in your favorite color to work with for an hour is so simple, but, oh, so refreshing. My favorite comments, though, are the ones that say "thank you for doing this" and "thanks for showing us something new." We often don't have the chance to try out new things on our own time, so having the opportunity to increase our crafting skills during the workday fulfills our desire to learn new things and opens up new avenues in creativity for each of us.

Conclusion

Maybe all you do after you've read through this essay is bring in a ball of yarn and a crochet hook to work on a cozy scarf during your lunch hour, but if you do, make sure you do it away from your desk, and hopefully where you will encounter some of your coworkers. Before you know it, they'll ask you, "What are you making?" Then they'll add that they should bring in their knitting and join you. Depending on your coworkers, a group could just happen naturally. However, to take it to the next level in which you encourage personal growth among library staff through creative crafts, you are going to need a plan, and we hope this essay will help you get started.

Appendix: National and Community Charities That Accept Handcrafted Items

NATIONAL

- Purple newborn hats for ClickforBabies.org
- Little Hats, Big Hearts, American Heart Association, heart.org
- Chemo Caps for the American Cancer Society, crochetforcancer.org
- Afghans and afghan squares for WarmUpAmerica.org

LOCAL

- Winter accessories (scarves, hats, gloves) for your local homeless shelters
- Pet beds and no-sew blankets for your local animal shelter
- No-sew fleece blankets for Hurricane Harvey area shelters
- Scarves and accessories for local women's shelters, empowered4pam.org
- Baby Blankets for the county hospital

The list could go on and on. These are just a few that have been brought up in our sessions. To find other organizations that need handmade items, do an online search using "handmade items for charity" as keywords.

PART IV

Writing and Publishing

Following in the Footprints
of the Master (Detective)

ROBERT PERRET

When the Student Is Ready the Master Appears

> "My mind," he said, "rebels at stagnation. Give me problems, give me work, give me the most abstruse cryptogram or the most intricate analysis, and I am in my own proper atmosphere."—Sherlock Holmes in *The Sign of the Four*

A funny thing happened when I hit a mid-career lull as an academic librarian. I discovered Sherlock Holmes, the famous fictional detective who shows chivalry towards gentleladies while pummeling Victorian ne'er-do-wells. Well, discover may not be the right word. The Great Detective is so firmly embedded in the Western zeitgeist that it would be impossible to say where I first encountered Holmes, perhaps in the Daffy Duck cartoon "Deduce, You Say!" (Jones 1954) or the Disney classic "The Great Mouse Detective" (Mattinson 1986). The first time I distinctly remember reading the original Sherlock Holmes stories was in high school, from a chocolate brown library bound edition of the 1960 Doubleday (Conan Doyle 1960). While writing this I was happy to discover that very copy is still in circulation. Holmes and I went upon our separate ways for fifteen years or so until the Guy Ritchie film of 2010. That sparked my interest enough to pick up the Costco edition of the Complete Sherlock Holmes (Conan Doyle 2011). I quickly read that cover to cover and my Sherlockian mania had begun, and also my transformation into a better librarian.

There are any number of aspects that make Sherlock Holmes remarkable, but I am going to suggest that the thing that truly sets him apart—from other private detectives like Mr. Barker, from the Inspectors at Scotland Yard, and even from Doctor Watson—is that Sherlock Holmes is a librarian. He calls his stacks a lumber-room and his catalog a commonplace book, but it is his deep collection of indexed knowledge that allows him to recognize patterns, recall precedents, and solve seemingly unsolvable crimes. Books are mentioned 243 times in the original stories, and Holmes poses as a book seller when he is in hiding from Moriarty. (There is only one mention of an actual librarian, sadly, that being a passing reference to Watson's friend Lomax the "sublibrarian" in *The Illustrious Client*.)

More than that, I am going to argue that Sherlock Holmes is a bit of an academic librarian, in that he regularly published the results of his research, creating such monographs as *Chaldean Roots in the Ancient Cornish Language, Malingering, Of Tattoo Marks, On Secret Writings, On the Polyphonic Motets of Lassus, On the Human Ear, On the Typewriter and Its Relation to Crime, Practical Handbook of Bee Culture, with Some Observations upon the Segregation of the Queen, The Tracing of Footsteps, Upon the Influence of a Trade upon the Form of the Hand, On the Ashes of 140 Different Varieties of Pipe, Cigar, and Cigarette Tobacco* and *Upon the Uses of Dogs in the Work of the Detective* (see appendix for source stories). He also planned to spend his "declining years" compiling his magnum opus, *The Whole Art of Detection*. It speaks to me that he was unable to focus his energies upon a particular specialty, or perhaps that he saw all specialties as having holistic cohesion. While my own research is nominally focused on student engagement, a quick look at my publication history will reveal my wandering inclinations (Perret 2018). One's curriculum vitae is also a kind of autobiography, and I appreciate one as rich and varied as Holmes'.

Sherlock Holmes also wrote fiction, or at least fictionalized true crime, depending on how far you are willing to carry the conceit that he was a living person. He reveals in the story *The Adventure of the Blanched Soldier* that he was compelled to write it in an attempt to show that he can write a story as compellingly as Watson while retaining rigorous factual standards. In his retirement he pens *The Adventure of the Lion's Mane*, a kind of epitaph to his detective career. He states that "Watson had passed almost beyond my ken" and therefore he was compelled to be his own chronicler. In that way Sherlockiana is a kind of Mobius strip; real people writing nonfictional scholarship about a fictional person doing real (fictional) scholarship documented via real fiction nominally written by fictional people who are writing fictional nonfiction. Is there any surer way to a librarian's heart?

Sherlock Holmes as a Role Model

> "You know my methods. Apply them, and it will be instructive to compare results."—*The Sign of the Four*

Among the things Sherlock Holmes has to teach librarians is the skill of the reference interview, particularly the skill of listening, for the Great Detective often began his adventures by sitting back in his armchair with fingers tented and eyes heavily lidded, prompting the client to give him every detail, no matter how minute or seemingly inconsequential. It is common knowledge among reference librarians that patrons rarely ask for what they actually want. They prevaricate, they hesitate, they ask questions that are far too broad, or worse, try to manage the reference interaction with a kind of conversational judo that leaves both parties bruised and exhausted. The prescribed solution is the follow-up question. Is there some part of this topic that interests you in particular? What kind of sources do you need? And so forth. The reference interview becomes a game of cat and mouse, the patron withholding, the librarian pursuing. It was a game I had played for years. I was quite surprised then to find the opposite strategy, prompting the patron to tell me everything, was often even more successful. Of course, as a librarian you don't get to say "lay out the facts of the case before me exactly as they occurred," but you can say, "tell me what you have already done." The results are nothing less than delightful. One gets a clear picture on the level of expertise of the patron, how much time and effort they have already expended, what kind of sources they are actually looking for, and along the way, as a matter of necessity, they have to reveal what their real information need is. All without the tension of a reference interview, which often takes the character of a reference interrogation, particularly with novice researchers. You have everything you need to know to move forward and the patron is engaging in the process with positive momentum.

As to research, Holmes takes a holistic approach to investigating a case. He searches the flowerbeds and looks for footprints in the carpet. He watches for the reactions of the servants, and knows the value of getting chummy with the gardener when the butler remains tight lipped. He begins assuming that everything is of value and whittles his investigation down from there. Holmes thinks laterally, and contrary to popular opinion, reasons abductively, that is from results to cause, which actually works well with undergraduates because, for better or worse, they are often trying to find evidence for their thesis, rather than truly testing it. If they have a poor pre-determined outcome, it is unsatisfactory if no supporting evidence can be found. They are left with the illusion that such evidence exists, they are simply unable to find it. If, instead, we can wring out the digital ephemera to find sources that say what the student wants to hear, those sources can then be subjected to scrutiny. So rather than remaining convinced that the perfect source is out there somewhere, they must grapple with the reality that the sources that share their opinion may be insufficient to meet the demands of an academic paper. At the same time, lateral theses can be generated, organically moving the patron from what they wanted to say to an adjacent idea that is supported by reputable materials.

The Librarian as a Researcher

"Data! Data! Data!" he cried impatiently. "I can't make bricks without clay."—*The Adventure of the Copper Beeches*

Like many reading this, I suspect, I was drawn to libraries by the joy of researching. In a pre–Internet childhood I would roam the stacks, pulling down interesting looking books and devouring those that proved worthy. I read through almost every *Time-Life* encyclopedia I could find. I exhausted the library's collection on UFOs. I did a middle school project about the assassination of U.S. President John F. Kennedy that could be described as excessive. These formative years would lead me to become a librarian.

And yet, as a librarian, I did basically no research of my own. As academic librarians, we teach our patrons how to be self-sufficient researchers, and so I rarely got past the initial steps of other people's research projects. Because I enjoy helping people I did not realize that I was missing the very joyful act that had prompted me to become a librarian in the first place.

When I began writing Sherlock Holmes stories I suddenly found I had a personal need for research again. I needed to avoid anachronisms, I needed historical events to anchor stories around, I needed to know what war a character would have served in, I needed to know when, say, telephones became commonplace. I needed to know about Victorian England and Canada, and even Victorian-era United States. I needed to know about sensational crimes of the day. I needed to know about period police methods. I needed to know! I was back in the stacks for myself. I was rifling through the now-digital catalog for minutiae that could inspire or enhance a story. Rather than a general sense of benign altruism towards my patrons I was feeling passion for library research again.

The Librarian as an Author

> "Oh, didn't you know?" he cried, laughing. "Yes, I have been guilty of several monographs."—*The Sign of the Four*

As a child I had wanted to write comic books like my hero Stan Lee. In college I majored in print journalism because that was the closest major available to me, and I spent years sending queries and treatments and manuscripts out to dozens of publishers, to no avail. I reached a point where the next step would have been to move to New York and start glad-handing editors and writers in person, which just wasn't practical for me. And so that dream got packed away with the rest of my college-miscellanea in a cardboard box which I assume still rests in my parents' basement.

And life went on, as it does, until I found my calling as a librarian. I had found my peace with not writing or creating, with being the helper rather than the author. And then I became obsessed with Sherlock Holmes. So obsessed that I quickly read through all of the original stories by Arthur Conan Doyle, and then all of the newer stories by famous authors, released by major publishers. Still ravenous, I ventured into the world of small press collections, finding hundreds of them. In addition to reading the stories I would peruse the biographical statements of the authors, and some had dozen of credits to their names and were eking out a living as "mid-list" writers who might crank out a novel a year and sell 10,000 copies. But then there were others, people who only seemed to have a couple of short stories to their name. And they had day jobs, non-writing careers, and they had created something wonderful purely for the joy of it. And they were getting published, and read by strangers who were buying physical copies of their work.

While I acknowledge there is a generational element to my thinking, this was "real" publishing in a way that putting stories on the Internet wasn't, at least to me. Editors were selectively choosing and editing stories, promotional campaigns were launched, books were printed; this was "real" authorship. When I signed up for newsletters and emails from the small publishers I began to receive calls for submissions, and almost on a lark I responded to one, and a few months later my first short story was accepted.

In *The Adventure of the Copper Beeches* Holmes declares that the rolling hills of the countryside fill him with "a certain horror," calling the farmsteads more dreadful than the vilest alleys of London. So, living myself on the rolling farmland of a predominantly rural state, I naturally pitted the Great Detective against his most despised environ, penning "The Canaries of the Clee Hills Mine" for the anthology *An Improbable Truth: The Paranormal Adventures of Sherlock Holmes*. Along the way I learned about Victorian era mining, including what kind of tools they would use. I looked at small mining towns from which I could cobble together Clee Hills. I researched era-appropriate pub names. I looked at eighteenth century train lines and time tables. I established what rural policing would have been like at that time. And then I sent Sherlock Holmes and Dr. Watson into the dark crags beneath the heath to discover the fate of missing miners. I did more research for this story than I had done for most projects in my two trips through graduate school, and I wanted more.

I researched safety coffins for "The Adventure of the Dead Ringer" (Perret 2017a). I studied the case of Lizzie Borden and Victorian inheritance laws for "A Case of Juris Imprudence" (Perret 2016a). I examined the development of poison gasses for trench warfare in the Great War to inform "For King and Country" (Perret 2016b). I made an allegorical study of the legend of the Catholic saint so that I could recapitulate it as a Victorian drama in "The Two Patricks" (Perret 2017c). I tutored myself in ancient chemistry for "The Adventure of the Pharaoh's Tablet" (Perret 2017b). I have written a few dozen short stories and a couple of novel drafts and for each I am digging deep into the library stacks, the online databases, the archives and repositories to extract the clay I need to make the bricks of my stories. I am grappling full-tilt with research resources in a way I rarely did as a librarian but much like my patrons do every day.

The Student Becomes the Master

> "Education never ends, Watson. It is a series of lessons, with the greatest for the last."—*His Last Bow*

So here I sit, seasoned Sherlockian and engaged librarian. I have accomplished my goal of being a published fiction author many times over. While the royalties may be pocket change, I have the joy of writing and the satisfaction of being recognized as a solid author, and sometimes even being solicited to submit stories, which is a source of great pride. More importantly, I have a new and lasting passion for research and teaching which I know has translated to better, more meaningful interactions with my patrons and students. My depth of reference knowledge is deeper and my knowledge of sources is wider. I had reached the point in my career where I had achieved all my goals and I had "nowhere" to go. Now I gleefully poke under the rugs and around the windowsills, finding new clues and new inspirations. It surely sounds a little silly that I discovered this fictional mentor well into my adult life, but it is the best thing that ever happened to me. In *A Study in Scarlet* Dr. Watson creates a list of all of the attributes he perceives in Holmes, from a feeble knowledge of politics to being an expert singlestick player. Taking that as inspiration, here is my list of Sherlockian Librarian traits:

1. Reference—patient and thorough, with a deep knowledge of the byways and back alleys of the information ecosystem
2. Instruction—enthusiastic with an occasional bent toward the outre, by turns infectious and wry
3. Research—eclectic, but not without a hint of method to the madness
4. Reading—manic and voracious, comes on in fits where he is simply inconsolable without a book
5. Fiction—variable in subject and quality, but prodigious in quantity

In short, I cannot recommend strongly enough indulging a mania now and again, particularly one that naturally scaffolds and reinforces your librarianship. It is only right to allow the Master the last word. To complete the quote this essay opened with:

"But I abhor the dull routine of existence. I crave for mental exaltation. That is why I have chosen my own particular profession,—or rather created it, for I am the only one in the world."—*The Sign of the Four*

Appendix: Monographs by Sherlock Holmes

Chaldean Roots in the Ancient Cornish Language—The Adventure of the Devil's Foot Malingering—The Adventure of the Dying Detective

Of Tattoo Marks—The Red-Headed League

On Secret Writings—The Adventure of the Dancing Men

On the Polyphonic Motets of Lassus—The Adventure of the Bruce-Partington Plans

On the Human Ear—The Adventure of the Cardboard Box

On the Typewriter and Its Relation to Crime—A Case of Identity

Practical Handbook of Bee Culture, with Some Observations upon the Segregation of the Queen—His Last Bow

The Tracing of Footsteps—The Sign of Four

Upon the Influence of a Trade upon the Form of the Hand—The Sign of Four

On the Ashes of 140 Different Varieties of Pipe, Cigar, and Cigarette Tobacco— The Boscombe Valley Mystery

Upon the Uses of Dogs in the Work of the Detective—The Adventure of the Creeping Man

The Whole Art of Detection—The Adventure of the Abbey Grange

REFERENCES

Conan Doyle, Arthur. 2011. *The Adventures of Sherlock Holmes, and Other Stories*. San Diego: Canterbury Classics.

Conan Doyle, Arthur, and Morley, Christopher. 1960. *The Complete Sherlock Holmes*. Garden City, NY: Doubleday. The specific copy is cataloged at https://chsd.ent.sirsi.net/client/en_US/OVERLANDWEB/search/detailnonmodal/ent:$002f$002fSD_ILS$002f0$002fSD_ILS:49621/one?qu=823.01+DOY&lm=OVERLAND&dt=list.

Jones, Chuck, Maltese, Michael, and Franklyn, Milt. 1956. "Deduce, You Say!" Accessed February 12, 2018. https://vimeo.com/88198010.

Musker, John, Ingham, Barrie, Price, Vincent, and Bettin, Val. 1986. *The Great Mouse Detective*. Burbank: Walt Disney Home Video.

Perret, Robert. 2016a. "A Case of Juris Imprudence." *Holmes Away from Home Volume 2*. CreateSpace.

Perret, Robert. 2016b. "For King and Country." *The MX Book of New Sherlock Holmes Stories Part VI*. 18th Wall Productions.

Perret, Robert. 2017a. "The Adventure of the Dead Ringer." *Sherlock Holmes: Before Baker Street*. CreateSpace.

Perret, Robert. 2017b. "The Adventure of the Pharaoh's Tablet." *The MX Book of New Sherlock Holmes Stories Part VIII*. MX Publishing.

Perret, Robert. 2017c. "The Two Patricks." *The Science of Deduction*. MX Publishing.

Perret, Robert. 2018. "Robert Perret Reference & Instruction Librarian." VIVO: Robert Perret. Accessed March 04, 2018. https://vivo.nkn.uidaho.edu/vivo/display/n1044275906.

Ritchie, Guy, Johnson, Michael Robert, Peckham, Anthony, Kinberg, Simon, Wigram, Lionel, Silver, Joel, Downey, Susan, et al. 2010. *Sherlock Holmes*. Burbank: Warner Home Video.

Rosario, Anne, and Thompson, A. C. 2015. *An Improbable Truth: The Paranormal Adventures of Sherlock Holmes*. Greensboro: Mocha Memoirs Press.

Poets and Scholars

Foregrounding Librarians' Creative Writing
In and Out of the University Classroom

ROCHELLE SMITH

When librarians share our writing with university communities, it is most often scholarly work in information literacy or other aspects of professional librarianship that we discuss (McCluskey 2013). We seldom if ever discuss or share our creative efforts outside our profession. Many librarians have education and experiences as creators: visual artists, writers, composers, performers. It is possible for us to reach beyond our own artistic output and inspire students as they work to express their own creativity. This essay explores ways that librarians' artistic experience, particularly with creative writing, can be invaluable to lower division, upper division and graduate students. It also suggests that sharing this experience is meaningful to our own lives as part of the larger creative community.

There are many direct ways in which creative practice can enhance the daily work of librarianship. Several authors in the library literature have pointed out that research is an essential component of the creative process. Julia Glassman, a novelist as well as an academic librarian, states that "the extent to which creative writing students conduct research—both formal and informal—for their work is still vastly underestimated" (Glassman 2014, 602). Librarian John Glover, also a novelist, echoes this point when he talks about the "combination of historical, investigative, image, and general research required to write novels" (Glover 2016, 274). Kasia Leousis makes a similar point about visual artists, stating that "developing artists conduct research to inform, inspire and stimulate their artistic practice" (Leousis 2013, 127). Any librarian working with students in a creative field can take advantage of this clear opportunity. David Pavelich among others has championed the role that librarians can play in fostering research on the part of writers, declaring that "writing historical fiction [for example] requires research skills, and librarians and archivists are in unique positions to provide this training" (Pavelich 2010, 296).

Creative writing, in my case essays and poetry, far from being a side interest or a separate part of my life, actively comes into play in my work as a librarian. My life as a librarian would be very different if I were not also a writer. I find concrete ways to interact directly with creative writing students who are sometimes underserved by libraries (Glassman 2014); discuss or share my writing with English classes or at campus readings; take a writing class or serve on an MFA thesis committee. The simple fact that I am an essayist fosters a way of thinking, and approach to research and inquiry that is wide ranging and omnivorous, and beneficial to the students I help.

I received a master of fine arts degree in creative writing from the University of Idaho (UI). In my third year in the writing program I began working as a reference and instruction librarian at the UI Library. Six years later I became the humanities liaison, which meant that the department of English became one of my liaison areas. I was fortunate to begin my work as a liaison to the English department having already formed relationships with much of the teaching faculty. This made it easy to persuade them that securing my help in their classes would be beneficial to students. In my time as liaison to the English department, I have provided information literacy classes for students at every level, from first year to graduate school. These classes, often one-shot occurrences, cover efficient searching of the library's catalog, JSTOR, MLA Bibliography, and other humanities databases. Teaching how to craft searches, make use of subject headings, and apply critical thinking skills is positive, rewarding work, but my working life as a librarian, and the lives of the students I interact with, are enriched when I get to do more.

Since faculty understandably associate academic librarians with traditional scholarly research, I am most often called upon by English faculty teaching business or technical writing, or literature. One member of the creative writing faculty, a novelist and short story writer, decided a few years ago that his 300-level fiction students would benefit from learning to incorporate research into their stories. So he made a researched short story a requirement. Unlike the other short stories written for this class, in which students drew the content purely from their experiences and imaginations, for this assignment the stories had to contain outside research of topics that intrigued the students enough to spark an idea. The thought that research could be an essential part of an imaginative work is a new one for many undergraduates. In this case, rather than asking me in for a classroom session, the professor strongly urged all of his students to meet with me one on one. He wanted his young writers to really think about what interested them and why, and to discuss and investigate those choices under my guidance, not simply hide out in a room of over twenty students and then Google the bare minimum later. He is himself an avid researcher in writing his own fiction, and wanted his students to discover the delight that well-integrated research can bring to a story, for writers and readers.

His students had chosen an eclectic range of topics for their short stories, among them, the lives of Marvin Gaye and Nikola Tesla, the assassination of RFK, alchemy, gladiators, LGBT communes, jousting, religious cults, bog bodies, Ruby Ridge, and Lord Byron. Some students needed specific details to flesh out their stories and make them more believable; others wanted to dive deeply into a particular time, location, or field, and were looking for substantive information. Some students were longstanding young writers already deeply immersed in their imagined worlds. Others were brand new to creative writing, knew only that they were interested in a particular topic, and needed to figure out how to approach it in a way that made a compelling, meaningful narrative possible. It was a great delight to go with these young writers wherever their imaginations and curiosity took them. The fact that I was a writer myself increased their confidence that I understood their needs and contributed to the feeling of camaraderie as I interacted with them.

Working with students on their story research also gave me the opportunity to talk about resources I seldom get to showcase to members of the English department, such as science and social science databases, image databases, primary source and historical newspaper resources, and back issues of magazines like *Life, Good Housekeeping*, and the *Saturday Evening Post*. This was just as true for graduate students, who were also often pushing themselves out of their humanities comfort zone. In one case I worked with an MFA student who wished to craft an extended conceit concerning bubbles for an essay. She wanted to describe their beauty and to use them as a metaphor for fragility and the fleeting nature of beauty; but she also wished to understand the physics of bubble formation in different substances, as well as viscosity, surface tension, nucleation, and other concepts that took her well outside her usual wheelhouse. As a librarian, I could appreciate the trepidation with which a new learner approached these subjects. As a fellow writer I could relate to the delicate mixture of rigor and whimsy that attends an essayist's particular approach to research in the sciences.

Working with faculty on their creative projects yields many of the same rewards. Faculty in creative fields don't always think to come to librarians when doing research for their own work, and in some cases their students have sometimes unwittingly led the way and emboldened faculty to contact me. I have worked with a professor in the English department on her research into Saudi Arabian history and the petroleum industry for a historical novel, and with a different professor, a playwright, who in the course of drafting a new play wanted to explore the question of why, evolutionarily, it can be advantageous to lie. Not having a psychology background, he had no idea there had been decades of research on this question by anthropologists, primatologists, psychologists and other scientists.

Conducting in-class and one-on-one information sessions on research for creative writing has been one way that my background positively influenced my work as a librarian and library liaison. I have been astonished do discover other ways my own creative work has allowed me to engage even more directly with young college writers. It began with a conversation with one of the English faculty who had been a graduate student at the same time as myself and knew my work. He was teaching intermediate nonfiction writing and asked me to talk with his students about my own work. This was unexpected, and I struggled to prepare. What could I tell them about my journey as a writer that would be useful to them?

I decided to share a part of an essay I had published about a trip to the Outer Hebrides in Scotland that I had taken years before. The professor sent the students the excerpt beforehand, and in my conversation with the class I discussed my approach to writing the essay, including research. This ranged from simple fact-finding (the distance between Oslo and London, for example) to more in-depth inquiry, like the history of British colonialism in the country of my birth, Trinidad, and the role that Scots played in that colonization. A few of the students in this class had met me before as the librarian who assisted them with their required first-year English composition classes. Unlike our past encounters which often were one-sided, teacher to student, as bibliographic instruction sessions tend to be, this talk became a conversation. Students and I talked about an essential and often baffling question in personal nonfiction writing: how does the writer move from her own interior, deeply personal and quirky musings to create something that holds a reader, allows that reader to trust her and the wanderings of her mind? How does careful attention to research, at all levels, from "basic background information [to] foundational knowledge on a subject" (Glassman 2014) increase the pleasure of the reader and the connection the reader feels to the author's experience?

I have given some version of this talk, featuring different essays, for classes from Personal and Exploratory Writing to Beginning Nonfiction, over the course of several years. I've shared my research process about Catholic saints, Grimm's fairy tales, mythology, the African diaspora, and more about Scotland—I never tire of writing and talking about Scotland. Of course, some of the benefits of giving this type of talk are straightforwardly connected to library work: it gives undergraduates an inroad into conversations with me, breaking the ice and ensuring that I am not a stranger when the time comes when they need research help for other classes. But the benefits of this go deeper, in terms of letting the students (and the professors) see a different side of the members of our profession. Creativity is a trait that librarians display with students all the time, in reference transactions and research sessions. This connects strongly to the "mazy mind" idea put forth by writer Cynthia Ozick, who describes the process of writing essays as "the movement of a free mind at play" (Ozick 2000). Not necessarily the first thing students and faculty think of when they think of librarians, which is unfortunate, because each time students observe how our own curiosity and intellectual flexibility lead organically to new approaches to a subject and to new, deeper questions, they learn how it is possible to do this research themselves. Letting students see us as fellow seekers and creators allows them to connect with us in richer ways.

Auditing classes, or taking them for credit, is another way for a librarian relatively new to a subject area to make inroads in relationship building. As part of my continuing writing practice, I take a graduate level nonfiction workshop every other year. This has proven to be a stellar way to make connections with students at the graduate level. Writing workshops tend to be conducted in a small group format, around a table. Writers take turns bringing in works in progress and having them discussed in detail by the entire class. We read, listen, respond to, and critique one another's work, and students see me as a fellow writer on a creative journey, which is, after all, what I am. My work is immeasurably improved by their feedback, as theirs is by mine.

These connections also mean that when these same students are looking for members of their thesis committees, I come to mind. In the UI English department, as in many other departments, students required to present and defend a thesis before a committee of three members, including their thesis advisor, a second faculty member from within the department, and a third faculty member from outside. Serving as third reader on creative writing thesis committees has been one of the most rewarding parts of my service as an academic librarian. As third reader, I spend time with the student's work, whether it is a novel or a collection of short fiction, essays, or poems, in advance of the defense. At the defense itself, I serve on a panel with the student's thesis advisor and another member of the English department faculty. We take turns asking the candidate to expound on their writing process, literary influences, history with the thesis project, and where they see their work fitting in the landscape of letters. We discuss the candidate's performance in private before giving a final assessment and signing off on the thesis. I have served on over twenty-five fiction, nonfiction, and poetry committees in my time at UI. This further strengthens my relationships with the English faculty, sharpens my own critical skills, and fulfills part of the teaching expectation on which I am evaluated every year.

Librarians' creative writing can even impact our scholarly output, which is for many of us a mandatory part of our work. A colleague at UI, Devin Becker, is a poet as well as a librarian. He has allowed his own creative writing practice to inform the kinds of scholarship he produces and the particular questions he chooses to ask in that scholarly writing, as in the case of one article investigating writers' (often inadequate) approaches to the digital archiving of their own works in progress (Becker 2012).

My hope in writing this essay is to show that academic librarians' impulses and output as creative writers need not be sidelined during their working lives at their institutions. Ways to integrate these two spheres are many, and include:

- Looking for opportunities to make connections with students about creative writing. This can hew closely to traditional bibliographic instruction, as suggested by Glover and by Glassman, extending outreach efforts concerning research instruction to creative writing students and faculty. It can also expand into discussions of your own creative process, and the idiosyncratic and interesting ways that you, as an individual writer, incorporate research into your creative output.
- Attending and participating in readings. Many colleges or college affiliated groups, such as literary magazine student editorial staff, hold informal readings throughout the year. These readings, often held off campus at a casual venue like a bar or coffee shop, are sometimes open to participants other than current students. Writers take turns reading short excerpts from their work, and get to hear the work of other writers rather than only see it on the page. If taking a writing class is too great a time commitment or otherwise unfeasible, participating in readings can be another way to connect strongly with students and faculty as a fellow creator, not simply as a service provider. Volunteering to help organize these events is also an excellent way to connect.
- Auditing classes or taking them for credit, whether writing workshops, studio art classes, or other hands-on creative sessions. This broadens your knowledge, builds relationships with students and faculty, and increases library visibility.
- Serving on thesis committees, whether for graduate students or senior honors candidates. Students are often required to secure third readers from outside their departments, and librarians with faculty status are eligible and in fact invaluable.
- Leading book talks and participating in other events connected with university common reading programs, and serving on the committees that choose the titles. In my experience, librarians' experience with fostering ludic reading can sometimes give them a keener sense of what will be a rewarding read for first year students.
- Urging the library's participation in other literary and creative programs, like National Novel Writing Month (NaNoWriMo), can also be a way to spark interest in the library as a creative space and "bring participants to an environment with copious resources for writing, revising, and researching outside of a commercial environment" (Watson 2012).
- Looking for opportunities outside the humanities as well, like field trips, service learning breaks, and citizen science projects. Even for established writers and artists, creativity can be defined and approached broadly, especially if the goal is to connect with students across disciplines.

I urge librarians who currently consider their creative efforts to be separate from their academic lives to think about all the ways that their artistic output, in whatever realm, feeds and is fed by their work as librarians, and about how they can bring these worlds closer together in ways that enrich both, to the benefit of their college communities and their own creativity.

REFERENCES

Becker, Devin, and Nogues, Collier. 2012. "Saving-Over, Over-Saving, and the Future Mess of Writers' Digital Archives: A Survey Report on the Personal Digital Archiving Practices of Emerging Writers." *American Archivist* 75 (2): 482–513.

Glassman, Julia. 2014. "Research Support for Creative Writers." *College & Research Libraries News* 75 (11): 602–609.

Glover, John. 2016. "Embedding Information Literacy in an MFA Novel Workshop." *Reference & User Services Quarterly* 55 (4): 273–276.

Leousis, Kasia. 2013. "Outreach to Artists: Supporting the Development of a Research Culture for Master of Fine Arts Students." *Art Documentation: Bulletin of the Art Libraries Society of North America* 32 (1): 127–137.

McCluskey, Clare. 2013. "Being an Embedded Research Librarian: Supporting Research by Being a Researcher." *Journal of Information Literacy* 7 (2): 4–14.

Ozick, Cynthia. 2000. "She: Portrait of the Essay as a Warm Body." In *Quarrel and Quandary*. New York: Alfred A. Knopf.

Pavelich, David. 2010. "Lighting Fires in Creative Minds." *College & Research Libraries News* 71 (6): 295–313.

Watson, Alex P. 2012. "NaNoWriMo in the AcadLib: A Case Study of National Novel Writing Month Activities in an Academic Library." *Public Services Quarterly* 8 (2): 136–145.

The Tenure-Track Librarian as a Scholarly Researcher

RACHEL K. FISCHER

Introduction

You are not alone if you began a master's degree in library science program with a desire to be an academic librarian without knowing that the path to tenure could include a requirement to publish scholarly research. Nor are you alone if you never planned to write another essay after you graduated but are now required to do so for the librarian position that you desire. Being able to meet the requirement for scholarly research, year after year, until you receive tenure, seems like a daunting task to many librarians. For those who just graduated, or will be graduating soon, the question of how to be successful at landing the first tenure-track job interview and being selected for a tenure-track librarian position weighs heavily on the mind. However, if you properly prepare and plan for a position that includes scholarly research, the job interview process and first couple of years on the job will be less stressful. Scholarly research and publishing articles in peer-reviewed journals are important for assisting future library students in their endeavors and for assisting future leaders in solving problems that were never discussed in library school. Reading articles about successful and innovative accomplishments lifts the spirits of those librarians who are faced with the numerous challenges in their field. Once that first article is published, and even more so after that article has been cited in another published work, the stress and preparation for a tenure-track librarian position will seem worth it. Your research really will have the power to make a difference in the field of librarianship.

This essay provides an introduction to the scholarly research component of being a tenure-track librarian. The first section explains the tenure-track requirement for scholarly research. This section is designed to assist a librarian when preparing for a job interview. The second section provides tips on how to prepare for a career as a tenure-track librarian who is required to publish scholarly research. It contains advice to assist students with making educational decisions, for the purpose of improving one's understanding of research methods and facilitating one's capability to publish articles. The next section includes tips to assist with the generation of research ideas. This will help one get over the initial hump of writer's block. The last section contains advice for a library science professor who may be interested in adapting the library science curriculum to better prepare students for a life of scholarly research. By following the suggestions in this essay, a librarian will be able to create a strategic plan that can set one on the right track towards more job interview offers, a tenure-track job offer, and help sustain good habits as a scholarly researcher.

Scholarly Research as a Requirement for Tenure

When reviewing job announcements for academic librarian positions, it is not always clear if scholarly research is mandatory, optional, or not required at all. The degree to which scholarly research is mandatory is contingent on the status of the librarians at the academic institution; the requirements vary widely. The Dean, Provost, and tenure-track committee create a tenure-track policy for librarians that is in line with the university's faculty handbook and comparable to the policies of peer libraries. Librarians with faculty status and tenure are frequently required to both conduct scholarly research, including the publication in peer-reviewed journals or presentations at conferences, and participate in association and university committees. Some institutions have a policy that will grant librarians tenure for having an excellent job record, even if they have not published articles. Librarians with faculty status without tenure may be required to either conduct scholarly research, for publications and presentations, or participate in association committees. Librarians with a staff status are frequently not required to conduct scholarly research, although at some institutions are given support for doing that, especially if they are staff with a tenure-like status.

Librarians who are required to publish scholarly research and participate in association committees are allowed "release time" for these activities to be conducted on the job. This time can be used for any steps of the scholarly research process, and for activities such as committee meetings and responsibilities. The current trend is for a tenure-track librarian to have a goal of publishing one peer-reviewed article per year. However, the required number may be different at some institutions, and may vary depending on the policy at the time a librarian was hired or the job title. Peer-reviewed publications can include articles published in academic journals and papers presented at conferences. Some academic institutions require tenure-track librarians to only publish peer-reviewed articles on a subject directly related to their job title. For example, a metadata librarian is required to conduct research related to the subfields of metadata, cataloging, and library technical services. Other institutions will permit tenure-track librarians to publish research on any topic, as long as the publication is peer reviewed. This allows one to publish in a field of a secondary master's degree.

This does not mean that non-peer reviewed articles are not important. Non-peer reviewed articles are typically seen as "extra credit." Additional articles look great on a CV when one is applying for a job for the first time or is under review by the tenure and promotion committees. Some promotion committees will count these extra articles for points towards promotion.

Not every institution has the same policy. It is important to thoroughly review and understand the specifics of the tenure and promotion policy before accepting a position. Before attending a job interview, it may be possible to find relevant policies on an institution's website. It is also acceptable to ask the hiring committee to email the policy before the job interview. Here is a list of questions to ask a hiring committee during an interview for an academic librarian position:

1. Can I see the tenure and promotion policy? (Ask for any clarification on requirements for tenure and promotion.)
2. How long does it take to get tenure?
3. Is publishing a requirement for this position?
4. How many peer-reviewed articles am I required to publish per year?
5. How many articles should I have completed before I am eligible for tenure?
6. How are non-peer-reviewed articles viewed?
7. How much time am I required to spend on association committees on the job?
8. How much time am I allowed to spend on scholarly research on the job?
9. Can I publish articles on subjects that are unrelated to librarianship?
10. What support does the institution offer for scholarly researchers?

Here are some questions you may ask during an interview meal:

1. What topics do you like to research and write about?
2. Have you published any articles or books recently?
3. Do you have a research project that you are working on at the moment?
4. Can you tell me about your experience presenting at conferences?

Tips on Preparing for a Career as a Tenure-Track Librarian

From a recruiter's perspective, it is important to select the candidates for interviews that already have demonstrated that they can meet the preferred qualifications for the job. It does not mean that one will not get hired if one has not previously published articles or presented at conferences. Professional experience is far more important. However, there is a greater chance of landing an interview and being offered a tenure-track librarian position for those who have previously published work, presented at conferences, or have an additional master's degree or a Ph.D. Publishing non-peer-reviewed articles like book reviews, conference reporting, and magazine or website articles is a great way to show a hiring committee that a candidate has the potential to succeed as a scholarly researcher. This can make it easier for one who is in the early stages of a job search to get interview offers. A goal of publishing at least one article, if not several, before applying for a tenure-track librarian position is easier to accomplish than one may think.

Taking the right courses in college is important to prepare for scholarly research. Quantitative and qualitative research methods and data analysis courses as part of bachelor and master's degree programs are highly recommended. Because these courses are not always required as part of a master's degree in library science program, a second master's degree or a Ph.D. that emphasizes research can really boost one's confidence and abilities in research and writing. Although a second master's degree or Ph.D. is not required for all tenure-track librarian positions, many tenure-track positions list it as a preferred qualification. A degree that provides an opportunity to do further library science research and improve understanding of quantitative and qualitative analysis can help successfully meet the scholarly research requirement for tenure. For example, degrees such as a MS in Management or Public Administration can help complete research assignments that are focused on library management, instead of just business management like an MBA.

Think of class assignments as more than just assignments, but rather as an opportunity to conduct original research that can be published. The essays may need to be later edited for publication, but changing how one thinks of an assignment will help meet the goal of publishing articles in journals. Case studies that are frequently assigned in library science courses may include site visits to local libraries, interviewing directors, and conducting original research. During this process, try to discover something challenging for the libraries, or innovative and successful about these libraries that deserves to be highlighted. Perhaps this assignment can be edited later or provide inspiration for a shorter article which can be submitted for publication. Collection Development and Reader's Advisory course assignments can easily be edited for publication in "The Reader's Shelf" column of *Library Journal*, or the "Alert Collector" column of *Reference and User Services Quarterly*. These are not peer-reviewed columns but submitting an article to these columns is a great way to publish for the first time, enhance one's resume, and gain experience working with an editor.

Take advantage of the time in an additional degree program to complete assignments in a manner that is focused on libraries. An assignment to do original research on management, for example, may be completed by conducting a survey of librarians on a management topic. Even a shorter essay assignment may be completed by answering it in a manner that applies to library science. Doing so will make research more relevant to one's career goals. Whether you follow proper research methods for writing a thesis or write a short response for a final exam essay, if you approach an assignment from the perspective of creating potentially publishable work, you will be able to publish at least one essay associated with your courses. Interdisciplinary research about librarianship coming from non-library-related degrees can be unique, desirable for publication, and may be impactful on future library leaders.

If an additional degree is not possible or desired, here are several continuing education options that are more affordable. These programs address the subject of research methods and data analysis in different ways. Some are geared towards librarians and others are general research methods courses.

1. Institute for Research Design in Librarianship (http://irdlonline.org). This is a week-long summer workshop in Los Angeles, CA, that includes additional virtual monthly meetings with a mentor for a year. The workshop covers all stages of designing a library science research project.
2. Library Research Round Table Mentorship Program of the American Library Association (http://www.ala.org/rt/lrrt/initiatives). This is a two-year mentorship program that pairs an experienced researcher with a librarian who would like to develop strong research skills. The program requires face to face meetings at ALA conferences and virtual communication. Participants present their research at ALA conferences.
3. "Your Research Coach" Program of the College Libraries Section of the Association of College & Research Libraries (http://www.ala.org/acrl/aboutacrl/directoryofleadership/sections/cls/clswebsite/collprogdisc/researchcoach). This program pairs an experienced researcher who has published articles and/or presented research at conferences with a person

who would like advice, support, and suggestions to improve the quality of research and scholarly projects. Communication is done via e-mail, telephone, or in person.

4. Library Juice Academy (https://www.libraryjuiceacademy.com). This program offers online courses on statistics, evaluating service quality, and patron surveys.

5. Free online courses from sites like Coursera (https://www.coursera.org) or edX (https://www.edx.org). Both sites offer courses on research methods, data analysis, and statistics that are relevant to the social sciences.

Tips for Generating Research Ideas

It is totally normal to have moments when you cannot think of a unique idea to write about or research, especially when it is not a specific and structured assignment from a professor. Once you graduated from college, it is normal to experience a writer's block. The good news is that even if it seems like everything has already been written about a certain topic, there still may be some part of it that deserves to be researched and reported on. Reviewing previous research is always the best way to start a new project.

A great time to think about publishing articles is after graduation and during a job hunt. Completed assignments are still fresh in your memory at this time. Start with the topics that are most familiar by reviewing previously completed academic assignments from a similar perspective as the previous section described. Case study assignments are great ways to uncover the challenges that librarians face for the purpose of pursuing further scholarly research. Here are some prompts for discovering research possibilities within previously completed assignments:

1. Make note of topics that were the most interesting to you.
2. Did any topic make you wish you had more time for studying it?
3. Did a topic, librarian, or library inspire you, and why?
4. Did any completed case studies report on challenges or problems that librarians or libraries experienced? Did they solve these problems, or do you have a suggested solution?
5. Did any completed case studies report on any innovative library practices?
6. Did you discover challenges, problems, experience successful problem solving, or witness innovative programming while on the job, as an intern, staff member, or volunteer?

When you start a new job or become a new member of a committee, fresh opportunities for research ideas will become apparent. Networking with coworkers and committee members to discuss their previously published work, discovering the strong writers, and discussing mutual interests can help find cowriters to work with. You do not always have to be the one burdened with generating new ideas. It is great to have a combination of solo and joint projects on your CV. If you are unsure of your next steps, announce that you are looking to co-write articles with others. Your coworkers may have ideas for projects that you can participate in while someone else is the lead investigator. Here are some prompts for discussion with your coworkers:

1. Can you send me a list of articles that you have published?
2. Are you currently working on any scholarly research projects?
3. Does anyone have future research plans that could benefit from a cowriter?
4. Have there been any challenges or problems that the department, library, or employees have experienced?
5. What have they done to solve these problems? If they are unsolved, what is needed to solve these problems?
6. Has the library, department, or employees done anything innovative or noteworthy?
7. Will any employees allow you to do informational interviews with them to discuss research interests and on the job experiences?

The idea of writing at least one article per year until tenure may seem a bit daunting. However, it can be accomplished. Brainstorming additional research topics by breaking down a general topic into subtopics can be helpful. For example, management includes many subfields, like human resource management, strategic management, and financial management. Human resource management includes subfields like staffing, compensation and benefits, strategic human resource planning, and employee law. Strategic management is reflected in strategic plans, decision making, and problem solving. Some of these topics can affect library departments differently. If the idea for researching a subfield came first, then brainstorm ideas of broader, narrower, and related topics. One research interest can easily turn into five to ten years or more worth of scholarly research. Each of these ideas could even lead to multiple articles.

Reading previously published research is very insightful when a topic has been published on frequently. Not only could it lead one to a publishable literature review on a topic, it can uncover gaps in research. Subtopics could be studied, or research designs could be improved on. When reviewing previously published research, make note of the following issues:

1. What were the results of studies and what do you think of the outcome?
2. How many studies can you find on a specific topic? If there are not many, would that topic warrant further research?
3. Did the research design seem flawed? If so, how would you improve it?
4. Did the author suggest that more research would be warranted on a specific topic?
5. Can I think of any additional solutions to a problem?
6. Should a subtopic of a previously published study be researched?
7. Did the research seem outdated?
8. Should the study be repeated at this institution to compare the results of previous studies to a new study?

If all else fails, and there is still a need for a new theme, skim through whole issues of a journal to discover a new and interesting topic. Try examining the articles of a journal that you have not spent time reading yet. There are multiple journals on every general topic of librarianship, in addition to interdisciplinary journals, and open access journals. While reading through a new journal, ask yourself the previous questions to generate new ideas. Skimming through unfamiliar journals may lead you to discover new research designs that could inspire future studies.

Following *A Library Writer's Blog* (http://librarywriting.blogspot.com) and list-servs for calls for papers and presentations can also help bring all of these ideas to fruition. If you have not decided on the best outlet for an idea, calls for papers may present the proper source. Consider a literature review, a survey, a case study of your own library, book review, or a how-to essay when perusing calls for papers and presentations that provide a diverse number of opportunities for publications and conferences to attend. You will assuredly not run out of opportunities or ideas by following these steps. The proper research design will become apparent as you become familiar with previously published studies. Ideas can be adapted to fit the needs of the different publications.

If you are unsure of the quality of an article, don't be afraid of being rejected. Rejection is bound to happen to everyone. It is an important learning experience. Rejection can happen because an article is not the right style for the publication, or because there are too many issues that need to be corrected before it can be published. When rejection occurs, it is important to ask the editor for feedback so that the article can be improved and resubmitted. Taking the time to revise the article and resubmit it will greatly improve your writing and increase your chances of getting published. If an article is rejected because it does not fit the style of the publication, send your writing to a different one. Don't give up. With enough patience and persistence, success is possible.

How to Enhance the Library Science Curriculum

Since most students do not come to class thinking that they should strive to publish articles related to their assignments, library science professors should actively help prepare students for tenure-track librarian positions by encouraging students to publish. By doing so, a professor can make the theory behind librarianship more practical. The curriculum can be easily altered to include assignments in the style of articles that can be published in journals. In some classes, students are required to read a number of trade magazine articles, websites, and academic journal articles each week. Instead of this, students can be assigned to read different styles of relevant articles, such as book reviews, published case studies, results of surveys, literature reviews, and bibliographies. The students could be given assignments to write in different styles.

Instead of just assigning a case study of a library, the students can be assigned to write about a library in the style of an article that could be published in a trade magazine like *Library Journal* or *American Libraries,* or an article on a case study in an academic journal, like *Public Library Quarterly.* As previously mentioned, collection development and reader's advisory course assignments can easily be altered to include an essay in the style of a publishable book review or bibliography of varying lengths. The students should be encouraged to include books in the assignment that have not been covered in a column recently so they have a greater chance of being published. Theoretical studies can include assignments to write literature reviews. Literature reviews can be submitted for publication in peer-reviewed journals, including *The Journal of Librarianship and Scholarly Communication.* By slightly altering an assignment to encourage students to write essays in the style of publishable articles, library science professors will be helping the students take an important step towards reaching a goal of becoming a tenure-track librarian. If they can have the experience of publishing articles before graduating, the students will be more likely to be hired for positions that require scholarly research and be more likely to succeed in meeting the requirement to publish peer-reviewed articles.

Conclusion

Even if the idea of accepting a job that requires scholarly research seems too stressful and undesirable, taking the time to prepare for a tenure-track position will be worth it in the end. Being a successful researcher is fulfilling by itself, but publishing research will be beneficial for all librarians and future library students. Although research methods and publishing are not always emphasized in the classroom, it is not too late to take a continuing education course or revisit old assignments for inspiration. You may find that an old assignment can inspire you to write an article, or a professor may find that an assignment can be rewritten to introduce a publishable style of writing to the students. There are many options for librarians to publish different styles of writing in order to gain the necessary experience for a lifetime of scholarly research.

The Writerly Librarian

Creativity and Writing

ADDISON LUCCHI

Librarians may not consider themselves to be writers. Just because we are surrounded by books, does not mean we write them. Regardless, writing of some form is an essential aspect of most or all librarians' daily responsibilities. Some types of writing are not practiced by all librarians—for example, academic librarians are more apt to participate in scholarly research. There are other types of writing that are more common in the library universe. Librarians often write grant proposals. Routinely, librarians have to write event summaries or reports. At the very least, we communicate information through writing—it is one of the primary ways we share our ideas (Smallwood 2010, ix). This essay looks specifically at some of the primary types of writing that librarians engage in—including scholarly research, grant writing, and daily written communication. Even if you do not regularly participate in one or more of these forms of writing, the hope is that through this essay, you will learn how each of these areas of writing is creative—and thus can help you grow creatively as a librarian.

On Creativity

Creativity is inherent to the library profession. Every day, we create in one form or another—whether creating new bibliographic records, lesson plans, library programs, or new research. To be innovative in our work, it is necessary to create new things and new ideas rather than simply copy what has already been done. To be effective in our work, it is necessary to create new methods of applying what has already been done in a way that fits our institutions' specific contexts and information needs.

It is helpful to be intentional about practicing creativity in our work. Developing new procedures to be more effective in ILL, experimenting with new teaching strategies, or planning a new library event are among the ways to practice creativity as librarians. Sometimes being creative means trying something new; sometimes it means refreshing and invigorating the work that we already do. Being creative in our work means not only caring about the work we do, but also how we do it.

Defining Writing

Writing is one outlet through which we can express our creativity as librarians. Let us explore the general definitions of three types of writing—professional, academic, and creative. These are often seen as entirely separate and unrelated. In many ways, this distinction is sensible. While academic and professional writing communicate facts and information, creative writing is generally fictionalized and is written to entertain. However, while there is certainly a difference between writing facts and writing fiction, neither form is more or less creative than the other—each simply has its own goals and standards.

Academic Writing

We are likely all familiar with academic writing. Academic writing encompasses college essays, scholarly journals, and some non-fiction books. Academic writing typically involves a great deal of research—finding, evaluating, analyzing, and synthesizing appropriate sources are essential components of academic writing. Academic writing is:

- factual and objective
- research-based or data-driven
- written in a formal tone
- well-organized

While there are certainly exceptions to these rules, these are some traits that generally describe academic writing. Pursuing academic writing can be beneficial to librarians in the following ways:

- increase knowledge on a specific topic
- enhance research skills
- provide opportunity for networking and scholarly communication
- improve resume or CV development

While not all librarians have a requirement to publish research or write academically, it can be a highly rewarding experience for any librarian. Writing academically has been an avenue for me and many of my colleagues to determine the areas of research which we were most interested in pursuing. Often, it is through the process of writing that we realize our full passions and specific interests within our profession.

Professional Writing

Professional writing is meant to complete daily tasks within our profession. It involves writing persuasively, producing cogent arguments, and making appropriate responses in professional situations. The realm of professional writing for librarians often includes creating:

- grant narratives
- reports
- LibGuides, library websites, and library newsletters

Professional writing is, thus, the most common daily writing task for librarians. Because professional writing is often mundane, it is regularly styled in a way that is dry and unexpressive. However, because of the ubiquity of professional writing in our day-to-day lives, it is the most essential aspect of our writing to imbue with creativity. Doing so will allow our grant proposals to be more successful, our reports to be more engaging, and our LibGuide descriptions to be more accessible and appealing to users.

Creative Writing

Creative writing is the type of writing most commonly seen as a form of artistic expression, drawing on imagination to convey meaning. Poetry, fiction, scripts, and screenplays all fall into the realm of creative writing. Creative writing is often:

- artistic
- original
- comprised primary of fiction, or fictionalized accounts of true happenings.

Naturally, most of our writing time will be spent on activities related to our work; thus, those activities will tend to fall into the academic or professional writing categories. However, it can still be beneficial to pursue writing on non-librarian topics. Creative writing can positively impact our librarian careers through:

- a better understanding of a "story" that can inform our library instruction
- the ability to make mundane topics compelling
- enhanced grant writing through storytelling

When we engage in creative writing as librarians, we open our minds to a whole new realm of creative expression. Writing fiction or poetry forces us to use parts of our brain that are not fully accessed in other types of writing. Additionally, spending time writing fiction or poetry can be an excellent way to practice eloquence as a wordsmith without the pressures of writing for work or the duty of accurately portraying facts. Whenever I return to academic or professional writing after some time writing fiction or poetry, I feel a greater inspiration to write and a greater sense of maturity as a writer.

Connections Between Modes

Even though each of these modes of writing has its own separate goals and standards, all three are interconnected and creative. Merriam-Webster defines creativity as "the ability or power to create"; it defines "create" as "to bring into existence" or "to produce through imaginative skill" (2017a; 2017b). When we write academically and professionally, we are bringing new material into existence through our imaginative skill in the same way as we would if writing fiction.

Why Write?

Writing should be essential for librarians. Through writing, we solidify our ideas and begin to reshape our unique understanding of our profession. Every librarian has a unique voice within the wider librarian community; often, it is through writing that those unique voices are found. Writing can help librarians to:

- solidify research interests
- express and develop innovative ideas
- develop their independent voices as librarians, teachers, and creators

I often draw on personal experiences and knowledge gained through the practice of research and writing to assist patrons in reference inquiries and reader's advisory. Writing forces us to be organized, and to be more precise and adept communicators; this has impacted my teaching, presenting, and daily interactions with colleagues and patrons. Writing can even teach us empathy for others, especially towards those who write. When we share our knowledge, experiences, ideas, thoughts, and feelings in a written format, it impacts us personally and professionally. Through engaging in the act of writing, we can become more creative in both our personal and professional lives.

Writing Well as Librarians

While writing is an essential part of most librarians' responsibilities, it is not a skill that is regularly taught and developed in library school. There, we write essays, research assignments, and practice writing grant proposals. What we are not taught, is how to write well. The result? Many published library research articles are dry and lacking in creativity. Many grant proposals are denied because they fail to touch an emotional chord, even though they include all necessary pieces of information. Many web pages, monthly reports, and even emails are never read in their entirety. How do we solve this problem?

First of all, it is important to know the mechanics of writing well. William Zinsser's book *On Writing Well* (2006), as well as numerous other books and articles, have already been written on this topic. However, I will share one specific strategy here: in order to write well, it is necessary to write succinctly. Regardless of the purpose and style of writing, we want our words to matter. We want our writing to be accessible to readers. We want it actually be read. To accomplish these goals, librarians should employ precision in their writing. Short sentences are often the best sentences.

To write well, we also need to be able to write professional and academic material that is creative. We can achieve that through diligent, methodical practice. It will produce better writing that attracts more readers and let us grow in our profession. Writing is experimentation. Writing is exploration. Writing engages our full beings; it integrates our hearts and minds, our ideas and facts, our professional and personal lives. Writing involves deep reflection and imagination. It allows us to think in new ways, ways we never would have thought of if not for the process of gathering our thoughts to write down. The act of writing is essential to reaching our full potential as professionals.

Making Our Writing Creative

While developing creativity in our writing takes time and practice, there are certain strategies that can help us make our academic and professional writing more creative.

Let us discuss writing creative scholarly papers. The scholarly paper is a research-heavy paper based on an author's original theory or ideas. It is written by an expert in a specific field, for an audience of peers in that field. But even though scholarly papers are research-heavy and targeted at other scholars (in our case, other librarians), they can still be written in a way that is compelling and interesting. Good writing is good writing; the same rules apply to scholarly writing as to other forms. When I suggest that scholarly articles should be creative, I am not implying that they do not need to follow appropriate structure and standards. Standards are important. However, to resonate with readers of our scholarly work, we also must tap into our creativity. While utilizing appropriate structure (an abstract, literature review, methods and results sections, and conclusion) is necessary to get accepted into most journals, an article will never reach its full capacity if it is not written with genuine curiosity and enthusiasm. How we write matters as much as what we write.

An example of creative academic writing is *How the How: The Question of Form in Writing Creative Scholarly Works* by Francesca Rendle-Short (2015). I would encourage you to read this entire article, as it is excellent both in content and style. This article, though scholarly and published in a peer-reviewed journal, is engaging, interesting, and innovative in its structure. The author employs vivid imagery, appropriate humor, and poetic subheadings. At several points, she even incorporates small pieces of original poetry within the text of the article. This creativity contributes meaningfully to the content of the article, which specifically discusses the idea of writing creative scholarly works. Also, these creative elements work to pull the reader into the article and make the content enjoyable for its own sake. Ideally, all academic writing should be engaging and enjoyable like this, due to the content it communicates as well as to way it is written. With a virtually endless number of potential articles to read on nearly any subject, it is increasingly important to write academic material that stands out creatively.

In academic writing, our greatest asset is our non-professional experience. As librarians, we all have an MLS or MLIS, so we all have a similar educational foundation. What distinguishes us from the crowd, is the rest of our lives. It is important to pursue the craft of writing well and seek opportunities to grow and develop writing skills. However, we should recognize that our unique backgrounds and ways of viewing our profession are our most valuable assets. It is when we draw from these unique backgrounds that we reach our greatest creative potential. It is not possible to create (bring into existence) something that already exists. Thus, it is essential that we bring something new to the table. When we write about our work, we are doing more than sharing our ideas with others. We are also shaping our own thoughts on a topic, and we are expanding our creative abilities. As we determine how to express our thoughts with written words, we unleash our creativity (Rendle-Short 2015, 92).

Through writing this essay, I am demonstrating this very idea. My personal background is in creative writing, and I have recognized the power of connecting this interest to my career as a librarian. My personal interest in creative writing influences what I write about as a librarian. It also influenced my other professional activities: I have presented at creative writing conferences, led a poetry reading event, and started a writer's group through my institution. All it took was recognizing the fact that I am most successful as a librarian when I also draw upon my non-librarian interests and experiences.

Even a process as tedious as writing grant proposals can become a creative expression. When writing grants, we need to share precise information and do so in a way that appeals to our readers' emotions. Good storytelling is at the heart of a good grant proposal. While all of the facts need to be in place, and the guidelines of the grant proposal followed to a tee, our proposals should be sprinkled with true stories. In "Storytelling for Grantseekers," Cheryl Clarke compares writing grants to writing stories in much detail (2009). Clarke provides thorough advice on how to enliven grants with stories by creating hooks and conflict, appealing to emotions, and describing people and places so that they can be clearly imagined by funders. She also cites examples of stories leading to successfully funded grants, and she quotes a former chair whose corporation donates more than a quarter of a million dollars a year to charities: "We'd love to see more proposals presented as stories. Those that do are easier to read and understand, and they are the ones that are more apt to be funded" (Clarke 2009, 2).

Stories enliven grant proposals. We can use stories to tell the specific reasons for our soliciting of grant money. We can use stories to share the innovative ways the funds will be used. We can use our own personal stories to communicate why a grant topic is important to us, and why it is important to our institution. It is helpful to remember that the reviewers of grant proposals are people; they can be persuaded with both facts and with stories. When we include both an emotional appeal and sound data in our grant proposals, we have the greatest chance of creating products that stand out amongst the others. Thus, we have the greatest chance of succeeding in our grant-writing efforts.

Every day, we write. Thus, every day is an opportunity to practice creativity. Even if you never write a grant proposal, or an academic article, or a work of fiction, you can still write creatively in your day-to-day work as a librarian. The tedium of monthly reports can be enlivened with stories and humor. The information presented in a LibGuide or library webpage can be creatively written and displayed. Our work-related emails can serve as expressions of our unique personalities and creative spirits. The potential ways for creativity to empower our daily work-related writing are truly endless.

Practical Steps to Becoming a Writerly Librarian

Regardless of your specific library position or setting, these tips will strengthen your skill as a writer-librarian.

Practice telling stories. Use stories to back up data in your reports and grant proposals. Include stories to make your instruction or presentations more effective. Facts capture minds, but stories capture hearts—endeavor to capture both. Whenever possible, I try to start my information literacy instruction sessions with a story. These stories are usually short and simple, but I use them to capture students' attention and connect them to what I am teaching. For example, I like to tell my experience entering Nebraska Furniture Mart for the very first time. I did not know how to navigate the store effectively to find the items I needed, due to its general enormity. When an employee noticed my confusion and handed me a map, I quickly and effectively found what I was looking for. After telling my story (and usually generating some nods of understanding from students), I relate it back to research by asserting that navigating databases and the internet is often like my experience at Nebraska Furniture Mart. Once we have a map of where to go and how to find the information we need, life becomes much easier. I then proceed to tell the students that I will be providing them a "map" during the remainder of the session to guide them during their research. This is just one example of how to use stories to enliven your work as a librarian. The possibilities are truly endless.

Read a wide variety of materials. While reading articles and books related to your work is vital, it is also important to expose yourself to viewpoints and styles that you may not be as comfortable or familiar with. Read articles from the perspectives of other disciplines. Examine scholarly sources, news articles, books, and informal blog posts. Peruse fiction and poetry. Writing creatively involves the integration and assimilation of a wide spectrum of ideas, angles, and thoughts. When I teach research as a librarian, I discuss the value of using multiple sources from a variety of perspectives. Using a diverse collection of sources and perspectives to inform a research project significantly enhances it. One source may add data, the second one—an emotional appeal, and the third may localize the research to a specific place. When these perspectives are combined, something new and interesting is created. In the same way, reading from a variety of perspectives and source types will add to and even change the way you think and help your writing become even more interesting, innovative, and creative.

Write regularly and widely. To become a good writer, you must write. The more avenues you can find for growing in your writing, the better. In addition to your work-related writing, consider starting a personal blog or experimenting with writing fiction or poetry. Two previous colleagues of mine, Jessica Williams and Danielle Wellemeyer, started a blog called The Roughly Right Way (http://theroughlyrightway.com), which is a blog discussing everything from librarianship, to career development, to favorite podcasts. This is an excellent example of a blog that fully integrates professionalism and creativity. I also actively manage my own blog, where I write regular posts not necessarily related to my work. My focus with this blog is more on my personal interests, philosophical thoughts, and original poetry. This writing, while informal, helps me grow as a writer in my academic and professional pursuits.

By pursuing these steps, you will grow as a writer, as a creative being, and as a librarian. Remember that growing in writing is a constant process for everyone; if you have not written much in a while, do not be discouraged. Anyone can become a better writer with time and practice.

Conclusion

If we are to be creative librarians, we must also be creative writers; not that we must write stories or poems or screenplays, but that we must write creatively. Every mode of writing involves choosing precise words to place on a page in specific ways. In addition to clarity, factuality, cohesiveness, and concision, our goals should also be creativity, artistry, and beauty. We must remember that the words we write (in a journal article, in a grant proposal, in our daily work) are being read by real people. These real people can be moved by beauty and artistry as much as by facts and clarity. To reach our highest potential as writer-librarians, we should write in a way that allows these two "sides" of writing to fully coalesce.

REFERENCES

Clarcke, Cheryl. 2009. *Storytelling for Grantseekers.* San Francisco: Jossey-Bass.
Merriam-Webster. 2017a. "Create." Accessed November 1. https://www.merriam-webster.com/dictionary/create.
Merriam-Webster. 2017b. "Creativity." Accessed November 1. https://www.merriamwebster.com/dictionary/creative.

Rendle-Short, Francesca. 2015. "How the How: The Question of Form in Writing Creative Scholarly Works." *New Writing: International Journal for the Practice and Theory of Creative Writing*. 12 (1): 91–100. doi: 10.1080/14790726.2014.983526.

Smallwood, Carol. 2010. *Writing and Publishing: The Librarian's Handbook*. Chicago: American Library Association.

Zinsser, William. 2006. *On Writing Well; The Classic Guide to Writing Nonfiction*. New York: HarperCollins.

The Process of Research
and Publication
as a Tool for Personal
and Professional Growth

Astrid Oliver

The process of research and writing in the field of librarianship enables library staff and librarians to engage with their peers on a different level than through the day-to-day tasks in which we are typically involved. In the act of performing research, you are able to discover the work that's been done and what the most current thinking is on any particular subject—something that might not normally happen in the everyday functioning of your job. By engaging on a larger scale with subjects that interest you, looking at a topic from a broader, more comprehensive perspective, you will gain insight into and more experience with the practice of librarianship that you may not otherwise have had the opportunity to develop.

The act of publication is, in fact, a contribution to the literature of the field. Publishers, particularly of peer-reviewed journals, will not print something that does not advance knowledge in some way. Contributing to the literature of the field is an act of creating original knowledge. It will not only enhance and deepen your own understanding of the practice of librarianship but will also serve to advance the knowledge of others who are interested in the same things you are.

The process of creating original knowledge may not be as difficult as you think. Chances are that in the day-to-day activities of your work you wonder about things—how things might work better or differently; have a new idea you'd like to develop; or have a question you'd like the answer to but haven't been able find. These kinds of thoughts are doorways to the research, writing, and publication process. Once you decide to answer your question, develop a new idea, or create a new process to make something work better, you've also created an opportunity to write about it and share it with others through publication.

Take the following steps to turn the inception of an idea into an article ready for submission.

Select an Area for Research

What have you been spending the majority of your time doing in the past year? Have you been working on any special projects? If you have spent significant time performing or thinking about an activity, this would be the area in which you would target your research. By conducting research closely related to the work you are already doing, you have the advantage of familiarity with the subject on your side. Ask yourself: *How can I frame what I've been working on into a question that needs to be answered? What has already been done in this area and is there a gap that I can fill with new, original information? Can what I've been working on be considered a case study? Have I developed a new process? Would others benefit from the work I've done or the process I developed?* When you select an area of research that you are familiar with and in which you've already invested your time, particularly for case studies, you have performed a great deal of the work that needs to be completed in the research and writing process.

Illustration

When I worked in Access Services, library staff needed to find a way to automate the billing process as much as possible. We did not have the funds available to purchase an expensive billing module for our integrated library system (ILS). We put our heads together to determine a means to connect our ILS with campus administrative software to convey billing and fine information back and forth. Looking in the literature, we didn't find direct answers to our needs, but discovered ideas that could possibly be applied to our situation. Library staff met with the Information Technology department to develop the outline of the project. A new process was created using scripts to convey information between our Library's ILS and campus administrative software, allowing the automation of much of our billing process. After the project was completed, several library staff decided to write about the work we had accomplished and share it with others who might also find themselves in a similar situation. In other words—we used the work we had already performed to develop a case study that could potentially help others and contribute to the literature of the field.

Perform a Literature Review

Before you can present new findings, you must discover what is already known about the topic and determine if what you have to share would be a contribution. *Is this new knowledge? Are you filling a gap in the conversation or creating a niche in a subject area?* A literature review covers the most significant highlights over time of the work that's been performed regarding that topic. Performing a thorough literature review will give you an understanding of how your research or case study might fit in with or advance current knowledge. Depending on your interest, there could already have been a great deal of literature generated and it may be more difficult to produce information that adds new knowledge. If there is an overwhelming amount of literature about your pursuit, you might want to consider shifting your focus to a tangential area where you can better contribute. A literature review will help you identify gaps in knowledge that you could potentially fill.

Illustration

When my colleagues and I were developing the new procedure using scripts to connect the Library's ILS to campus administrative software, we found that not a lot had been written about this topic or of billing procedures in general. In identifying our needs we had also exposed a gap in the knowledge. Billing processes are something almost all libraries perform. This was an area ripe for generating original information that could be shared with others. For the literature review, we gathered subject-related articles to create the context in which our project came to be. We utilized articles pertaining to campus accounting, accounting interfaces, and library software. One writes a literature review to tell a story, establishing the context for the work you are preparing to do. The best way to write a literature review is to read the literature reviews of other articles and model yours after them. You can even use the literature review of a previous publication and build on that to create your own.

Construct the Framework of Your Research

What is it you propose to do? Do you want to query a particular population to find the answer to a question? Do you want to develop a new process for performing some kind of work and determine how successful it is? Think about how to best use the work you've been doing in your library and reframe it into a question that can be answered or a process that can be shared. The framework of your research will define itself based on your intentions.

Illustration

Recently I realized that there has been a great deal of discussion in the literature about non–MLS-holders holding professional positions in libraries. Researchers had looked at the topic from demographic points of view and job function perspectives, but I didn't see any information derived directly from non–MLS job holders. This looked like a good opportunity for research and discovery. A colleague and I made a plan to query job holders in libraries, particularly academic libraries, performing professional-level work who did not have a graduate degree in library science. We devised several questions based on what had been discussed in previously published literature. Creating questions that refer back to prior data allows the researcher to compare and contrast new data with established information, enabling him or her to confirm trends or demonstrate deviation. We also formulated a variety of other questions to capture new information that could only come directly from non–MLS job holders and as such had no counterparts in the prior literature. An example of these types of questions were whether or not they intended to obtain a library science degree in the future, or not, and why. To get the answers to the questions we had, we determined that the framework of a survey was the best tool to use.

Perform Research and Collect Data

Perform the work that needs to be done to collect the information you need: send out the survey to your target population, develop your new work process with your partners or stakeholders, or implement whatever new project procedures you have developed.

Illustration

When my colleague and I decided to survey non–MLS-holding professionals working in academic libraries, we had to determine how best to reach them. Because we were interested in academic libraries in particular, we targeted American Library Association (ALA) and Association of College and Research Libraries (ACRL) academic library listservs. We distributed our survey on all applicable academic library listservs. The online survey tool we used stored the survey responses for later inspection.

If you are developing a new process or procedure, it is important to document in detail the steps you took from beginning to end. You will need this documentation later to describe your methodology and progression.

Organize Your Results

What does the data tell you? Organize your raw data and start looking for meaning.

Illustration

With our survey of non–MLS-holding academic library professionals, there was a lot of raw data that needed to be organized and categorized. Demographic information gathered such as age and length of time in academic libraries had to be grouped in ways that could be used for analysis. As an example, for age, we put responses into groups used in prior literature, such as 25 or younger, 26–30, 31–35, and so on. For length of time in academic libraries, we also followed previous practice; we grouped the data into groups of 5 years or less, 6–10 years, 11–15 years and so on to make the results comparable with previously published information. Organizing the data in the same manner as previously published literature allows comparisons between data sets that highlight similarities and differences in results.

For case studies, review your documentation to ensure all steps are in logical order and detailed enough to be followed by someone who has little knowledge of the subject area. Writing out proper procedure allows a means to assess the level of success of each step in the process.

Analyze Your Data

You've performed your research, recorded and categorized your data. It's time to analyze the results. Do you see trends emerging from the data? Do your results agree with or refute what you found in prior literature? Was the process you developed successful, or did unexpected problems or challenges arise? Explain in detail what you determine is the meaning of your collected information.

Illustration

In case studies, an analysis often means determining the level of success of your efforts. Several years ago, I met with an Art Department faculty member to develop a Library student art competition in partnership with the Art & Design department. We developed a process for the competition, a timeline for applicants, a rubric for scoring proposals and other documentation. We conducted our first annual student art competition. The Library received multiple proposals and a winning proposal was chosen and funded. Library and Art Department staff were pleased with the results and an artwork was created and installed in the Library. After the competition concluded, stakeholders discussed what worked well and what could use improvement. We measured the degree of success by the usability of the documents created for a student to complete a proposal and for judges to score proposals; we also measured success by the ease with which procedures were able to be followed by both student applicants and administrative staff. Based on user experience, we found that some documents and processes could be improved with minor modifications, and included this analysis in our conclusion.

In research, analyzing data means drawing meaning from the findings and discussing them. In the case of our survey of non-degree holding library professionals, we compared some of the data to earlier findings: Did our data confirm earlier literature stating that younger age groups tend to hold positions hired without the MLS? (Yes); is the cost of obtaining the MLS a major factor for those who have chosen not to pursue an MLS? (Yes); is there a trend for particular job titles not to require an MLS? (Maybe). Beyond grouping the data in ways that make sense, you need to go one step further to identify the meaning of the data.

Develop Conclusions

Based on the literature in the field, and based on what you discovered in your research and data analysis, at what conclusions did you arrive? Is your newly developed process successful and appropriate to share? Does the data collected from your research indicate a change in trends? Does your investigation provide information that can be replicated in some way? Does more research need to be performed to dig deeper into something you discovered? Discuss what you think is the end result of the work you've performed.

Illustration

In the case study concerning the development of a new process to automate the Library's billing process, the IT department was able to successfully write a number of scripts to connect campus administrative software to the Library's ILS. We were able to share these scripts for others to modify and apply, and also shared the limitations of what we had accomplished.

For the survey directed at non–MLS-holding academic library professionals, we were able to confirm and/or question certain prior trends identified in the literature as well as identify current intentions and attitudes of non–MLS job holders to better understand how academic libraries are changing and in what ways employment gaps are being filled. We concluded that additional work can be continued by investigating the attitudes and thoughts of library leaders who develop job descriptions and make hiring decisions.

In the case of the student art competition, we were able to supply documentation for others to adapt and modify, determine measures for success, identify sticking points that needed improvement prior to another competition cycle and provide recommendations based on our experience.

Write It All Down

You've conducted a literature review, developed your idea, performed your research, collected your data, and documented and analyzed your results. It is time to write it all down and format it for publication. You may find that you will write pieces of the future article as your work is progressing. You don't need to wait for the entirety of the project to be completed to begin the writing process. Format your piece to agree with the general format of a research article:

   a. *Introduction.* What is your article about? Describe what was examined and what questions have been answered. What prompted you to perform this work? What did you hope to achieve in performing this research?
   b. *Literature Review.* Put your findings together in a narrative that makes sense, either thematically or along a timeline. Write about what you have discovered in the literature—what are the most important or interesting pieces of information? Arrange your narrative in a way that best makes sense to you and complements the theme of your article.
   c. *Process or Methodology.* How did you perform your research? What did you do? Explain your process here. Often, the survey or other documentation is attached at the end of the article as an appendix.
   d. *Data Analysis/Discussion.* Provide the results of your research. Deliver the organized data and explain the meaning of the results. What are your findings?
   e. *Conclusion.* Based on your findings and analysis, identify your conclusions and tie them back to your original intentions as stated in your introduction to make sure you've come full circle in the research process.

Review and Edit Your Work

Read and re-read your work. Make your work as error-free, clear and concise as possible. Review your work several times to give yourself the opportunity to edit. Have someone else read your work and provide suggestions and comments. Make any changes needed and then read your article again. Put it away for a week and then review it again for style and clarity.

Submit Your Article

You do not need a publishing agreement before performing research and writing an article. Go ahead and do it. Then, find the journal in which you think it would be a good fit and submit it.

How do you find appropriate journals to which to submit your article? You can easily Google it. Perform searches such as: *library journals, or peer reviewed library journals,* or *professional library journals*. Wikipedia maintains a list of library science journals for scholarly work and library science magazines for non-peer-reviewed publications. Look at the scope and description of the journals whose titles interest you. Review the content of the articles published in the journal to see if your article would fit in.

Identify a few journal titles whose scope fits the content of your article. Prioritize the journals as to which you will submit to first, then second, and third. Each journal will have its own submission guidelines on their site. Find them and follow them precisely, including formatting the paper in the required style. When you submit an article for consideration, you cannot submit it to any other publication until you hear back from the publisher to which it is already submitted. You can only submit to one publisher at a time. It can take from several weeks to several months to hear back from them.

Through hard work and preparation, your article is accepted! You may need to re-edit the article based on an editor's suggestions or a peer-reviewer's comments. If you are submitting an article to a scholarly journal, do not be daunted by the peer-review process. Peer-review is a time-honored method that serves to strengthen your piece and ensure high quality literature.

Once the final edits are done, congratulations! You will soon be a published author. Your professional cachet will be enriched with publication. Even better, you have contributed to the literature of the field and enhanced and deepened your personal knowledge of a subject area about which you care and in which you are invested. You have initiated and actively participated in a growth process, both professionally and personally. These are skills you can take with you wherever you go in the future.

PART V

Innovative Business Practices

Small Steps, Big Impact

Professional and Personal Growth and Development

Robin R. Breault,
Brooke McDonald Shelton *and*
James Ritter

The rise of the industrial era brought a major shift in the way we work and live. Technological and structural changes to the way we organized labor and learning shifted the very nature of institutional and individual lives. Institutions were designed in the vein of mechanical systems, which by nature are fixed and bureaucratic rather than responsive. Individually, less than 40 percent of the workforce is engaged at work, (Gallup 2017) yet workers are expected to be more productive, efficient, and responsive than ever before.

Today, organizations are changing and redefining how employees connect and engage within their organizations and with their community. Concepts of embeddedness, openness, and connectedness have given way to the traditional transactional and industrial-based systems model, and this requires that the librarian is aware and cognizant of more than what's on the shelves—library services must meet the needs of its community. This shift also requires the library—as an organization—to provide the platform for library employees to adapt as they strive to meet these needs. To do this, the organization must develop personal leadership at all levels by supporting creative exploration, embracing community connections and relationship building, and prioritizing equity and social justice.

To this end, we present a framework to support the professional growth and leadership of library staff. This framework highlights four strategies for personal and professional development:

- *Develop personal leadership.* Create opportunities for staff to practice and develop skills that promote both personal and organizational growth.
- *Support creative exploration.* Establish an organizational mindset that supports staff participation in creative activities that feed innovation.
- *Embrace connectedness.* Foster a culture of boundary spanning where staff at all levels play a role in organizational growth through participation and developing relationships internally and externally.
- *Prioritize equity and inclusion.* Place social justice at the center of organizational culture, strategy, and decision-making.

This framework is rooted in theory and articulated through the experience of the library staff interviewed for this essay. Each section of the essay shares one strategy and brings it to life through the stories of staff who contributed their first-hand accounts of leadership and learning. With intent to capture staff across different levels and varying points in their careers, we conducted in-depth interviews with three individuals.

Meet Debbi. Debbi is a Library Associate at the Martha Cooper Library in Tucson, Arizona. Starting out as a volunteer with the "book bike," Debbi is an active member of the library and the greater community. With a knack for identifying needs and working alongside others to find creative solutions, Debbi describes herself as a helper and someone who helps make things happen from the sidelines. Most recently, Debbi helped launch Kindred, a group of like-minded library staff members who reach, support, and celebrate the Black community.

Meet Jennifer. Jennifer is the Digital Scholarship Librarian at the University of Arizona, and co-director of the UA Libraries' pilot makerspace, the iSpace. She collaborates with faculty and students to integrate digital scholarship tools into their research and teaching, and creates programming for campus and the larger community to support learning new tools and novel applications of technology. Jennifer is passionate about creating inclusive environments for learning, and connecting people to one another.

Meet Tim. Tim is a Library Support Specialist at Maine InfoNet, which is an organization that began in the late 1990's when the Maine State Library and the Fogler Library at the University of Maine created a partnership to help deliver library services through new and emerging library systems. With more than 25 years of library experience in an IT environment, Tim specializes in electronic resource and software management support, as well as management of authentication systems and library catalog systems available to libraries in Maine.

Develop Personal Leadership

The foundational strategy for promoting organizational learning is to provide the tools and resources for individuals at all levels to grow as self-directed professionals within the organization. Since libraries have taken a more traditional top-down approach to leadership, creating an environment that fosters personal leadership at all levels is a deliberate process that should be grounded in three components that manifest as both mindset and actions: Mix It Up, Eliminate Roadblocks, and Failure Is Learning.

Mix It Up

Organizations must purposefully seek to create environments for individuals that get them talking to, and learning from, one another. "Frans Johansson, author of *The Medici Effect*, described his finding—based on interviews with people doing highly creative work in many fields—that innovation is more likely when people of different disciplines, backgrounds, and areas of expertise share their thinking. Sometimes the complexity of a problem demands diversity..." (Amàbile and Khaire 2008, sec. Open the Organization, para. 1). Leaders and organizations benefit from processes that foster divergent thinking and problem solving, so ensuring that the right mix of people are tasked to help solve problems around identified needs is critical.

Eliminate Roadblocks

Get out of the way! At times, it's important for leaders to simply get out of the way and help ensure that processes are not constricting the natural flow of business. Finding ways to eliminate unneeded and burdensome bureaucracy is important. Managers, "must act as a shepherd … executives must protect those doing creative work from a hostile work environment and clear paths for them around obstacles" (Amabile and Khaire 2008, sec. Provide Paths, para. 2). Leaders must also recognize when it's wise for them to distance themselves from the process to gain perspective. Hearing fresh ideas, absent of the process, and allowing time to digest and ruminate upon those ideas allows leaders to grow in their own thinking and see the bigger picture.

Failure Is Learning

Easy to say, hard to accept—failure is part of the learning process and an individual's ability to grow professionally. Organizations that make it safe to fail and learn in small ways find that employees trust that it's okay to try new things. Empirical creativity allows individuals and organizations to test ideas on a smaller scale before they launch larger initiatives (Collins 2011, 23–27). If these smaller initiatives don't succeed, the impact to the organization is limited, but more importantly, individuals involved in the smaller initiatives are more informed when they attempt to try something different.

At the Library

The Maine State Library established a strategic initiative team to fully examine Maine's virtual content library called *MARVEL!*, and Tim was selected to chair the team with the full support of his manager and the leadership team of the Maine State Library.

Tim's team was intentionally designed to ensure that individuals from other libraries, other backgrounds, and other professional experiences could participate and embody the tenet of 'mixing it up.' To create autonomy and ownership, the State Librarian and other senior leaders served as champions, but not active participants in the team's work.

Tim saw the benefits of diverse input; one of the major elements that emanated from his team's work was to create three new sub-groups with additional people, independent of management's input, to shepherd parts of the strategic initiative through. Tim was able to step outside his direct IT and systems support responsibilities, which enabled him to more effectively weave his creative vision into the process.

Support Creative Exploration

Shifting the culture of a library towards that of a learning organization that supports librarians like Tim requires leverage. One point of leverage for change comes from new ways of thinking (Senge 2006, 62–63).Simply put, libraries need to get creative, and this requires staff to seek opportunities for change and creativity and to be creative without being directly told (Kaufman and Sternberg 2010, 166).This premise demands that the organization's leadership establishes and embraces a culture and climate of trust to help foster an employee's ability to do something new and useful. When the right environment is created, individual needs can be met and aligned with the desire to help others and meet organizational goals. This dynamic creates the foundation for creative exploration.

Research disproves the myth that creativity is innate and is at odds with organizational productivity. In fact, a generation of research shows just the opposite: Everyone Is Creative; Ideas Matter; and Creative Fulfillment = Productivity.

Everyone Is Creative

You don't need to be born a genius to be creative. In fact David and Tom Kelley's research underscores that we all have creative potential, and that developing creative confidence "is a way of experiencing the world that generates new approaches and solutions" (Kelley and Kelley 2013, 5). If we all have the capacity for creativity how can an organization and its leaders help nurture and develop it?

Part of the answer resides in a diagnostic tool created by Frederica Reisman that distinguishes 11 individual attributes we rely on when engaging in exercises requiring creative thought. These attributes are: Originality, Fluency (generating ideas), Flexibility/Adaptability, Elaboration, Tolerance of Ambiguity, Resistance to Premature Closure (not shutting down possible ideas), Divergent Thinking, Convergent Thinking, Risk Taking, Intrinsic Motivation, and Extrinsic Motivation. (Reisman, Keiser, and Otti 2016)

An organizational environment that supports the development of the Reisman's attributes is able to build the trust needed for individuals to better understand themselves and the ways they can effectively explore.

Ideas Matter

Ideas are the building blocks of creative exploration and innovation. Throughout humankind, our ability to adapt and use ideas to meet basic needs is evident—think of the caveman and fire. Successful organizations empathize and relate to the genuine needs of their communities or customers; they enable processes that encourage numerous diverse ideas (divergent and non-domain specific) as a way to meet such needs. Can there ever be too many ideas? Not really! However, as organizations enable divergent thinking and idea generation, they must also have processes in place to filter those ideas by finding similarities, trends, and workable solutions (convergent). This divergent/convergent process can take root in both single ideation exercises as well as long-term strategic processes. It enables evolutionary creativity and establishes a solid process for underscoring how important ideas are to the organization.

Creative Fulfillment = Productivity

The easiest way to conceptually understand creative fulfillment is to consider it an extension of enlightenment associated with Maslow's hierarchy of needs. Dan Pink clearly articulates this through a trifecta of intrinsic motivators: Autonomy, Mastery, and Purpose, and is able to marry our desire to be self-directed, with a desire to improve and contribute to something bigger than ourselves, and in doing so inextricably ties our creative fulfillment to productivity (Pink 2009, 83–152).When we are intrinsically motivated (a key attribute of Reisman's), we feel comfortable to explore. This allows us to better understand ourselves and our potential, enables us to embrace the many contradictions in life and our jobs, and lets us persevere as we seek creative solutions to needs and problems. A creative workforce is a productive workforce when the organization is able to support an individual's innate desire to creatively explore.

At the Library

Tim's team engaged in activities to help foster creative exploration and trust. An important initial exercise was to identify the collective styles and shared values of each member on the team, which enabled them to understand the unique perspectives they could bring to the initiative.

As the team advanced, they conducted an empathy mapping exercise, which required them to identify key user segments of *MARVEL!* (i.e., K-12 students, teachers, academic researchers, public at large, etc.). This empathy map was used to help the team reimagine *MARVEL!* through the lens of different constituents.

The most successful library organizations will create and foster the environments for their staff to explore, and the most successful librarians will cherish that environment so that they can be fulfilled in the work they do. The creation of the strategic initiative teams, like Tim's team, reflect an approach that connects numerous individuals within an organization and allows them to explore creative solutions to problems.

Embrace Connectedness

Providing opportunities for library staff to build new connections inside and outside the library provides exposure to different people and perspectives, and enhances individual and organizational well-being (Pentland 2012). Relationships are not only essential for emotional health and getting things done, they also strengthen an organization's capacity to remain relevant by exposing it to new perspectives. In today's knowledge economy, the most successful organizations are those with relationships spanning traditional organizational boundaries (demographic, geographic, horizontal) (Lee, Horth, and Ernst 2014, 3–6).Libraries that seek to build boundary spanning connections and empower employees at all levels can begin by championing staff projects and activities that promote internal collaboration and facilitate community connections.

Promote Internal Collaboration

Research on employee collaboration highlights the benefits of increased creativity and innovation when staff are given the tools, autonomy, and authority to engage in collaborative meaningful work (Sawyer 2007, 39–58).When staff have the opportunity to collaborate and participate in organization-wide initiatives and decision-making processes, they have an increased sense of belonging and a greater commitment to the library's mission and goals. Both public and private organizations are incorporating collaborative strategies in their day-to-day operations. For example, sporting goods retailer, REI, facilitates an online "company campfire" where employees from across the country can connect, share, and learn from one another. These relationships strengthen internal networks and support cross-boundary relationships within the library (among branches and staff levels).

Facilitate Community Connections

As community-centered organizations serving different stakeholders, libraries need to provide ample opportunities for staff to build meaningful connections beyond the library walls. When staff are supported in building boundary spanning relationships, the library and its patrons are the beneficiaries. As libraries reconsider inward facing institutional structures and seek to meet the changing needs of diverse communities, boundary spanning strategies range from embedded librarians to creative community, public, and private partnerships. Chicago Public Library's "Punk Rock and Donuts" is a great example of mutually beneficial community connections. Supporting local bands and businesses while providing a safe space for neighborhood youth to catch a show, the library launched this series of events in partnership with a local coffee shop, musicians and artists.

At the Library

There was a common theme in the stories of our library staff interviewees. They valued the connections in their own libraries as well as the broader community. When Jennifer began her career at the library, she quickly found the value of connections with community partners. As a teen/adult librarian, Jennifer wanted to empower youth to bring their own passions and interests into the library. Partnering with a local behavioral health agency, Jennifer was able to seek shared funding and resources to launch a Teen Board. Later she would go on to partner with a variety of local artists, web developers, photographers, and storytellers who helped youth take ownership of their own learning and skill development.

From Debbi's story, we learned of an internal collaboration that was beneficial for both time-strapped staff and the greater community. Debbi and her library team members saw a growing need to support the houseless and reentry population that was frequently visiting the library. Seeking services to secure a job, find housing, or obtain health insurance, many of these individuals were relying on librarians for this support. Debbi and a cross-functional team of staff were given the opportunity to work together to identify and test solutions to this challenge. The team began by interviewing social service agencies in the nearby area. They found that many of the library services were being duplicated. The team then decided to create informal partnerships that would connect patrons to the appropriate services.

Fostering these types of collaborations both inside and outside the library requires a commitment of time, space, and training. The most effective organizations begin by strengthening their internal networks through mutual respect and safety. As trust in the organization and each other emerges, effective staff collaboration develops, allowing the library and its staff to reach further, build new relationships, and grow with the communities they serve.

Prioritize Equity and Inclusion

Equity and inclusion have been identified as indicators of organizational commitment and employee job performance (Cho and Barak 2008, 109–11).Equitable inclusion requires libraries to develop a culture and climate where employees feel both a sense of belonging and individuality (Shore et al. 2010, 1265–66). However, inclusive efforts fall short when the library and its staff do not confront implicit biases, the unspoken attitudes, and stereotypes that reinforce inequitable action. To emerge as inclusive learning organizations, libraries need to address historical biases and eliminate legacy organizational structures that continue to privilege white, male, heterosexual employees. The Equity Design Collaborative offers a simple approach for organizational redesign: See (Situate the Organization), be seen (Act with Intention), and foresee (Understand Process as Product) (Hill, Molitor, and Ortiz 2017).

Situate the Organization

All systems are unique: they are situated in context, bound by time, space, and environment. In other words, libraries are as unique as the individuals who staff them and communities they serve. To overcome explicit and implicit biases, libraries and individual employees must acknowledge the unique set of circumstances that inform current relationships, and these circumstances (both pleasant and unpleasant) must be accounted for as the library creates more equitable systems.

Act with Intention

To acknowledge inequity in context is not enough to facilitate inclusion. Organizations and their leaders need to be intentional about bringing diverse stakeholders together to build relationships across boundaries. To be clear, racial and gender 'representation' is not sufficient. Efforts to act with intention must be rooted in community engagement and the ceding of power in decision making.

Recognize Process as Product

If efforts to promote equity and inclusion are to stick and support organizational transformation, libraries must recognize the process as product. In other words, organizations must treat the process of including diverse stakeholders in decision making and creation as the end goal, rather than the means to an end. This approach diverges from conventional success metrics of end product outputs and outcomes. Organizational change is a long game. An equitable, inclusive process is the ultimate goal.

At the Library

To make the equity design framework tangible, we share two stories from our interviews with staff whose personal career growth and creativity has been facilitated by opportunities to design for equity and inclusion.

Debbi is a member of Kindred, a collective of seven library staff at PCPL who seek to reach, support, and celebrate the Black community. Kindred was established in 2017 to meet a need internally at the library and externally in the community. Kindred's goals are to improve black representation, break down prejudice, and promote and articulate the goals and desires of the black community in Pima County.

In 2013, Jen received a planning grant from the MacArthur Foundation. For three years, a youth design team (YDT) worked alongside Jen and fellow library staff to design and launch the 101 Space in the library under the direction of a youth advisory council whose vision is to empower and connect youth.

Kindred and the 101 Space are solid examples of equity and inclusion in action. Checking who and what has been overlooked in the library, the Kindred members and the 101 Space youth design team asked how they might come together with intentionality to eliminate barriers. Through the process, each initiative has created space for individual staff member growth and positioned the library to implement creative solutions, establish new internal and external connections, and develop more equitable and inclusive programming.

Conclusion

In his book *The Fifth Discipline,* Peter Senge, defines "learning organizations" as places where people are continually enhancing their own capacity to create the outcomes they desire (Senge 2006, 3).While actions required to adapt and grow into a learning organization differ from library to library, implementing this type of organizational change requires a similar set of strategies that support the growth and development of the people working in the system.

With the pressure of budgets, policy changes, and multiple agendas, library leaders often seek quick solutions for staff development. Many assume that a few conferences, online courses, or one-day workshops can do the trick, but these are not sufficient. Since learning is not a one-size-fits-all process, we suggest a short list of "do-it-now" activities for the strategies we have discussed in this essay. Although not comprehensive, it is a compilation of simple, action-oriented activities that have a low barrier for implementation. The activities are organized below for quick reference and adaptation by you, your team, or your library.

	Support Creative Exploration	Embrace Connectedness	Prioritize Equity and Inclusion	Develop Personal Leadership
Weekly stand ups		x	x	x
Speed dates	x	x	x	x
Community cafes	x	x	x	
20 percent time	x	x		x
Idea breaks	x	x	x	x
Participation tools	x	x	x	x

- *Weekly Stand-ups.* Promoting shared knowledge, trust, and relationship building, the stand-up is a brief meeting where staff come together (standing up) and share a brief (60–90 sec) update or topic of interest since the last meeting. Stemming from the startup community, the Weekly Stand-up is designed to be brief and informative. The format is designed to be inclusive, because all attendees are required to report out and take ownership of their work and progress.
- *Speed dates.* Encouraging cross-functional knowledge and collaboration, staff across different departments and levels are paired together to learn about each other and their work. Through "speed interviews" or organized coffee conversations, staff can build meaningful connections, expand organizational

knowledge, and often dispel previously held assumptions about departments or positions. This helps build boundary spanning relationships horizontally and vertically throughout the organization.

- *Community Cafes.* Inviting business and community leaders to connect and share their knowledge, passions, and experience at a regular gathering is a smart strategy for staff to expand their networks while opening opportunities for collaboration around shared interests. Pima County Public Library piloted a similar concept when librarian Lisa Bunker created the "Catalyst Cafe" and invited community catalysts to come to the library each month and share their talents and experiences.

- *Twenty percent projects.* In hi-tech organizations like Google, providing opportunities for staff to explore projects of interest to them is standard practice. Employees are encouraged to spend 20 percent of their time at work pursuing passion projects. Counter to the conventional command and control approach, opportunities for creative exploration empowered staff to step-up on new initiatives that can improve the organization as a whole.

- *Idea breaks.* Encourage learning. Just as many successful teachers encourage their students to take brain breaks to promote effective learning, organizations can provide structured ways for staff to reflect and contemplate ideas. Contrary to stereotypical images, librarians spend the majority of their day interfacing with the public in customer service of one sort or another. Offering ways for staff to have some quiet reflective time can provide needed respite for creative thought.

- *Participation tools.* Shake-up meetings and routine activities with participation tools that help facilitate alternative interactions between staff members. Simple tools can be found online (see mindtools.com) and in facilitation or teaching guides. Simple activities that encourage participation can change the dynamics in a meeting to be more inclusive, empowering, and productive for everyone. An example of one such tool is the empathy map used by the Maine State Library. It was a simple activity that shifted perspectives in complex ways.

Learning and development do not happen in a vacuum, they require a deep commitment to organizational growth and change. Starting with small actionable steps that reinforce larger strategies can help shift practices and mindsets without major disruptions or resource investments. In other words, small actions can help organizations adapt and grow in organic ways that respect the time and contributions of individual staff members. For all growing leaders, and for all those wishing to find satisfaction in their jobs and careers, understanding the element of time and contributions as they relate to personal and professional growth will help maintain sanity and ensure the necessary perseverance in our quest to make a difference.

REFERENCES

Amabile, Teresa, and Khaire, Mukti. 2008. "Creativity and the Role of a Leader." *Harvard Business Review,* October. https://hbr.org/2008/10/creativity-and-the-role-of-the-leader.

Cho, Sangmi, and Mor Barak, Michàlle E. 2008. "Understanding of Diversity and Inclusion in a Perceived Homogeneous Culture: A Study of Organizational Commitment and Job Performance Among Korean Employees." *Administration in Social Work* 32 (4):100–126.

Collins, Jim. 2011. *Great by Choice.* New York: HarperCollins.

"Gallup Daily: U.S. Employee Engagement." 2017. News.Gallupwww. Accessed January 5, 2018. http://news.gallup.com/poll/180404/gallup-daily-employee-engagement.aspx.

Hill, Caroline, Molitor, Michelle, and Ortiz, Christine. 2017. "Racism and Inequity Are Products of Design. They Can Be Redesigned." *Medium*. November 5. https://medium.com/@multiplyequity/racism-and-inequity-are-products-of-design-they-can-be-redesigned-12188363cc6a.

Kaufman, James C., and Sternberg, Robert J. 2010. *The Cambridge Handbook of Creativity*. New York: Cambridge University Press.

Kelley, David, and Kelley, Tom. 2013. *Creative Confidence: Unleashing the Creative Potential Within All of Us*. New York: Crown Publishing.

Lee, Lance, Horth, David Magellan, and Ernst, Chris. 2014. "Boundary Spanning in Action Tactics for Transforming Today's Borders into Tomorrow's Frontiers." Center for Creative Leadership. https://www.ccl.org/wp-content/uploads/2015/04/BoundarySpanningAction.pdf.

Pentland, Alex. 2012. "The New Science of Building Great Teams." *Harvard Business Review*, April. https://hbr.org/2012/04/the-new-science-of-building-great-teams.

Pink, Daniel H. 2009. *Drive: The Surprising Truth About What Motivates Us*. New York: Riverhead Books.

Reisman, Fredericka, Keiser, Larry, and Otti, Obinna. 2016. "Development, Use and Implications of Diagnostic Creativity Assessment App, RDCA—Reisman Diagnostic Creativity Assessment." *Creativity Research Journal*, vol. 28 (2): 177–187.

Sawyer, Keith. 2007. *Group Genius: The Creative Power of Collaboration*. New York: Basic Books.

Senge, Peter. 2006. *The Fifth Discipline: The Art & Practice of the Learning Organization*. New York: Crown Publishing.

Shore, Lynn M., Randel, Amy E., Chung, Beth G., Dean, Michelle A., Ehrhart, Karen Holcombe, and Gangaram Singh. 2011. "Inclusion and Diversity in Work Groups: A Review and Model for Future Research." *Journal of Management* 37 (4): 1262–1289.

Transparency and Subterfuge

Encouraging Creativity in Academic Libraries

Jack Maness, Erin Elzi *and* Shannon Tharp

Introduction

Libraries have long aspired toward a humanistic, value-centered mission through analytical planning and strict orderliness. Descriptions of libraries throughout the centuries often evoke the language of poetry and religion, yet this rhetoric is not often used by library employees. Whether due to cultural norms adhered to in most workplaces, or the simple necessity that libraries must initiate and follow standards if they are to be libraries and not piles of books, this dichotomy is one that libraries as institutions must manage if they are to encourage the creativity of their most valuable asset: their people.

Linked data, collection analysis, information literacy assessment, bibliometrics, data curation, discovery platforms, organizational structure, the finer points of analog and digital preservation—these are the issues librarians contend with on a daily basis, issues about which scholar-librarians research and write. Alongside this work, many of us write poetry, novels and zines; we paint, dance, play instruments, and sculpt. Some of us are art or literature librarians, of course, but many are administrators, catalogers, and science librarians with "secret" degrees in literature and philosophy. We are, essentially, talented humanists with a desire to create and transform. We're also social scientists with an equal desire and mandate to preserve and persist. And in many academic libraries we contend with complex institutional politics and the expectations of promotion, reappointment, and tenure.

This essay outlines the challenges in encouraging the creativity of library staff in academic libraries, and it offers strategies for overcoming those challenges. It addresses: (1) facilitating healthy organizational cultures, (2) finding and integrating work-life balance, and (3) seeking buy-in for experimental projects. In some cases, openness and transparency works; in others, a subtler approach may be necessary.

Ultimately, creativity in academic librarianship means managing risk and the pace of change. It also means being courageous and empathetic. It means understanding our comfort zones, why they exist, and when and where they should—or should not—be breached.

Facilitating Healthy Organizational Cultures

Challenges

The very nature of academic library organizational structure and culture can act as a challenge to creativity. Steeped in centuries of tradition, the institutions in which academic libraries operate are not given easily to change. Librarians in these institutions are often expected to conduct research, an area where perhaps their creativity could be more fully realized, but this research is predominantly analytical and pragmatic. Indeed, often it must be so if administrators and review committees are to give librarians credit for it.

Librarians, then, often turn to their librarianship as a creative outlet, or undertake creative endeavors outside of their profession. But libraries are inherently avoidant to risk and have not changed much in three centuries. Libraries work, and they work very well. Expectations researchers have for libraries are tied to rigid traditions of tenure and promotion. Libraries provide what researchers need efficiently. Throughout their existence, libraries have shown just as much creativity as is necessary to meet expectations.

Fostering a culture that encourages, even allows in some cases, librarians to exercise creativity in their professional and personal growth can be exceedingly difficult. Simply put, libraries inspire creativity in others, but struggle to properly encourage and allow it in their employees. Embedded in state, municipal, or private university organizations, they often adhere to traditional standards of workplace expectations, strict organizational structure, and librarians are asked to simply "do their job."

But libraries need inspired employees with deep levels of engagement in order to continue adapting.

Strategies

Providing institutional support for creativity, with goals for both personal and professional growth of librarians, requires a re-thinking of traditional library management. Thankfully, such a re-thinking has already begun. Early stages of the digital revolution, later compounded by economic recessions, demanded that library leaders in institutions across the country explore alternative structures and approaches to library operations and talent management that attempt to foster creativity in librarianship. The turn of the twenty-first century was marked by a variety of resulting reorganizations.

What is missing is a unified theory of management, an approach that embraces librarianship as a service profession, and the confident application of the feminist ethic of care to organizations that have evolved in the fundamentally patriarchal culture of the academy.

We propose two broad aspects of management, adapted from business research, that can inform library leadership in a more comprehensive understanding of fostering creativity: 1) holistic engagement of employees, and 2) focus on a broad mission purpose (Capelli et. al. 2010).

Holistic Engagement of Employees

Library managers can encourage creativity by simply acknowledging that the personal lives of employees are important to the organization. They can go further by accommodating those lives. They can model it. Transparently and openly discussing personal challenges with work-life balance, allowing others to do the same if they so choose, looking for ways to align work with personal passions, library managers can offer institutional support by providing personal care. Creating policies that allow for flexibility, built-in "free time" to explore new concepts, and, ultimately, feeling an obligation to employees as the organization's most important asset, will create a culture of curiosity, exploration, and creativity.

Managers can also use subterfuge. Allowing, for example, productive employees to bend workplace rules, flex their work time and place as appropriate, take space to reflect, recover, and inspire themselves, or be vulnerable and not fear failure, fosters a culture of trust and understanding. These are not things that can be codified in policy manuals. If libraries seek to encourage creativity, they must be creative themselves.

Of course, balance and boundaries are still necessary. But a little bit of blurring can create another picture altogether. In many respects, satisfying users may be most employees' primary motivation, but library leaders should be driven in large part by the holistic success of library employees.

Broad Mission and Purpose

Engaged and creative employees have a strong sense of the organization's mission and purpose. They see how they support it. They conduct their work not only within the field of their career, but in the concentric circles that expand out from it, through the library, the university, the broader community, and, ultimately, to the greater society and its history. They feel that they are a part of something larger than themselves.

Libraries and their leaders must reiterate these alignments, repeat them, remind employees of them, and openly discuss the larger values and ethics-based decisions they must engage in on daily basis. Engaging employees in these discussions and listening to their thoughts can help create this sense of purpose.

Libraries, and universities, are values- and service-driven institutions. Their employees often chose their careers because they were inspired by this mission. The whole of them, their passions, interests, and creative capacities, influenced their choices. By engaging library employees holistically and fostering conditions for them to feel the broader purpose and mission of their work, we amplify the reasons for their choices.

Work-Life Balance

Challenges

Work-life balance is a significant challenge in academic librarianship, especially where creativity is concerned. Life isn't linear, work isn't linear, creativity isn't linear; one demands more than the others on any given day depending on whatever unfolds. We need to welcome uncertainty—a key element of creativity—and adapt to it, while allowing room for the animating and shaping force that is life to exist in our library work. We need to recognize that it's difficult, if not impossible, to compartmentalize work, life, and creativity, which is another reason to engage library employees holistically.

Librarians who work in an academic setting are complicated, purposeful humans who catalog, configure, troubleshoot, instruct, assess, develop collections, steward budgets, acquire and process materials, register patrons, perform readers' advisory, communicate with prospective donors, maintain resources and spaces, and meet many other responsibilities. Often we forget to care for ourselves and each other in the same ways we care for our patrons. In "Vocational Awe and Librarianship: The Lies We Tell Ourselves," Fobazi Ettarh cuts straight to the point: "You may impress your supervisor by working late, but will that supervisor come to expect that you continually neglect your own family's needs in the service of library patrons? The library's purpose may be to serve, but is that purpose so holy when it fails to serve those who work within its walls every day?" (Ettarh 2018).

One of the major challenges presented by navigating work, life, and creativity in an academic library is learning to say "no." Contrary to decades of library and information science rhetoric, we can't do everything, and we can't be everything to everyone. Therein lies the road to burnout, which is the enemy of creativity and well-being. Significant organizational support—the support of library management, in particular—is necessary in order for people to feel they can say "no" without reprisal.

For example, a librarian who's a junior faculty member is working toward tenure and promotion, and is invited to present at a conference. She's currently working on two book chapters, carrying out her day-to-day responsibilities as a librarian, and preparing a presentation for another conference. She might feel obligated to accept the invitation out of pressure, which may be a side effect of fearing failure, all of which has been instilled in her by a tenure and promotion system that upholds prestige, impact metrics, and perpetual busyness (another enemy of creativity).

This is where organizational support enters the picture. A perceptive, creative manager would have found ways to help the librarian set boundaries and protect her time. Think back to the managerial subterfuge that allows for bending workplace rules, exploring flex time and place, and you'll get the idea.

Another challenge presented by navigating work, life, and creativity in an academic library is the aforementioned perpetual busyness, which is directly tied to one's ability to make room for creativity. The mutable nature of libraries and the resources they acquire makes for a near-constant current of troubleshooting (databases, e-journals, e-books) and configuring those resources. Then there's keeping track of those resources, which can be puzzling. There is also budgeting for those resources, figuring out what resources to purchase with what's budgeted—the list goes on and on. Where in this list, which is only a small part of the day-to-day functioning of a library, is room for creativity? It's easy to say that creativity exists in there somewhere, that one simply has to find it, as though just looking around for it makes it transpire, but the truth is that often we have to make room and find time for creativity. In the workplace, that making has to be allowed. For what it's worth, one of the definitions of "allowed" is "appreciate the value of."

Elaine Scarry writes, "Recognizing our own capacity for creating is again a prerequisite for working for justice: while beauty can be either natural or artifactual, justice is always artifactual; it always takes immense labor to bring it about. So anything that awakens us to our own power of creation is a first step in working to eliminate asymmetries and injuries" (Scarry 2012). It's not a far stretch to say that libraries play a role in awakening people to their own power of creation, and that those of us who work in libraries are, in our own ways, contributing to the elimination of the asymmetries and injuries of which Scarry writes.

So how do we, as academic librarians, go about first recognizing our own capacity for creating, then making room and time for creativity? How do we stop sidelining creativity in favor of everything else our days demand? What follows are strategies that are intended to be more suggestive than prescriptive, more adaptable than fixed.

Strategies

WELCOMING UNCERTAINTY

Creativity, an act of the imagination, can't be forced. Welcoming uncertainty and getting away from perfectionism requires patience. As librarians, we are trained to find information, have answers, just *know*, and yet we are rarely told that not having an answer or not knowing is valid too.

We're not omnipotent, and perpetuating that idea does us a disservice; what if, instead, we admitted that we require some time to figure out the puzzles in front of us? What if we were granted time (within reason) to look and listen? There's not one right way to go about welcoming uncertainty, no timeframe for getting comfortable with it, but cultivating an environment in which improvisation and adaptability are valued is a start.

TIME ALONE

While our work as librarians lends itself to collaboration, it's critical that we have time to ourselves. This strategy might require some resolve at the outset, as perceptions surrounding absence, or even a closed office door, vary depending on the library. But subterfuge shouldn't be required in order to take a break and leave the library.

Part of time alone has to do with recognizing that library work will always be there—whether it's in process, nearly finished, or nowhere near being finished—in one form or another. By taking time alone, we're granting ourselves permission to turn away from what's in front of us for a while. In that process, we recognize that we're better colleagues when we have room and time to think through complicated aspects of a project, difficult discussions, and the general plot of our days. Also, keeping a notebook and a writing implement around throughout the day, but especially during time alone, works wonders for capturing fast-moving ideas.

OUTSIDE OF THE LIBRARY

Our interests outside of the library inform our library work. Take a look, for instance, at the biographies of this essay's authors; writing, roller derby, and photography (among other interests) play significant roles in our lives. If work, life, and creativity aren't linear, certainly our interests aren't linear; employing those interests in our profession can have substantive, positive long-term effects on the communities in which we live, work, and create. As with the other strategies mentioned, this one requires patience and time. It also requires one to be brave when gaining buy-in from colleagues.

Gaining Buy-in

The concept of supporting creative endeavors in the workplace is not new or unique. Yet it can still be a struggle to gain buy-in to the idea of allowing space for it in the library environment. At first look, it might not align with SMART goals, or strategic plans, or the need for analytics that justify our budgets each year; it takes time, it may appear like a reduction in productivity, it can force some employees to step out of their comfort-zone, and not everyone responds well to that (after all, we're library scientists, not library artists). As Donnelly wrote, "what is creativity really, but the ability to set and transform ideas, materials and objects into new and original forms?" (Donnelly 1994). What if we changed that language to say "creativity is the ability to set and transform ideas, collections and services into new forms that better meet changing user needs?" Libraries, like many other institutions, benefit from creativity in the workplace. There is plenty of existing research and literature that champions those benefits.

Yet, because libraries are distinctive institutions, different from profit-based sectors, it can be easy to write off the literature that focuses on those sectors as not applicable. However, with a little bit of jargon juggling, we find that the benefits of promoting creativity in the workplace already exist. This wordsmithing, or taking the language and examples used in the other professional sectors, forms the foundation for gaining buy-in. A perfect example of this is IDEO, a popular leader in design thinking. In additional to their publications that are broad in scope and intended for application by various sectors, IDEO created a unique document just for the application of design thinking in libraries. The theoretical underpinning of the design thinking process remains the same in all of IDEO's publications—a three step procedure of inspiration, ideation and iteration. The only real differences between *Design Thinking for Libraries* and IDEO's other, more general publications is that the definitions, verbiage, scenarios and activities cater to the library environment (IDEO 2015b) (IDEO 2015a). Julie Evener does something similar in arguing for innovation in the library. She presents a number of success stories from well-known corporations that have designated time and space for their employees to explore creative new ideas, and then shows how these methods can be applied in the library setting (Evener 2015).

We can also look at the culture and practices that exist in art libraries—those that cater to scholars and students in the fine arts, art history, and design. These libraries are often staffed by both paraprofessionals and MLS-holders who have additional art-related degrees; second jobs as creative professionals, or even just highly-polished creative hobbies. In these institutions, there is no need to advocate for the space to explore new ideas, or to bring the creative process to work. It is not only acceptable practice, it is highly encouraged. These libraries maintain low rates of staff turnover, operate in a low-stress and positive work environment, and manage to complete elaborate projects with less funding and fewer staff than traditional academic libraries. They may have the same pressures as other libraries, but the greater value placed on building a creative environment at work may help them respond positively to those pressures and truly figure out how to do more with less (Wolf and Gottlieb-Miller 2017)

In short, the literature proves creativity works (pun intended). Yet, it is understood that the literature about what worked in other institutions, or even other industries, is not always accepted at face value when making the argument in one's own library. Even the culture that exists in many art libraries might seem difficult to translate into a public or academic institution. To that extent, we offer ways to get colleagues, staff, and administration to warm up to the prospects of letting creative juices flow: establishing proper environment, building strong relationships, creating low-barrier projects, and being persistent and positive.

Establishing Proper Environment

A proper environment must be created where all employees feel like their ideas are welcomed and respected, and where, in turn, they'll be more open to the ideas of others. This defines the difference between forcing creativity and allowing for it. Not everyone will want to flex those muscles, but everyone needs to accept creativity when other people do. According to Evener, a "key element of innovation is a library culture that cultivates creativity, encouraging employees to stretch their abilities, experiment with new ways of doing things, and accept and even celebrate mistakes" (Evener 2015). This may involve a culture shift, which is no easy feat. It will not happen overnight, but is more likely to occur over time and in small increments.

Due to the incremental nature of a culture shift, it's probably going to happen in a way that resembles a domino effect. The likelihood of employees exploring radical ideas, taking time to fail, or incorporating their creative passions into the workplace increases after they have witnessed their peers do so, especially when the library administration is supportive of these endeavors. It's about opening up to vulnerability without feeling like it's a risk. This kind of buy-in works in two ways, both in accepting the creative process in others, and in taking the plunge to allow it for themselves.

Building Strong Relationships

The stronger your relationships are with other library employees, the more likely they are to consider your new idea. Broadening your circle of participants also helps build support. Seek out not only those whose professional duties make them prime stakeholders, but also those whose professional aspirations or personal interests could be applied. This will build a stronger team, with a greater variety and depth of skill. It also increases each member's dedication to the project since they are getting the chance to apply passions of their own. This is another example of the aforementioned domino effect, where gaining the support and confidence of the team members will trickle outward and gain the buy-in of others, as they go back to their own departments, supervisors, and other colleagues, and speak positively about the processes (Zaboski, Dierberger and Douglas 2016).

Creating Low-Barrier Projects

The best way to get everyone on board is with some low-barrier projects—projects that will not require large amount of time taken away from other tasks; where failure can be shrugged off; where there is no negative impact on users or staff; projects that promote creativity and learning among employees without initially taking them too far out of their comfort zone. This can start with something as simple as trying a new way of running a meeting or offering a workshop using innovative forms of pedagogy. While such projects may seem inconsequential, that's because in some way they are. If they fail, it is less detrimental than it would be if a large-scale project has snags. On the other hand, existing leadership methods highly suggest that incremental steps forward lead to the most effective and long-lasting big changes (Kouzes and Posner, 2003). Low barrier projects that foster creativity and accept failure are great examples of the incremental steps that lead to the acceptance of creative endeavor on a larger scale.

Keeping Persistence and Positivity

Gaining the trust and support of colleagues may not happen right away. Even if the administration has built room for failure, that doesn't mean that your first few attempts will be received well by your colleagues. The first meeting where attendees are asked to brainstorm, create prototypes, or participate in ice breaker activities (all low-barrier jump-starts to creative thinking) may not result in engaged, active dialogue and new ideas. Don't give up, try again—each time being more prepared and polished than the last (Evener 2015). There will be a project, method, or meeting that will finally pull them in. Optimism is infectious; the more highly you can speak of successful creative processes, the more likely others are to try them, or at the very least, be more supportive when you do.

Conclusion

Creativity is not something that can be forced on a person, an institution, or a profession. No manual, initiative, or linear process exists that demonstrates how ideas can be formed, flourish, or synthesized with others. Encouraging creativity requires creating conditions, fostering culture, patience, and a broad view of what is important to people and organizations.

In academic libraries, there are good reasons for the pace of change to be moderate. Reliability, consistency of experience, and preservation of the scholarly record are vital qualities for libraries where teaching and research are the primary missions of the community. By fostering healthy cultures, acknowledging that creative endeavors outside the profession inform and enrich our librarianship, and learning the nuances of persuading our colleagues to try something new, we can balance creativity with stability.

The creativity of library staff is there, and in many respects, needs no encouragement. It needs the time, permission, and occasional nudge to flourish.

REFERENCES

Cappelli, Peter, Singh, Harbir, Singh, Jitendra, and Useem, Michael. 2010. *The India Way: How India's Top Business Leaders Are Revolutionizing Management.* Harvard Business Press.
Donnelly, Brian. 1994. "Creativity in the Workplace." *The Journal of Technology Studies* 20, no. 2 (Summer/Fall): 4–7.
Ettarh, Fobazi. 2018. "Vocational Awe and Librarianship: The Lies We Tell Ourselves." *In the Library With the Lead Pipe.* Accessed June 1, 2018. www.inthelibrarywiththeleadpipe.org/2018/vocational-awe/.
Evener, Julie. 2015. "Innovation in the Library: How to Engage Employees, Cultivate Creativity, and Create Buy-In for New Ideas." *College and Undergraduate Libraries* 22, no. 3–4 (The Business of Libraries): 296–311.
IDEO. 2015a. *Design Thinking for Libraries: A Toolkit for Patron-Centered Design.* IDEO.
IDEO. 2015b. *Design Thinking for Libraries Activities Workbook.* IDEO.
Kouzes, James M., and Posner, Barry Z. 2003. *The Jossey-Bass Academic Administrator's Guide to Exemplary Leadership.* San Francisco: Jossey-Bass.
Scarry, Elaine. 2012. "Poetry Changed the World: Injury and the Ethics of Reading." *Boston Review.* Accessed June 1, 2018. www.bostonreview.net/archives/BR37.4/elaine_scarry_poetry_literature_reading_empathy_ethics.php.
Wolf, Eric Michael, and Gottlieb-Miller, Lauren. 2017. "The Small Easy: Budget-Neutral Digital Projects at Small Libraries." *Art Documentation* 36, no. 2 (Fall): 332–344.
Zaboski, David, Dierberger, George F. and Douglas, Ryan. 2016. "The Alchemy of Creativity: An Operating System for Innovation, Collaboration and Enhanced Creativity." *American Journal of Management* 16, no. 3 (September): 66–81.

Creative Accommodations

Finding the Best Solution for Library Employees with Invisible Disabilities

Joy M. Perrin *and* Carrye Kay Syma

Invisible disabilities are symptoms that are not visible but still affect an employee's ability to work. Examples from the Invisible Disabilities Association list fatigue, pain, cognitive dysfunctions, mental disorders, and hearing and visual impartment (2018). Some estimates say that up to 10 percent of those in the workforce have an invisible disability (Disabled World 2017). This means that even in a library of only ten people, one person may have an invisible disability.

Invisible disabilities can be frustrating to managers because they are not readily apparent and often require employees to disclose their disabilities. Employees might be reluctant to do that out of fear; or they may not realize that accommodations can be made for invisible disabilities the same way that they can be made for more apparent ones. However, managers and Human Resources (HR) personnel may have to get creative to find reasonable accommodations that meet the employees' needs while respecting their privacy.

It becomes even more challenging when a manager or HR personnel suspect that an invisible disability may be the root of performance issues, but the employee has not disclosed any disability. Proceeding with these cases can be challenging; it requires managers and HR to dig deep into their well of ideas to find solutions to help employees reach their full potential.

This essay presents a few real-life cases of invisible disabilities and the creative solutions to their unique problems. The names have been changed to protect the identities of those involved. Genders have been occasionally avoided, also for identity protection. In the organization where the cases from this essay were present, there are currently around 150 employees, and these cases span a wide time period. They represent only a small portion of the invisible disabilities in this organization that have had to be addressed by both managers and HR. These cases are examples of successful resolutions.

Case #1: *Managing Depression and Anxiety*

Sam, like 18.1 percent of the population, developed depression and anxiety (Anxiety and Depression Association of America 2016). Sam, an otherwise productive and happy employee, suddenly had problems completing tasks, reporting out, and generally getting through a day. Sam's situation is not at all uncommon. Sam, unlike most people suffering from depression and anxiety, was seeking treatment.

However, Sam is not the actual focus of this case. Sam needed no more reasonable accommodations than what was already provided. The focus of this case was Sam's supervisor.

The supervisor did not know how to work with someone with depression and anxiety. Reasonable accommodations aside, the supervisor did not know how to communicate in a way that would not stoke Sam's anxiety. Sam would shut down during meetings, and the supervisor was left with a feeling of helplessness, not knowing how to work with the employee smoothly.

Sam's supervisor talked to HR about the issue and posed the question: how do you give an employee dealing with an invisible disability enough space to work through it, while also holding this person accountable for performed work? The supervisor and HR together conceived a unique solution. The supervisor would go to therapy specifically to talk to the therapist about the ways to be a better supervisor to Sam.

The supervisor was able to address specific problems with the therapist and receive constructive feedback on how these issues could be handled. The supervisor learned a lot about anxiety disorders and how they manifest. The therapist also suggested specific communication techniques and explained ways of making expectations clear. This conversation resulted in changes of the supervisor's own behavior and communication style, making them clearer and less reactive. When Sam got visibly shaken, the supervisor would stop and give the employee time to calm down and work on the words to explain rising concerns. The supervisor had to learn to be less defensive, focus conversations on the specific tasks, and listen more and ask questions to get clarification when Sam seemed anxious.

Supervisors often forget that everything managers say or do have greater weight with employees. For employees with depression and anxiety, a supervisor's gentle correction can feel like a strong reprimand and elicit a strong response. However, with the help of a therapist, Sam's supervisor could communicate more appropriately, and Sam was able to remain productive while working through health issues.

If employees are doing their best to work with their invisible disability, and are still having problems, it is important to remember that the problem may sometimes rest with the supervisor and not necessarily with the employee. As in the case of Sam, the employee was doing everything possible to deal with the problem, and it was the supervisor who needed correction and help.

Case #2: Harassment of an Invisible Disability

Val had a long history with her invisible disability. As a child, she was diagnosed with Auditory Processing Disorder (APD). APD occurs when there is a problem between the ears and the brain. The person with APD can hear but struggles sometimes to make sense of what they are hearing. People with APD tend to struggle with early learning as they work through reading, spelling, and figuring out how to understand the world around them. As an adult, Val had adapted to her condition, learning to make light of the way she heard things, and brush it all off as being hard of hearing. At work, the only symptoms of APD that were still visible were spelling errors or an occasional joke that was misunderstood. Usually, the spelling errors were easily enough explained or avoided using modern technology. However, occasionally, a misspelled word would make it into a document or an email because the word was a correctly spelled word, just not the right one. Val had spent a whole year sending out "project summery" instead of "project summary" to the chagrin of her coworkers. When someone pointed this out to Val, Val made a joke about it and changed the spelling for the rest of the project.

It was the weirdly misspelled words that caught the attention of another coworker who worked under the same supervisor as Val. Jerry was older and had become a mentor to Val. Jerry tried to mentor Val even when Val did not care for Jerry's help. Once Jerry became aware of the spelling issue, suddenly, it was a problem to be solved. Jerry told Val that no one would take her seriously if she couldn't spell. It would seriously destroy her credibility and needed immediate corrective action. If this had been an employee/supervisor relationship, Val would not have felt comfortable talking about her disability since Jerry had made it so clear that it was unprofessional. Keep this in mind as a warning about how you talk about other people's behavior, especially about employees.

Jerry brought up the spelling problem in almost every interaction. Jerry researched voice typing software and would send Val emails about how Jerry thought it might help. Jerry would go to Val's presentations, watch like a hawk for misspelled words, and make sure Val knew that Jerry was carefully looking for problems.

Val, who felt like she couldn't go to her supervisor to discuss the constant harassment caused by her invisible disability, went to HR. HR was presented with a dilemma. Jerry's intent was to help, but the level of involvement and interest was well beyond what a coworker should have, and Jerry didn't know about the invisible disability. Val didn't want Jerry to know. She was afraid that Jerry would act negatively toward her because of her inability to fix this "terrible flaw" of not being able to spell correctly. HR had to come up with a solution that would stop the harassment without letting Jerry know why. They worked through a few possibilities, but most of them required either telling Jerry, or telling the supervisor about the disability, and Val was not comfortable with either option.

The HR staff had a very simple question for Val. Was it necessary to work with Jerry? Were they required to talk or work together on projects? When Val said that it was not necessary, HR had a reasonable solution. Val had to try not to engage Jerry. If Jerry insisted or harassed Val, then Val was to send an email straight to HR describing the harassment. If the harassment continued, HR could handle it without talking about the disability by citing the specific instances in which Jerry would be acting inappropriately. Meanwhile, HR would talk to Jerry's and Val's supervisor. It was not necessary to disclose a disability to request that Jerry and Val not be put on projects together. The supervisor was surprised and didn't understand, but complied and didn't request further explanation from Val, Jerry, or HR.

Val was relieved. There was a path forward, support of both Val's supervisor and HR, and no reason to make public her invisible disability.

Interactions between coworkers are an important part of the workplace, and people can sometimes overreact to behaviors that seem abnormal to them. If Jerry had known about the invisible disability and was told that the behavior, even with the best intentions, came across as harassment, Jerry would have likely felt embarrassed for these actions.

This is why employee education and awareness of invisible disabilities is important. General awareness may help people understand that sometimes, different behaviors exist because people are differently-abled than they are, and they should not assume it's a character flaw.

Case #3: A Manager with an Invisible Disability

Ash was a middle manager who was suffering from major depression related to a life event. The specifics of the event are not important. What is important are the consequences of the depression for Ash's direct reports. There was a ripple effect. While dealing with the physical and emotional consequences of the depression, Ash was unable sometimes to respond to employees' needs and requests. An unresponsive, disengaged boss creates unresponsive disengaged employees. Sadly, supervisors (and especially middle managers) are more likely to suffer from depression than their employees because supervisors often do not have as much authority as the upper management or as much autonomy as their subordinates (Burkus 2015).

Ash's reasonable accommodations included a more flexible schedule with a stipulation that Ash sets up access to email on a personal phone and responds to emails from employees if needed. The library business needed to continue. Ash was also given time to go to therapy during the day but only when it did not conflict with important meetings. Ash was given a quieter office, which was an easy accommodation since Ash was responsible for the area's office assignments. Ash was coached on how to use apps that helped keep track of assigned tasks and received help on developing a schedule to get the most essential tasks done during the time of the highest productivity. Ash was allowed to have natural light in the office, with full spectrum lighting, with the stipulation to be in the office more often and more available for employees to talk to.

Ash's reasonable accommodations were not unusual for someone with depression, but the extra requirements were. Ash's case is a clear example of how every case is different. A cataloger with depression would and should be handled differently than a circulation librarian with depression. A supervisor with depression should be handled differently than a non-supervisory employee. Someone with depression should be treated differently than someone with bipolar disorder.

Case #4: Supervisors Make All the Difference

Dylan was diagnosed with major depressive disorder, borderline personality disorder, bipolar tendencies, obsessive compulsive disorder, and anxiety several years ago as an adult. This may seem like a long list of conditions, however, this is a result of the way in which mental health professionals officially evaluate patients for psychological issues. When someone is diagnosed officially, they are evaluated on five dimensions that include things like clinical conditions, medical conditions, and environmental stressors. The reason for this is to capture the complexity of disorders to get a better sense of the needs of the patient. It also means that someone who may be suffering from depression may be diagnosed with other corresponding disorders.

Dylan chose not to disclose these invisible disabilities to the supervisor for fear of judgment or lack of confidence in the employee's ability to do the job. The medications for these conditions made Dylan often be late for work. These medications made it difficult for Dylan to wake up in the mornings and make it to work on time. This came to the attention of Dylan's supervisor. The supervisor did not ask why Dylan was late, just asked what they could do to help Dylan get to work on time. After some discussion, it was determined that Dylan's schedule could be modified so that Dylan worked 8:30–5:30 rather than 8–5 as the rest of the department.

Some of Dylan's coworkers questioned Dylan about this change in schedule. Dylan responded to these inquiries with the statement that it was between the employee and the supervisor. This appeased the coworkers to a degree. Dylan felt uncomfortable confiding to coworkers about the diagnoses.

In this case, a simple change in schedule allowed the employee to get to work on time. Dylan's example is a great way to illustrate how sometimes employees are afraid to come forward and disclose an invisible disability to their supervisors or coworkers. Fortunately, in this case, Dylan's supervisor did not require a disclosure to work with an employee to figure out a way to accommodate the disability. Supervisors should be coached on when to evaluate their own expectations of their employees and make accommodations for those who work differently. If this were more common practice, invisible disabilities would not be a problem as often as they are because supervisors would already be trying to help when problems arise.

Case #5: The Bare Minimum

Alex is a librarian with a nerve condition called neuropathy that affects balance and ability to type, and it's been getting worse. Alex's colleagues know that Alex uses a cane (a visible indicator of disability), but may not realize that this specific condition affects more than just walking, and that there are invisible aspects of Alex's disability. Colleagues and supervisors are far more likely to casually accommodate a visible disability, such as having meetings closer to Alex, but they are less accommodating of the invisible aspects. Alex is a busy researcher who finds it increasingly more difficult to type or use a keyboard. It is scary for Alex, because so much of the job has to do with using a computer. Thankfully, Alex has had good experiences with supervisors understanding the condition and making accommodations such as providing an ergonomic mouse and keyboard. Alex also realizes that more accommodations will need to be requested as the condition gets worse. However, because Alex's condition is so comprehensively integrated into his whole life, he has had to deal with other ADA compliance issues. In Alex's own words:

> Accommodations have been made for me, but I've noticed more and more that institutions give lip service to accommodating disabilities, but in reality only give the bare minimum of ADA compliance. It's little stuff like the fact that the ADA-compliant bathroom stall is at the end when it should be in front. The doors sometimes don't open very well. This world is not ADA-compliant, and the laws don't help people the way they should. I notice this, and my disability isn't nearly as prominent as some of the folks I've seen. But I've become increasingly aware of how difficult it is, and how it's the bare minimum that's being accommodated. I don't think we go far enough in the world in general to really help those who have visible and invisible disabilities. Because it's very expensive, so I think a lot of institutions and businesses, public places, only do the bare minimum because it's cheaper. That's something that I have noticed whether in practically every city I've traveled to. It's really kind of sad.

Alex's case is a good example of why creative solutions for accommodations are necessary. With the world being hard enough for people with disabilities to move and work in, libraries should be doing what they can to accommodate each employee and help them achieve peak performance.

Discussion

These five cases have presented an argument for why creative solutions for invisible disabilities are important. In order to increase the innovative approach to solutions for work problems, those in the workforce need more information.

Employees need more guidance on when and how to disclose an invisible disability and the kinds of reasonable accommodations available for their conditions. Coworkers may see reasonable accommodations as favoritism without understanding the context. The general population of the library needs to be educated on potential manifestations of invisible disabilities and the types of reasonable accommodations they may encounter. Supervisors need more training on what kinds of invisible disabilities may exist and how they can be accommodated. Supervisors and HR should also create a work environment where invisible disabilities are not stigmatized.

Invisible disabilities require creative solutions because there is no clearly defined set of actions that will work in all cases. With visible disabilities, reasonable accommodations can sometimes be obvious or at least a little better defined. Employees who have trouble walking need access to elevators and may need their job responsibilities adjusted so they don't have to walk as much. Invisible disabilities will rarely be so direct and clear. Those involved should take each case as a completely new situation that requires completely new approaches as there is no "one size fits all" solution with invisible disabilities.

Acknowledgments

We would like to thank Heidi Winkler for her help with editing this essay.

REFERENCES

Anxiety and Depression Association of America. 2016. "Facts & Statistics." Accessed January 31, 2018. https://adaa.org/about-adaa/press-room/facts-statistics#.

Burkus, David. 2015. "Why Managers Are More Likely to Be Depressed." *Harvard Business Review*. Accessed January 31, 2018. https://hbr.org/2015/09/why-managers-are-more-likely-to-be-depressed.

Disabled World. 2017. "Invisible Disabilities List and Information." Disability World. Accessed January 18, 2018. https://www.disabled-world.com/disability/types/invisible/.

Invisible Disabilities Association. 2018. "How Do You Define Invisible Disability?" Accessed January 18, 2018. https://invisibledisabilities.org/what-is-an-invisible-disability/.

Contagious Creativity

Leveraging Staff Talents and Interest to Find Career Satisfaction

SHELIA GAINES *and* CASEY PARKMAN

Introduction

The music is from *Starsky and Hutch*. The scene fades in on the student's footsteps as he walks up the outside stairs to the front door of the building. He slings his backpack over his right shoulder and opens the door with his left hand. As he glances back with an imploring look, the shot pauses and the caption, *Calculations*, appears on the screen. No, this is not the opening scene from a 1970s movie. It is the promotional video for circulating technologies at the University of Memphis' McWherter Library. This and four other videos are the result of contagious creativity. In my position as Circulation department head, I have been intentional in modeling and encouraging creativity to my staff and the library as a whole.

You may be familiar with the concept of a contagion. A disease that can be widespread by close contact with an infected individual, and one isolated case can become an epidemic. This may seem like an odd comparison because it normally refers to something debilitating. However, I am referring to a more positive impact. Contagious creativity occurs when one staff member has an idea that jumpstarts opportunities for other employees to be part of a new concept or collaborate on an existing project. This is the epitome of the assertion often attributed to Albert Einstein that creativity is contagious and it is up to us to pass it on (O'Toole 2017).

One new idea, such as creative videos, can inspire a community, or, in our case, a department, to seek innovative ways to showcase their particular skills and talents or to contribute to the overall development of new ones. Such was the case with our Reserve Room manager, Casey Parkman, who has tapped into his substantial professional creativity to become the circulation department's resident Tech Guru and Movie Producer.

Casey enlisted the help of a regular cast of staff members from the circulation department. The role of each member is discussed repeatedly throughout the essay, but this brief introduction to their creative potential will help set the stage for what is to come.

Javin is a member of the collection maintenance team. He was a theater major in college and has several local acting credits as well as one national motion film appearance as an extra. Not only does he play the role of the student in the previously mentioned

Calculations video, he also portrays a student in all but one of the videos that Casey has produced.

Delaine is our Student Worker Supervisor. She co-starred with Javin in the first video and appeared with him and other circulation staff members in the *Calculations* video. Her dramatic flair and Javin's theater training were a big part of Shelia's inspiration for the first script.

Greg is our special projects assistant and local display design extraordinaire. He brings a creative flair to displays that the Outreach Committee spearheads as well as to special occasions installations, such as Banned Books Display and Finals Week Student Relaxation Zone. He is a supporting cast member in the previously mentioned *Calculations* video.

The Creative Contagion Effect (as Explained by Casey Parkman)

I would not necessarily think of Shelia as "patient zero" in the creative contagion flowchart, but she was the "patient" in whom the creative stimulus developed. Our similar backgrounds in writing often popped up in our conversations, and she has always seemed tolerant of my propensity to "geek out" when talking about movies or TV shows. I assume that tendency made me susceptible to catching the creative bug she was harboring. One day she talked about a video project she had in mind for the department and asked if I would like to make the videos. I had never made a video in my life, hardly ever touched a camcorder or video camera, and had no idea even where to start when editing a film. So I said, "Sure, sounds fun."

The first video we made was about our basic checkout procedures, with the script written by Shelia and starring Javin and Delaine. We filmed the video using a Flip Camera—one technology item we have for checkout. We hoped for a dual promotional benefit by using our wares: to create the videos and publicize the circulating equipment at the same time. Putting the video together was a lot of fun with a ton of learning experiences in the filming and editing processes. The script was well written, the acting part was well performed, but I was not thrilled with the production quality. I had to do better. The creative contagion had fully taken hold of me.

Javin ended up being my muse and also my main source of good-natured contention. He has a theatre background and often requests repeated takes of lines after finding his performance to be "ugly." He has been the star of every video since the first one, along with Greg who has proven to be his "straight man" and a great source of ideas for the skits. The three of us have formed a partnership in making these videos and doing our best not only to create different concepts for each one, but also to try to learn and apply new filmmaking techniques. The contagion was spreading.

The next video, *Calculations,* was our opportunity to spread out and bring in more cast members. Greg, Javin, Delaine, two other library employees, and I booked one of our library instruction rooms and went in with a concept and a few found props. We had no script, only a fantastic chemistry we knew would produce a cool little video about graphing calculators we have for students to check out. Javin played a student unable to purchase an appropriate calculator for his trigonometry final, so he brought in a massive 1970s-style ribbon-fed printing calculator—one that makes a ton of noise. Greg played the out-of-touch and narcoleptic professor hollering "Who let a cat into the room!" when awoken by the noise. The other employees played annoyed students who finally informed the hapless Javin that our library had modern and quiet calculators he was more than welcome to go check out.

Six of us bounced around ideas on lines, timing, blocking, and other film-sounding words, and went with what seemed to work, or just redid the shot if it didn't. It took us an hour to finish the whole thing, even without the script, and it was one of the most creatively fulfilling times I have had. We later added opening and closing credits, title cards, and music, all inspired by 70s films and television to give the whole thing a slick vibe. The fun we had while working on this video inspired us to get bigger and better. Our next video was about an impromptu movie theater where Javin set up a screen, chairs, popcorn maker, and refreshments right outside of our library to impress his date. The video was meant to promote our circulating mini projectors. It featured a cast of twelve people, including my toddler son. We plan to do a promotional video disguised as a horror movie trailer for our next project. I have also filmed events, presentations, and speakers for the library as we work towards amassing a digital collection of library-related video content.

Similar to how I was approached to make videos despite my lack of experience, I was asked to teach workshops in the library on our 3D printers after the previous instructors accepted other positions. I watched these machines before as they printed three-dimensional objects, such as horse figurines, chains, and tiny robots, but I had no idea how to use them. I had never even seen a 3D printer before working at the library, but now I was going to teach others how to use them? Sure, sounds fun.

The summer before I was supposed to start the workshops, I spent nearly every day printing toys, cookie cutters, phone cases, and puzzles just trying to learn all I could about the process. It taught me how to troubleshoot, what little quirks the printers had, and gave me ideas on what to emphasize in the workshops. I started the workshops in the 2016 fall semester, and by the 2017 spring semester, I had to double the number of classes I was teaching to keep up with the demand.

My creative partnership with Greg continued as we discussed bringing board games into the library for checkout and for programming possibilities. At almost the same time, we came up with the idea of 3D-printing our own games and started with a checkerboard. Each checker piece had to be printed, as well as each square of the board, which would interlock like a puzzle. We made it roughly 4 times the size of a standard checkerboard—similar to the checker sets guests play on the front porch at Cracker Barrel restaurants. Between Greg, a student worker, and myself it took over 200 hours of printing time, which we completed in about two months. We set it out in our lobby during finals week, along with coloring pages and candy. We soon realized that we had a big hit on our hands as the board was almost constantly utilized. We have put it out for each finals week since, along with a chess set we started, and even left it out into the next semester as students were still using it. Due to the high interest, we began talking with various departments about starting an actual board game checkout program, proving just how contagious creativity can be.

For several years Greg has installed enormous detailed interactive book displays in the library's rotunda for Banned Book Week. Soon after I was hired at McWherter, he recruited me to help him realize his grand designs and build the displays. During our first year working together we set up a full-sized skeleton at a podium with chairs for an audience. We connected a wireless microphone to a laptop that continuously played the audio book version of *V for Vendetta* through the podium's speaker. Many students would stop for a while to listen to our skeleton "read." The next year Greg built a book cave out of shelves and stacked books; it took up a large percentage of the rotunda; and students could walk through several paths in the cave to look at challenged books layered within its walls. For our next display he envisioned and built an elevated platform in the middle of the rotunda, with a scene of a busy office space with desks, shelves, and computers playing videos from the Banned Book Week website. Our skeleton returned to this display as the overworked office employee. Our two most recent Banned Book Week displays won the Tennessee Library Association award for best display. We also help put up other displays or set up other events for the library like a display and art event for Women's History Month. We added books shelves and reading areas to frame in the display and event in the rotunda. Typically the rotunda floor is free of any furniture or shelving, but the setup for the display proved so popular with students and library employees that we now keep it in the rotunda space year round. We regularly alternate books in the area depending on significant dates, local events, or library happenings. We have since added the tables for students to be able to play our 3D-printed board games or sit and take their minds off school with coloring sheets.

Through all of this, I have learned skills and technologies I never thought I would have the chance to use, much less teach to others. I have learned a lot about my own talents in the process. The quality of the work I am producing is not for me to judge, but I have enjoyed and still am enjoying doing it all. I get to learn and share and use my creative skills in ways that make work fun. Because of Shelia's initial creative contagion, I realized I was in the career field I needed to stay in, but I wanted to learn and do and be more. I was accepted into the Information Science program at University of Tennessee Knoxville, where I plan to focus on the technology that has defined much of my career in the library field. And that sounds fun, too.

Leveraging the Creative Flowchart (Shelia's Creative Concepts)

I have always enjoyed allowing my own creative side to shine though. For instance, each year at the library's annual staff retreat, our former dean allowed each department head the option of choosing any presentation format to share accomplishments from the previous academic year and the plans for the upcoming one. Our department's first report was an audio recording of me singing our stats and goals to the tune of *Seasons of Life*, from the musical *Rent*. The lyrics from that song ask "How do you measure a year in a life? In daylights? In sunsets? In midnights? In cups of coffee?" I changed the words to "How do you measure a year in circulation? In check-ins? In check-outs? In billings? In weekly schedules?" I also included lyrics about gate counts, reserves and collection maintenance. My concurrent PowerPoint slideshow reflected statistics, goals and other department accomplishments strategically arranged to this newly created library-related song parody. The stage was set. Each year since, the library staff came to expect something different in the Circulation department's report that would add a little extra flair to the retreat. I enjoyed sharing the report in a unique way and the staff benefited from a little bit of extra effort and creative thinking.

Similarly, as Casey's work moved beyond circulation to include filming library-sponsored events, other departments within the library were able to take advantage of his new skills. It wasn't long before he caught the attention of the head of Systems. The end result of collaboration between Casey and the head of Systems was a new makerspace. This new creative space, the auxiliary rooms for video and audio production as well as presentation practice, will benefit staff professional development and the library as an organizational marketing tool. Our hope is for students to start creating their own films, podcasts, and artwork, and to spread the creative bug out into the world.

The goal of creativity is not to take anything away from anyone else but to add momentum or interest in your own area. Find a good balance between creativity and purpose. Years of practice have helped me, for the most part, not to make the mistake of having too much creativity and not enough concrete information concerning the specific project or assignment.

In order to be most effective, creativity in the library should be both refreshing and informative. For instance, when Greg installs a display in the library rotunda in recognition of and as submission to the Tennessee Library Association's statewide Banned Book Week display contest, it is always aesthetically pleasing. However, if you look closer, it also has a cohesive theme throughout. The purpose and goal of this project are seamlessly interwoven. One year, the display was set up to resemble a courtroom. There were placeholders on all the chairs with the names of banned book authors. The defending lawyer mannequin was presenting a slideshow on a widescreen TV that showed examples of banned and challenged books along with the 'crimes' they had been challenged for. Artfully arranged banned books left observers with a visual image of what a literary trial would look like. Likewise, when, Javin uses his theater voice for the closing announcements, the customers know it's time to start packing up to leave but they are also treated to his channeled "Morgan Freeman" in the process. It can be challenging to find the perfect mix of creativity and information, but sometimes it turns out just right.

We were able to be both entertaining and informative at a former institution when one of my colleagues convinced our library director to host a Murder Mystery Night in the library. I wrote the script for the "murder plot" and coached our "victim" as she recorded her "in case of my untimely demise" monologue. Many freshmen students received an introduction to the academic library in a fun way, and the creative contagion had caught on. Our director was not a fan of games, but by show time he was fully on board and even created his own "persona" for the event. He welcomed the students to the library and the mystery night using British accent. When we hosted the event again the next year, he showed up in a trench coat and top hat as Benny "The Bookman" Balducci, The students and the staff were equally impressed by his "mafia" mystique as they were with his previous year's royalty routine.

During my time at that same institution, I was also the supervisor of the library's student workers. I encouraged the ones with dramatic tendencies to assist us in the mystery night. Of course, once they found out what we had in mind, it did not take much convincing. Student workers can be your biggest supporters in creative projects. They will often bring ideas that appeal to their peers. Don't worry if a little tweaking is necessary to make their ideas work within the parameters of your organizations. Just knowing that their creative energy is appreciated often fuels their desire to contribute more. I believe it was actually our students who gave us the idea to ask if professors would be willing to offer any additional credit to students who attended the event since the mystery would be solved by using resources from all areas of the library. Additionally, our students let us know that they would be willing to stay as long as we needed them that night (as long as they could clock in for work, of course). Interestingly enough, several of the students who worked for us during Mystery Night and future creative endeavors spent their entire college career working in the library, and are now full-time librarians. Naturally, I concluded that the interest we showed in their professional potential beyond their normal work duties helped shape their career goals.

Paying attention to staff members' current interests is an excellent way to tap into creative energies that they might already have. For instance, when another circulation staff member here at McWherter Library submitted a request to take a computer class, I talked with him briefly about his objectives. I learned that the popularity of the 3D printer class inspired him to teach a HTML class because that was the subject in which he was interested. Similarly, Casey's developing interest in all things tech led to his selection as the Circulation department's designated service provider (DSP). This means, in addition to his Reserve Room duties, he is responsible for general computer troubleshooting within the department and determining if an IT service ticket is appropriate. It was a natural extension of his current interest.

Furthermore, as Casey mentioned in his section, the first video he produced was about basic circulation checkout procedures. Even though Casey was dissatisfied with the production quality of it, it was still very beneficial to us. Casey was able to learn from his mistakes and groom his skills with each subsequent video produced. Additionally, I saw the creative potential in both Javin and Delaine and was happy to discover a unique outlet to showcase their creative energies while promoting the services and resources of the Circulation department.

Another step I have taken in encouraging staff creativity to the next level was suggesting for Greg to create a conference presentation on his creative techniques of display design. The videos, rotunda displays, and end of semester activities for students are perfect material for that professional development opportunity. He has already developed a session on simple, creative, low-cost book repair solutions that he presents regularly at local conferences.

This would be a good time to mention that Casey, Greg, and Javin are members of the Outreach Committee. They are tasked with assisting the Community Engagement Librarian in coordinating outreach programs/activities and in advertising and highlighting the library's resources, emerging technologies, and collections. The responsibilities of the committee tie in perfectly with their creative interests.

With a little creative thinking, supervisors can easily use simple guidelines to broaden new concepts and ideas into potential professional skills:

- Look for and find ways to appreciate creativity and initiative in all staff.
- Find out what their passions are and see if they match current or possible future job responsibilities.
- Find outlets such as programs or special events in which a more outspoken or outgoing person may channel their creative juices or frustrations.
- Publically recognize creative efforts.
- Allow staff autonomy to exercise their creative interest as it pertains to their professional responsibilities.
- Remember that not all creative ideas will work in all professional settings.

The exciting thing is that while not all creative ideas will work everywhere, creativity can still be utilized anywhere. Creative contagion flowcharts can be and should be as diversified as are each organization's goals and objectives. Even if some staff members cannot write a script themselves, a good script written by someone else can inspire them to act in it. A staff member who has little interest in the latest electronic gadgets may be the perfect person to host a board game session. Leverage staff talents, interests, and skill sets with your creative goals. If, as the supervisor, you don't feel you have the time or interest to be "a patient zero," consider the previously mentioned guidelines and see if you can find staff members who are. You might be surprised at how quickly their ideas become contagious.

Conclusion

By allowing employees to tap into their creative energy, managers can increase productivity, improve employee morale, and develop new skill sets within the staff. Creative autonomy is simply a space in which to create, be it physical or virtual. The implementation of new technology as circulation material in McWherter Library led to the development of promotional videos that introduced the technology and its benefits to students and staff. Acquiring a 3D printer prompted the necessity for Casey to learn how to use it, which inspired him to want to teach others what he learned and to learn as much as he could through the MLS program.

This opened opportunities for staff to showcase natural and newly acquired skills and talents. It also led to a plan to repurpose library space to establish video and audio recording suites for podcasting, interviews, and presentations. This is giving us yet another creative outlet that will open staff development opportunities for the entire library. Other departments already have staff members learning to use the 3D printer and teach classes because the demand has grown so that additional help is needed for instruction.

The best way to empower staff to develop professional creativity is by modeling and encouraging it. Pay attention to staff interest beyond their current responsibilities. Pass along webinar and conference specifics that may be of interest to them. Suggest new ways to marry talents and interest of the staff with the objectives of the organization. Be creative. It's catching.

REFERENCES

O'Toole, Garrison. 2017. "Creativity Is Contagious. Pass It On." Quote Investigator, May 15. https://quote investigator.com/2017/05/16/contagious/.

Parkman, Casey. 2015. "Video Games in the Library?" Filmed December 2015 at McWherter Library in Memphis. Video, 3:48. https://www.youtube.com/watch?v=Q_gU4X4zrus&list=PLrg_dpZ2-LywUpvnjMFQvk-c2hXjX9chL&index=3

Parkman, Casey. 2016a. "Calculations." Filmed November 2016 at McWherter Library in Memphis. Video, 4:09. https://www.youtube.com/watch?v=U5E40B84eDI&list=PLrg_dpZ2-LywUpvnjMFQvk-c2hXjX9chL&index=1

Parkman, Casey. 2016b. "The Great Library Chase." Filmed May 2016 at McWherter Library in Memphis. Video, 4:04. https://www.youtube.com/watch?v=VaS5MmPauIk&index=2&list=PLrg_dpZ2-LywUpvnjMFQvk-c2hXjX9chL.

Developing In-House Support
for Early Career Staff

PAULA ARCHEY, MAGGIE NUNLEY *and*
ERIN E. PAPPAS

As mid-career librarians at a large, occasionally siloed, and oftentimes perplexing institution, we know how difficult it can be to find your feet at a new place, particularly when it happens to be your first professional job. Even for the more seasoned among us, each change of position or institution comes with concomitant setbacks and confusion. Second-career librarians, alternative academics, and non–LIS professionals who simply happen to work in libraries face similar issues.

While individual circumstances undoubtedly differ, we can identify some key needs that crosscut those differences. First, there is an overarching need to become oriented to the new workplace as physical location(s) and as a culture, and learn how it functions organizationally. Many people may be new to librarianship as a profession, and thus unclear about what may be unique to that organization and what may be shared. Yet even if they are not novices, many library employees still require help in navigating the different expectations that will define and shape their careers.

To this end we created an in-house support group at the University of Virginia Library (hereafter, "the Library") specifically meant to reach early- and mid-career library staff. In this essay, we walk you through our process: explain how we formed the group and why, and describe how we now keep momentum going. We discuss the reasons we established the group and what needs we found that were best addressed through such an informal community rather than administratively. Following that, we lay out what types of outreach we did to include both new and existing library staff. We touch upon projects and proposals that worked as well as those that did not. Finally, we offer some specific lessons learned and point out potential pitfalls in undertaking a similar endeavor at your own organization.

Background and Structure

To better understand our motivations and process, it is necessary to have some background on our library, its structure, and recent organizational history. Like many large institutions, the Library maintains multiple categories for staff. The clearest divide in terms of status is between faculty and staff appointments, with faculty having assigned rank and tenure. In 2013 the University stopped hiring librarians as faculty. This meant that any librarian hired after 2013 would be classified as university or professional staff. For further context, the Library underwent a major administrative reorganization in 2013 where all departments were restructured. Six existing staff members, the Senior Leadership Team (SLT), were selected to oversee each newly formed unit. Other staff members chose the new unit in which they wanted to work. Most, but not all, staff were placed into the units of their first choice. SLT was also given the responsibility of dividing the units into smaller teams and appointing supervisors to the smaller teams as they saw fit. The effects of this reorganization are impacting relationships and operations even now, nearly five years later at time of writing. As units' and individuals' roles changed, many responsibilities were lost in the shuffle. In many cases, what were once clearly defined responsibilities were taken away from specific units or individuals, but never reassigned to new ones. This continuing uncertainty means that gaps in communication still remain.

Two years after the reorganization was undertaken, the library conducted a climate survey to assess its impact on our workplace. The climate survey had between a 60 percent and 80 percent response rate, hovering between 115 and 150 responses for each question. The survey asked staff for feedback on nine aspects of their jobs post-reorganization: job satisfaction, acknowledgment, supervisor relations, library leadership, communication, organizational values, resource availability, staff development, and reorganization. Staff responded to questions using a five-point Likert Scale. A key takeaway from the survey is that staff did not feel that the Library was adequately supporting their professional and career development goals. In a sample of the questions related to issues of career, advancement, and job development, the highest percentage of responses (25–39 percent) were neutral about the support and offerings coordinated by the Library. For instance, when asked whether their library work helped achieve career goals, the most popular response was "neutral" with 28 percent. When asked if there are opportunities to advance in the library, the most popular response was "neutral" with 25 percent followed by "strongly disagree" with 23 percent. Although deficiencies were identified after the reorganization, such as a lack of understanding of the relationship between current library work and career goals, the Library has yet to chart a unified way to address these needs.

Part of the problem may be with the structure of the survey itself, as the responses lack any context. For instance, the survey revealed that 39 percent of respondents feel that Library training is not relevant to their personal and developmental goals. The question itself is problematic as it assumes that all staff establish specific personal and developmental goals and that they are aware of the Library's training opportunities. Without context, it is impossible to know if the issue is that training is not relevant, or if staff are unclear on why or how to set goals. Similarly, it is unclear whether they lack awareness regarding Library training and development or simply have yet to take advantage of it.

The nature of the survey and many of its findings also underscore a fractured communication system. Communication within the Library is drastically varied by frequency and method, and between and across units. Because of this, staff do not always receive the same messages, depending on how and when they get their information. Granted, the Library is not unique in this regard, as any large, diffuse organization may struggle with effective communication. To give a few examples:

- depending on the unit, in-person meetings may be held frequently or hardly at all.
- multiple Library-wide listservs are maintained but only one of these is mandatory, often leading to important information being shared on a listserv that does not reach the whole staff.
- multiple, different library-wide content-sharing platforms are operating simultaneously (Confluence, Staff Library Site, Springshare, Collab, Box), and not all units use the same platforms

Existing Support for Professional Growth

The Library provides support for professional growth, primarily in the form of monetary reimbursements for professional conference participation. Though time allotted for research and writing differs between faculty and staff, the Library extends the same monetary professional development benefits to all full-time employees: $1,000 a year to be used for conference registrations, transportation, lodging, and other costs associated with professional travel. New employees may use up to $1600 per year for two of their first three years of employment with the Library.

Internally, staff often host webinars, offer talks or discussion forums on subject-specific topics, and provide information sessions on new or innovative tools and services. Our Learning Coordinator maintains a list of professional development opportunities, along with other external opportunities, and posts them to the staff learning calendar. This calendar is maintained on the staff website and distributed bi-weekly to the all-staff listserv. Pre-registration for events is encouraged but not mandatory. Typically events touch upon a wide range of topics, are voluntary, and open to anyone interested in attending.

In addition to fostering a culture of learning from colleagues and offering monetary support, the Library offers one directed professional development opportunity. The Library Fellows' Program, which began in 2015, is a two-year program for extremely small cohorts (2–3 each year) of self-selected applicants. This program aims to develop future library leaders through staff development, "by allowing participants to gain both conceptual insight and practical knowledge on how to function as an effective library leader" (University 2015). Fellows are given exposure to each organizational area and to the existing leadership teams. As the outcomes state, the program is intended for employees to gain skills and experience in organizational leadership or to develop possible new directions for library services. Although the program is only open to employees who are not directors or on leadership teams, it is too small to assist even a fraction of the people who need workplace and professional support. Replicating some of the stated goals of the Library Fellows program while making them accessible to a wider group was a determining factor in our decision to start the Early- to Mid-Career Group.

Forming the Early- to Mid-Career Group

While we did not initially seek out formal structures for the career support group—codifying it organizationally, or making it bureaucratic, burdensome, or onerous in terms of time commitments—it quickly became evident that we would need administrative support in order for the group to be established. To that end, we opened up the group to anyone on staff at the library who fit a very loose set of criteria. Our goal was to create an internal community for staff with similar levels of professional experience who could provide support to one another directly. We specifically did not want the group to be limited by whether or not an individual had an MLS. Rather, we envisioned a forum that would represent all areas of the library, connecting people who may have not had many opportunities to interact. The following criteria were all we required for involvement:

- professional focus
- open to paraprofessionals
- not dependent on holding an M.L.S.
- between 0–15 years of experience
- non-supervisors

Publicity was primarily achieved by word of mouth, personalized emails, and promoting our meetings in the staff learning calendar. We also formed an internal listserv and included individuals who wanted to be looped in to our communications. Several mid- and second-career staff felt this was a better use of their time than attending meetings. As for frequency, once a month was sufficient to start building a cohesive group.

As this was a grassroots effort rather than a top-down directive, it seemed appropriate to ask participants to articulate a shared vision. We did this through several initial in-person meetings and by conducting a survey using Google Docs. Not surprisingly, it turned out that many people had overlapping concerns and interests. Among these the most commonly articulated concerns and areas of interest were:

- gaining familiarity with the organization
- sharing and retaining institutional history
- having a place for informal mentoring
- establishing best practices on the job
- managing upwards
- forming relationships across units and departments
- fostering research partnerships
- building awareness of opportunities for funding, leave, and projects
- highlighting professional development opportunities
- onboarding new staff, especially early career staff
- introducing staff to the profession and its structures
- raising awareness of professional organizations

Initially, we expected that the group would have plenty to discuss without a formal agenda or planned structure. Conversation about things that were lacking or areas of confusion came easily enough, but merely providing this space for discussion did not seem sufficient as a long-term goal. Thus as our group developed, we found that it was better to use the allocated time to make headway on specific projects, to work on shared documentation, or to bring in outside speakers to discuss administrative policies in place or those being developed Library-wide. These collaborative projects have been extremely useful in several ways. Most importantly, they have helped us establish a baseline of organizational knowledge among group members. When we had our initial meetings, there were many overlapping questions from group members in different departments: particularly regarding education benefits, conference funding, the way onboarding works, travel planning and funding, and so forth.

When we began the support group, we sent out a survey to everyone who was on our initial email list. It was meant to gauge professional affiliations, experience with research, writing, and publishing, and interest in finding partners and collaborators. To that end, we asked the following questions:

- What professional organizations do you belong to?
- Have you published before? If yes, where?
- Do you have any ongoing projects or research? If so, what are they?
- Are you interested in collaborating with others in this group?
- Please list your areas of interest.

Based on the results from this survey, it would appear that many of our early- and mid-career staff are somewhat untethered from their professional organizations. A third of the respondents belong to no professional organizations, whether regional or national, at all. Others belong to multiple organizations, but even so, half of these have never published before. Thus it would appear that there is a disconnect between professional affiliation and ensuing research and publication amongst our group. Some of this can be attributed to the fact that the Library is not a faculty system, at least not amongst the newer cohort of those who were hired as staff. That being said, we hope that creating an informal community of practice will allow us to make headway on issues of professionalization. At the very least, it allows staff spread across disparate departments and buildings to come together to establish support networks and a designated place for development.

We are in the early stages of this project and find many areas for continued growth and improvement. Both the group itself and the practice of colleagues informally, yet intentionally, supporting one another are new ventures. As a result of the documented need for and interest in topics related to career and professional development, we received immediate interest from those who were initially contacted about the group. Yet curiously, that interest did not span evenly across departments. We found that those in departments more recognizable for performing "traditional" library work (e.g., subject liaisons, teaching and instruction librarians) have been more actively involved than those who were not (e.g., user experience, data, digital humanities). Working on common issues, such as onboarding, has also alerted us to the vast difference in approaches from departments within the library. While there is no unified effort for supporting early- to mid-career staff, some departments have created support and documentation for their individual staff that range from incredibly comprehensive to bare basics. The same is true for mentoring within individual departments, as well as allocating monies for travel and conferences. Again, this points up the need for shared and consistent documentation that can be easily disseminated across departments and among new employees.

We did find that the group had many shared needs. As mentioned above, a common theme to come out of our early conversations was the sense of feeling adrift within the Library itself. This may have meant different things to different people, but it bears repeating that—whether as a set of buildings, as interrelated and overlapping processes, as an organization, or some combination thereof—the Library can be difficult to navigate. After coming together and talking through our shared issues, we discovered that many new, and even some existing employees, had only partial knowledge about these underlying foundations. Thus it made complete sense for us to begin by building that foundation, making the implicit and tacit knowledge about how to navigate the Library and the University as explicit and known as possible. Foundational information, such as important contacts, communication platforms, workflows, etc., is currently housed in multiple locations and unevenly distributed to new employees. It may be distributed via email from an HR representative or supervisor, located on private or public University-maintained websites, passed down through conversation, or be housed on one of the Library's many communication platforms.

Several members had begun working at the Library quite recently, so the onboarding process seemed like a logical starting point. Creating streamlined documentation for onboarding was one of the first tasks undertaken by the group as a whole, since this information was piecemeal and often not accessible. The Scholars' Lab, the Library's digital humanities lab, was able to provide us with their comprehensive onboarding materials. The materials include both general and Scholars' Lab-specific information, but they make explicit the internal knowledge usually passed down by managers or fellow employees. We combined these with the varying onboarding checklists that many of us had received from our managers when we ourselves started. Each member of the group searched their email for onboarding information. Individuals in the group volunteered to mine the staff website, their own email archives, and Confluence for checklists, threads, comments, and unmoderated conversations pertaining to onboarding. Coming together, we found that our collective knowledge was greater than any one individual's experience. We shared challenges, remembered missteps, asked questions, and described successful strategies for becoming oriented to a new place. In the end, we compiled that collective input and created a living document to be shared with new staff moving forward. It will also be used for onboarding new fellows hired under the Library's ACRL Diversity Residency program.

As we discussed onboarding and all that it entailed, we unearthed further questions about how to best navigate the administrative structures of the Library. These ranged from the practical—how to request research and professional development funding, and access to benefits such as the educational benefit—to the more abstract—such as what future organizational structure might look like, the impact of organizational history, and the ongoing discussion regarding faculty status. While many of these are beyond the capacity of our group to address, it has made sense to bring in senior leadership to clarify areas of concern and clear up confusion. To that end, we invited the Deputy University Librarian to discuss Library administration's long-range goals for mentoring and professional development, to answer questions about these subjects, and to help inform them about the mission of the group. The Deputy University Librarian was able to shed some light on the Library's organizational structure and on the systems for accessing professional development and educational benefits, thus providing the group with a better foundation for identifying our goals and mission. Additionally, two spontaneous calls emerged from that meeting. First, a desire to provide mentoring for new employees and second, the discovery that though Library outreach is decentralized, many people contribute to it. As a result, we are now developing a way to share processes, ideas, contacts, and so on to make outreach a more unified effort.

The mission of the group is evolving in response to the participation of active members. Because this was a grassroots effort, we have not been tasked by administration with carrying out specific charges. Currently, we are concerned with providing support for development and a community of practice above all else. Like with so many other things, time, or lack of it, is an acute issue for this group. It may be due in part to the fact that career development and professional involvement are not immediately pressing issues for group members, especially if they have not yet considered their long-term professional goals. Also, while professional development and educational funding are available to all staff, the support and time required to serve on a committee, chair an initiative, or to undertake research, publish, and present is uneven. Nor is it required for many of those in the group since they are classified as staff, rather than faculty. This compounds the difficulty of focusing on those areas of development. Our future efforts will likely focus on in-house mentoring and maximizing professional development benefits rather than activities more commonly required for promotion and tenure.

We recognize that our approach does not fit the needs of everyone involved in the group. As noted above, there is still a great need for one-on-one mentoring, whether formally sanctioned through administrative channels, or informally through other channels of connection. Though we have made some headway in this area, we have not yet implemented either approach. Many of our group members mentioned, in the survey and in conversation, that they would benefit from having a mentor, yet have not made overtures to individuals either within the Library or their own professional networks. In the coming months, we plan to reach out to colleagues who have been involved with in-house mentoring elsewhere to see what insights they can offer. It may turn out that creating pathways for formal relationships will provide a way to connect more seasoned colleagues with their early career counterparts.

That being said, the formation of our group has enabled informal relationships to spring up organically among those who share immediate and long-term career interests as well as experience. The most successful so far has been a conference proposal that came about because of related conversations regarding research interests. Instead of developing multiple, competing submissions, we formed a collective including members from both inside and outside the career group and across Library departments, with experience ranging from one year to over a decade.

Conclusions: Takeaways and Lessons Learned

One unexpected reaction to forming the early- to mid-career support group was getting pushback from managerial staff regarding its existence. Specifically, we heard concerns about age (people in the group tended to be under forty years of age) and the fact that managerial staff were not invited to take part. Our thought was that it would be inappropriate to ask junior staff to share their personal and professional concerns with supervisors present in the room. There also was a fair amount of back-and-forth conversations regarding definitions and terminology. What did it mean to be 'early- to mid-career' staff? What about 'professional'? Did someone's degree make a difference? What about their seniority in terms of years of service, even if they had not yet been in a professional role during that time? While we recognize that mid-career and middle managers have their own sets of concerns, at least some of which might overlap, we ultimately thought it would be counterproductive to include them in our cohort. What is more, the managers and supervisors at the Library have their own regular meetings, and thus have a built-in network of their own to tap into.

Ultimately, we would suggest that regular meetings, which are as open and informal as possible, can go a long way towards creating an inclusive community that spans multiple departments. We also decided that while we did not need to totally transform the character of our group and its meetings, it would help to have some more accountability. Thus we now have a standing agenda item to collectively identify individuals who are new to the Library and to send them personalized invitations to our meetings. We are also establishing a web presence using Confluence, in order to make our work transparent to the Library at large. We hope that this will alleviate some of the critiques that came from administration. The creation of this specific group also highlighted the need for support to be distributed throughout the organization. While we focused on new arrivals to the library, we unwittingly hit upon a universal need to have larger conversations about a variety of issues: becoming familiar with new responsibilities and expectations; setting and achieving professional and personal goals; navigating the culture of an institution and a profession. The early- to mid-career group assumed many topics that were unique to their cohort, including imposter syndrome, confusion about the course of a career path, and lack of access to mentors. This has sparked a multiple rewarding conversations about the need for informal sources of support and encouragement among a variety of groups such as first-time managers, those moving into their second careers, and those who are late into their careers. While it is beyond our capacity to establish each and every one of these support networks, we hope that providing a transparent and ongoing support structure, flexible enough to accommodate the needs of many people at different stages in their careers, will begin to make inroads in this direction.

REFERENCE

University of Virginia Library Fellows Steering Committee. 2015. "University Library Fellows Program." Accessed November 15, 2017, from private UVA Library intranet.

PART VI

Visual and Performing Arts

Music to My Ears

Using Amateur Music-Making
as a Means of Vocational Specialty

BRUCE R. SCHUENEMAN

This essay examines how violin lessons, concurrent with a first professional position, blossomed into a specialization in the French Violin School. This led to books, articles, numerous book reviews (over 60 for *Library Journal*, nearly all on music), prefaces to scores (a recent activity), Naxos Records essays (over 20 essays to date, many concerning French School composers), presentations at conferences, and book chapters, including an academic European book publisher. My avocation resulted in a Kennedy Center podcast and interviews with the *Houston Chronicle* and the *Wall Street Journal*. The essay discusses the symbiotic relationship between vocation and avocation, and how librarians can make an avocational specialty work for their career.

A Musical Avocation

In 1979 my wife and I moved from California to Texas for my first professional library position at Texas A&I University in Kingsville, Texas. One of my very first purchases was a student violin. I had taken piano lessons as a teenager, but the violin was new to me. The sound, no doubt, was awful at first, but my musical avocation would lead to the discovery of Pierre Rode, which would in turn have a major impact on my career. I did not plan for my avocation to directly influence my career. As I look back, I consider it fortunate that my avocation could be integrated into my career, and that the ability to marry a creative endeavor with one's vocation is both satisfying personally and useful professionally.

By 1979 the strings program was on the downslope at A&I. An orchestra, active until the mid–1970s, had been allowed to die. Still a member of the faculty, however, was Dr. Thomas Pierson, an Eastman School educated violinist. I began taking lessons with Dr. Pierson in 1980. Like any enthusiast, I read extensively on my new love, and habitually purchased scores above my level of expertise. Dr. Pierson lent me his copy of *Nurtured by Love* (Suzuki 1983). Suzuki's primary message is that any child possesses the ability to learn the violin, just as any child can learn their native language. Moreover, that playing an instrument is (or should be) about love. When Dr. Pierson left the university for a year while pursuing research associated with an NEH grant, his substitute organized a string quartet and recruited me for summer musicals. My violin career was on its way.

While reading a "teach yourself violin" book (Rowland-Entwistle 1973), I discovered a reference to Pierre Rode (1774–1830), a violinist/composer active in the late 18th and early 19th centuries. Rode was said to have written violin concertos accessible to intermediate players. I learned that several of Rode's concertos, especially numbers 6 and 7, were still in print. As soon as my abilities were (more or less) equal to the task, I began practicing Rode's Violin Concerto No. 6 in B-Flat. My enthusiasm sparked a desire to purchase different editions of Rode's work, and, in my pursuit to find as many Rode works as possible, to contact the music publisher Peters in New York. Peters had published concertos 4,6,7,8,11 in 1930 or 1931, often with editor supplied cadenzas (none by Rode himself were ever published). Peters was able to supply me with the 4th concerto, whose slow movement I would later play publicly.

An Avocation as Scholarly Pursuit

During the mid–1980s, Texas A&I began tightening scholarly requirements of tenure-track faculty. Librarians, as tenure-track faculty, were expected to engage in scholarly pursuits. Finding little material on Rode, scholarly or otherwise, I thought that Rode might be an appropriate subject for an article. I searched for a suitable platform and found *The Violexchange*, a journal published by the Department of Music at Carnegie Mellon University. Since I was working on Rode's Violin Concerto No. 6 and was familiar with it, I decided to write an article on this concerto. My consideration of Rode's "minor masterpiece," including a sidebar on whether Thomas Jefferson may have heard Rode play, was published in 1990 (Schueneman 1990).

At this point in my career, I began to think seriously of concentrating my scholarly endeavors on music, and specifically on Rode and the French Violin School of which he was a member. I was able to do this in part because at the time library administration accepted scholarly endeavor in any field as legitimate research for librarians. This was unusual. One history professor, who had published little in his field, had published more extensively in his avocation (ornithology). None of his ornithology scholarly publications counted in his department.

My next project was to obtain and translate one of the few biographies of Rode, Pougin's *Notice sur Rode* (Pougin 1874). With several university colleagues assisting in the effort, my translation was self-published in 1994 (Pougin 1994). Currently WorldCat lists 29 holding libraries, including Harvard, Yale, Cambridge, and Julliard. To publish the work, I created a publishing company and obtained ISBNs, as well as a Texas sales tax permit.

As I continued my slow labor on Pougin's text, I became aware of *Strings* magazine, a popular magazine for string players. I submitted a proposal for an article on Rode, and it was published in 1992 (Schueneman 1992a). Because I now had a reputation as being knowledgeable on French School composers, *Strings* asked me to review Rode's colleague Baillot's *The Art of the Violin* (Schueneman 1992b), as well as music of Rode's teacher Viotti (Schueneman 1993).

In tandem with efforts to produce articles, I put my name forward to write book reviews for *Library Journal*. From 1992 to 1998 my six reviews concerned history, literature, and politics. Beginning in 2001 my LJ assignments became exclusively musical. From 2001 to present I have written over 65 reviews on books with musical subjects. While many of these reviews concerned classical music (Beethoven, Brahms, Rachmaninoff, Cliburn), some reviews dealt with popular music: Tin Pan Alley, Frank Sinatra, Richard Rogers, Paul Dresser, Jerome Kern, Stan Kenton, and Lorenz Hart, among others. Reviewing is a means of keeping familiar with a field in the widest sense and to read books one might not have read otherwise.

I proposed another article on Rode in 1993, this time to the editor of *Music Reference Services Quarterly* (MRSQ), William (Bill) Studwell. This was accepted under the title "The Search for the Minor Composer: The Case of Pierre Rode" (Schueneman 1994). Bill liked the format of the article and solicited six additional articles in the same format in the following two years. My "searches for the minor composer" included Charles de Beriot and Maria Malibran, Samuel Coleridge-Taylor, Felicien David, Giovanni Battista Viotti, Riccardo Drigo, and Fritz Kreisler.

Bill suggested several collaborations, which would be both books and double issues of MRSQ. Our collaborations concerned minor ballet composers, college fight songs, state songs, circus songs, and unappreciated songs from the late 19th and early 20th centuries. This offered scope for another skill: use of music notation software. Bill provided text and I supplied the notated scores. I contributed a limited amount to several prefaces and wrote most of *Minor Ballet Composers* (Schueneman 1997). Of lasting consequence were books on state songs (Studwell, Schueneman 1998b) and two volumes on college fight songs (Studwell, Schueneman 1998a and Studwell, Schueneman 2001). Until his death in 2010, Bill (a cataloger at Northern Illinois University), regularly participated in media events, usually concerning college fight songs or Christmas carols. After his death (despite our collaboration, we never met), I inherited some of these events, which included interviews with the *Houston Chronicle*, *Wall Street Journal*, and most recently *The New York Times* (Tracy 2018). The most interesting event was the opportunity to participate in a Kennedy Center for the Performing Arts podcast on college football songs (Kennedy Center ArtsEdge 2010). I was interviewed and recorded through the kind auspices of the local PBS affiliate, and waxed lyrical discussing Faulkner's mention of football in *The Hamlet*, among other effusions. Only several soundbites were used, none of them Faulkner material.

I worked throughout this period on a French Violin School book. I discovered that Paul Gelrud had written both a thesis (Gelrud 1940) and a dissertation (1944) on the French Violin School, altogether comprising over 500 pages and a veritable gold mine of information. Also important was continuing research into Rode and the French Violin School. During my researches references to the French Violin School suddenly appeared in various sources; one example is a reference to Rode in the letters of Mendelssohn's mother (Klein 1993), which showed that Rode and his German-born wife were intimates of the Mendelssohn family during Rode's seven-year stay in Berlin. My book was self-published in 2002 (Schueneman 2005). Later the book was revised as an ebook.

Now a collector of Rode concertos and an owner of several versions of Rode's violin concerto number 6 in my possession, I was able to compare various published editions. Rode's 6th concerto, while certainly not well-known, has been in print since its first publication in 1800, and a number of various versions are available for purchase or through libraries. It became clear that the version edited by Sam Franko, published in 1916 by

Carl Fischer, was unusual in several respects as compared to other published versions. Essentially Franko had shortened some passages, changed the location of the first movement cadenza, and made other editorial changes which appear in no other published version. The more I explored the violin repertoire, the more such editorial high-handedness became apparent. This generated an idea for an article on the necessity for libraries to collect various versions of the same musical work. While major composers may have urtext and other scholarly examination related to published scores, for many minor composers, comparison of different published versions may be the only way to discover the composer's intentions. Franko's edited score is unique among sixth concerto published scores, and so shows clearly his editorial bias. In other cases, such as Tchaikovsky's *Violin Concerto*, the departure from Tchaikovsky's original score is well known but countenanced by tradition. An analysis of some published versions of Smetana's *Aus der Heimat* showed massive cuts in Smetana's beautiful singing line: simply an editorial decision to shorten the score. This analysis relied on my skills as a librarian (what is the provenance of this document and what role did the editor have in its creation?). The resulting article was published in 2001 (Schueneman 2001a).

The French Violin School and Pierre Rode also provided opportunities for conference presentations. As a member of the Texas Library Music Association, I learned of a conference celebrating the 500th anniversary of printed music (Schueneman 2001). Working with a library colleague, I looked for a new angle on Rode and the French Violin School, finding it in Rode's business partnership. Rode and several of his colleagues tried to gain better control over their artistic output and capture more of the fruit of their labors by forming a publishing firm. A primary purpose of the firm (inelegantly called La magasin de musique de Cherubini, Méhul, R. Kreutzer, Rode, Nicolo Isouard, et Boïeldieu) was the publication of their own works, but the firm also published works of other composers and operated a shop in Paris. This business angle provided an opportunity to explore the economics of music publishing in the first decade of the 19th century. This material was used in a later article (Schueneman 2004). Several years later I gave a presentation on a theme that Rode had borrowed from another violinist/composer (Giornovichi), tracing its use by Beethoven and others (Schueneman 2010).

In 2004 I wrote an article for the Sound Recording Reviews section of *Notes* (Schueneman 2004). The review article examined "The French Violin School: From Viotti to Bériot." Journals often seek submissions for such ongoing sections, and the recorded legacy of the French Violin School was a natural fit for the sound review section and my particular expertise.

My amateur music-making continued, and by a stroke of good fortune symphonic music returned to Kingsville after the absence of 30 years. I had the opportunity to perform in the Kingsville Symphony Orchestra for nearly ten years. Being a player, even an average one, was immensely satisfying, though I was never more than the least of the second violins. This experience worked to advantage as I discussed music as part of my scholarly profile.

In 2005 I was contacted by Massimiliano Sala, an Italian scholar putting together a book on Giovanni Battista Viotti, considered the father of the French Violin School (though an Italian) and Rode's great teacher. My contribution was a chapter on the relationship between Rode and Viotti (Schueneman 2006).

Naxos Records, one of the largest classical music labels in the world, contacted me in 2008 to ask if I was interested in writing CD notes for recordings in their series entitled 19th Century Violinist Composers. This effort began with notes for Benjamin Goddard's

Violin Concertos, and my work currently includes notes for over twenty recordings, ranging from Bazzini, Hubay, Bériot and Ernst to Hermann, Servais, Kreutzer, and Vieuxtemp. Five sets of notes accompany recordings of Rode, including nearly all the 13 violin concertos, as well as his most famous work, the *Twenty-Four Caprices for Solo Violin.* Rode's concertos had been unrecorded till these Naxos recordings were released, and given my avocational and scholarly interest in Rode, I was doubly honored and excited to write the notes for the Rode works.

Musikproduktion Höflich (mph), a German group part of whose mission is to publish unjustly neglected music scores from the past, regularly solicits Music Library Association members with opportunities to write prefaces for newly-reminted classic scores. I volunteered to write several prefaces, including the preface to Godard's *Concerto romantique,* and prefaces to three Granville Bantock works: *Dante and Beatrice, Vanity of Vanities,* and *Atalanta in Calydon.*

Go for It or Wait for It

Experience taught me that opportunities to use avocation as vocation consist of both sought opportunities and opportunities that fall in one's lap. At first, opportunities must be sought. I had to contact *Violexchange* and submit an article idea "cold turkey" as I was unknown and music was not my primary field of expertise. The following lists show the opportunities I actively sought and the ones that came to me unbidden.

Sought (Go for It!) Opportunities

- Translation of *Notice sur Rode* (late 1980s, early 1990s)
- Creation of Lyre of Orpheus Press
- *Violexchange* article on Rode (1990)
- *Strings* article on Rode (1992)
- Initial review for *Library Journal* (1992)
- *Music Reference Services Quarterly* article on Rode (1994)
- *Legacies: 500 Years of Printed Music* presentation (2001)
- *The French Violin School* (2002)
- *Notes* article on French Violin School recordings (2004)
- Preface to new edition of Goddard's *Concerto romantique* (2017)

Unsought (Wait for It!) Opportunities

- Regular reviewer for *Library Journal* (1992–current)
- *Music Reference Services Quarterly* journal and book projects (1994–1998)
- Article in *Fontes Artis Musicae* arising from *Legacies* conference (2004)
- CD essays for Naxos Records (2008–current)
- Kennedy Center podcast on college football songs (2010)
- Prefaces to three works by Granville Bantock (2017–current)

Lessons Learned

From the time I graduated from library school and began my career, I wanted an avocation as well as a career. No matter how much we love our work—and library work is entirely satisfying on many levels—it exists on the plane of necessity and compulsion. We all need a realm of love, something we are interested in for its own sake and not what we can extract from it. Perhaps avocation never leads to vocational use, but many avocations are suitable partners for our careers. The only danger is that avocation may take on a tinge of necessity and a bit of our first love may grow cold.

Sought and unsought opportunities have a symbiotic relationship. Once you have a foot in the door, both your confidence and your reputation will grow. The avocation as adjunct to career will flower with proper nutrition. First opportunities are sought, and then they come to you unbidden on the wings of previous work—on your reputation. When opportunities appear, you will be ready.

The initial challenge is discovering what elements of avocation are suitable for use in vocation. A music avocation centered on Beethoven may not generate much traction since Beethoven is one of the most discussed persons in the history of music. Either one will need to search for a niche in Beethoven's output or life, or one will need to choose a more obscure subject within the broad realm of music. Rode and the French Violin School were ideal. Though hardly known to the public, Rode played an important role in music history and his music has remained in print for over 200 years. Even so, his life and music remained mostly obscure, and my task was to become an expert on the obscure. By creating a knowledge base from Pougin's biography and other sources, I was led step by step to a useful and fulfilling annex to my career.

The continuing challenge is to "keep the ball rolling" by looking for ways to integrate career and avocation. Like the initial challenge, this will require effort, but increasingly it also involves decisions related to, or growing out of, opportunities from previous projects. on opportunities that are generated from the work that has gone before. Sometimes opportunities will have to be declined, but the shape of avocation as related to vocation is entirely in one's hands and limited only by one's imagination. One delightful aspect is that many such opportunities are far afield from narrow expertise—I had little sense of the richness of college fight songs before given the opportunity to explore this field of music. My goal has been to live an integrated life, where both aspects of normal existence—private life and work—are joined together. Such integration is not only possible but should be sought as a means of joy and satisfaction with both life and work.

References

Gelrud, Paul Geoffrey. 1940. *Foundations and Development of the Modern French Violin School*. Cornell University MA thesis.
_____. 1944. *A Critical Study of the French Violin School (1782–1882)*. Cornell University Ph.D. dissertation.
Kennedy Center ArtsEdge. 2010. *Touchdown Songs—Music and Football—Fight Songs*. http://artsedge.kennedy-center.org/multimedia/series/AudioStories/touchdown-songs.aspx.
Klein, Hans-Günter. 1993. "...dieses allerliebste Buch: Fanny Hensels Noten-Album." *Mendelssohn Studien* 8: 144.
Pougin, Arthur. 1874. *Notice sur Rode: Violoniste Français*. Paris: Pottier de Lalaine.
_____. 1994. *The Life and Music of Pierre Rode*. Kingsville, Texas: Lyre of Orpheus Press.
Rowland-Entwistle, Theodore. 1973. *The Violin*. London: St. Paul's House.
Schueneman, Bruce R. 1990. "Reconsideration of a Minor Masterpiece: Rode's Sixth Concerto in B Flat Major." *The Violexchange* 5 (3&4): 11–13.
_____. 1992a. "The Life and Times of Pierre Rode." *Strings* 7 (2): 68–71.
_____. 1992b. "A Philosophical Method: The Art of the Violin." *Strings* 7 (3): 12,14.
_____. 1993. "Three Viotti Rarities." *Strings* 7 (4): 14.
_____. 1994. "The Search for the Minor Composer: The Case of Pierre Rode." *Music Reference Services Quarterly* 3 (1): 37–48.
_____. 1997. *Minor Ballet Composers: Biographical Sketches of Sixty-Six Underappreciated Yet Significant Contributors to the Body of Western Ballet Music*. New York: Haworth.

_____. 2001. "The Importance of Being Various: The Necessity of Collecting Various Editions of the Same Musical Work." *Humanities Collections*. 1 (4): 19–34.

_____. 2004. "The French Violin School: From Viotti to Bériot. *Notes: The Quarterly Journal of the Music Library Association* 60 (3): 757–774.

_____. 2005. *The French Violin School: Viotti, Rode, Kreutzer, Baillot and Their Contemporaries*. Kingsville, TX: The Lyre of Orpheus Press.

_____. 2006. "The French Violin School: Viotti and Rode." In M. Sala (ed.), *Giovanni Battista Viotti: A Composer Between the Two Revolutions*. Ad Parnassum Studies 2, Bologna: UT Orpheus Edizioni. 199–218.

_____. 2010. "Metamorphosis of a Theme: Gionovichi's *Rondo a la Russe* and Its Use by Haydn, Wranitzky, Beethoven, and Rode, 1789–1799." Texas Music Library Association Annual Meeting, October 9.

Schueneman, Bruce R., and Ayala-Schueneman, María de Jesús. 2001. "The Composer's House: the Publishing Firm of Cherubini, Mehúl, Kreutzer, Rode, Isouard, and Boieldieu." Legacies: 500 Years of Printed Music Conference, Denton, TX, October 25–28.

_____. 2004. "The Composer's House: The Publishing Firm of Cherubini, Mehúl, Kreutzer, Rode, Isouard, and Boieldieu." *Fontes Artis Musicae* 51 (1): 53–73.

Studwell, William & Bruce R. Schueneman. 1998a. *College Fight Songs*. New York: Haworth.

_____. 1998b. *State Songs of the United States*. New York: Haworth.

_____. 2001. *College Fight Songs II*. New York: Haworth.

Suzuki, Shin'ichi. 1983. *Nurtured by Love: A New Approach to Education*. Athens, OH: Ability Development.

Tracy, Mark. 2018. "Recognize That Tune? It's the Northern Accent of Georgia Football." *New York Times*. January 8. https://nyti.ms/2Ekx3rc.

A Shutterbug in a World of Bookworms

Photography as a Creative Outlet in Academic Librarianship

Michelle P. McKinney

Librarians are often called on to be creative in their work in a variety of ways such as developing programming (e.g., book clubs), planning events, or creating displays. Unfortunately, academic librarians rarely have creative activities rooted in their day-to-day duties. Tenure-track requirements, research, teaching and liaison work leave little time for inventive and inspired personal pursuits. Having worked as a tenure-track librarian for over a decade, I have been fortunate to have the ability to exercise my creativity through photography as part of my responsibilities. Photography provides fun and clever ways to interact with faculty and students and helps avoid burnout by keeping me engaged in my work.

Photography Interests

I have always been drawn to photography. I have very few photos of myself as a child and I would pore over them to take in every detail. While working at Burger King during high school, I won my first camera in an incentive contest. It was a small, pocket-sized Panasonic that required film. Throughout high school and college, I drove my friends a little insane with my demands to take their photo. While in library school, I treated myself to a Pentax camera which introduced me to the world of digital photography. As a graduate assistant assigned to the library's marketing department, I was able to use my camera to capture photos in and around the University of South Florida's Tampa Library. Some of those photos were displayed on the library's graduate assistant website as well as in my online ePortfolio that I used to host my resume and promote my educational and work experience. That Pentax traveled with me to my first professional job and around the country to various library conferences throughout my career. I constantly sought opportunities and created ways to incorporate my camera into my day-to-day activities at my library and beyond.

I have no formal photography training aside from the new owner's class provided by the store where I purchased my camera and a one-time continuing education class on the basics of digital photography. Everything beyond that is self-taught. I read photography books and articles when time permits. The best way I have found to improve my skills is to shoot lots of photos as often as I can. When my schedule allows, I take photo walks alone or with friends and other hobbyists. I also participate in photo challenges where I can. At some point I would love to obtain a degree in photography and pursue it as a post-library career.

How I Use Photography at Work

Job Responsibilities. A portion of my job responsibilities is focused on marketing library events, services and resources via the web. This includes managing our campus library's website, collaborating with our central library's marketing director and other web-related personnel, and creating content for our blog and video message monitors. Although it is not explicitly stated, there is enough room in my job description to imply a need for photography activities. I took that as an opportunity to pursue photography-related tasks wherever I could.

Our college has a communications department and an official college photographer. This person typically takes photos for all major campus events, official faculty and staff portraits, and candid photos around campus. I depend on these photos when in need of images for print materials, such as the library's annual report. Other times, I need simple shots of library materials like new books or library displays. These are ideal opportunities to take my own photos. In doing so, I don't have to submit a request for a photographer or wait until the photos are edited and sent to me, which can take several days depending on the photographer's workload.

From the Desk of Blog Series. As the coordinator of our library blog, LiBlog, I am responsible for identifying and creating ongoing content. I created a variety of getting-to-know-you features highlighting faculty and staff. One series, *From the Desk of*, highlights the workspaces of library faculty and staff. I photograph the person in their workspace (at their desk, writing on their white board, etc.) and specific items of interest they are willing to share, such as a bookish souvenir or a piece of art. This series allows me to be a bit more creative with my photography as I help our blog readers learn more about our faculty and staff. As I show parts of their personalities through photos I also I get to know my colleagues better.

Promotion of the library, college, and university. I often snap photos with my phone to share on our institution's various social media sites. I take quick photos as I walk across campus and use related hashtags to share it with others. Our college includes a "Photo of the Week" segment in the weekly newsletter, and my goal is one day to have one of my photos highlighted there.

College and University Events. I have become the de facto library photographer for campus events. Every year, library faculty, staff and student workers pose for our annual group photo. During these sessions I usually capture several professional photos and at least one or two silly shots of everyone shushing or taking on superhero stances.

I capture photos of library faculty and staff during college and university events as well. The library regularly participates in campus-wide events. For several years, our college hosted a 5K run. It was my task to get the library faculty and staff assembled for a group shot and take candid photos throughout the event. I also photograph other events such as Convocation and the college orientation program.

Library Space. Our library was completely renovated in 2013. I photographed the space throughout the different phases of the renovation. The photos created a historic reference for our old space. It also recorded a major event in the life of the library. The college's official photographer was able to document major events, but I was able to show the behind-the-scenes of the renovation such as the cleaning and packing that took place as faculty and staff prepared to move their offices.

Our shared space, the Learning & Teaching Center, has movable tables. Since non-library faculty and staff can use this room, we wanted to provide a photographic visual for people to reference when changing the space configuration. The photographs allow people to see the different ways the tables could be rearranged. They also serve as a reference for how to return the room back to the original set-up. I regularly update photos that depict various activities in the library for use on the website or other web spaces. These photos are usually staged using a student assistant posing as a visiting student. These types of photos include a staff member assisting a "student" at the printing station or a librarian helping a "student" at the information desk.

Library Faculty and Staff Portraits. My colleagues are aware of my photography hobby and use it to their advantage. Over the last few years I have been asked to take portraits for professional use. These pictures are utilized to update profile photos in places like Outlook, Gmail, Facebook and LinkedIn. Colleagues have also used my photos for LibGuides and presenter information for conferences and other professional activities. When I get a request to take personal photos, I offer my services to all library faculty and staff. A time is scheduled for their photo shoot and on that day, they bring makeup for touching up their face or an accessory to change their look. We move around the library and the college to take advantage of lighting and scenery. Once I have captured the photos, I edit them as needed and forward copies to each person to use at their discretion. I also save copies of their edited photos to the library's image collection in our SharePoint site. Additionally, I photograph new employees as part of a welcome email that our library director shares with the college community.

Benefits

As I explored photography at work, I had not initially considered its potential benefits. After some consideration, I realize there are several advantages.

Engaging with colleagues. Taking photos around campus and the university gets me out of my normal day-to-day activities. I'm able to interact with college faculty and staff in a more casual way while learning about their interests outside of their classrooms or departments. During these times I often discover another shutterbug and we chat about photography. We discuss the type of photography we pursue, our equipment, and favorite photography sites or apps, among other things.

My institution hosts an annual day dedicated to volunteering in the community. Volunteers come together from all areas of the university to work on a team project. I always take my camera and make sure everyone is aware that I will be photographing our activities. We normally get together for a few group shots. During the event I post selected photos to social media using dedicated hashtags. Following the event, I edit and post them all online via Flickr or Google Photos and then share them with my fellow volunteers. I give them permission to download and use the photos as they wish.

My overall enthusiasm for photography propels me to encourage colleagues to take and share their own photos. I ask colleagues to take photos of library-related events and places when they travel to conferences and workshops, or during personal travel if they are so inclined. Upon their return, I draft blog posts about their travels using their photos. This creates more robust content for our blog feed. When appropriate, I share information about different sites and projects that may be of interest. I also try to follow their photography on social media.

Staying connected to my camera. Life is busy which forces me to frequently abandon my camera for long periods of time. I have a Canon Rebel T2i that I love to use but I have yet to master all of its bells and whistles. Once I find time to return to my camera, I have to reacquaint myself with its features. I have to retrain myself to think about light settings and moving between automatic and manual features. It can take me several wasted shots before I remember to change settings for the ideal photo. Using my camera for work-related projects has me actively engaged and keeps my skills sharp.

Creating a relaxing workspace. I enjoy the atmosphere that photos create in my office. I do not print my photos as often as I would or should but I do enjoy viewing my own work. A distant goal of mine is to create a gallery of my photos for my office. Such a gallery would allow me to share my work with others in an off-line format.

Artistic Pleasure. The *From the Desk of* blog series is centered primarily on photos. I am taking photos purely for the art. I take a few staged photos of the faculty or staff and the rest are taken as I visually wander around their office. I am able to show a side of their personality through my photos.

Challenges

These issues pertain to the hobby in general and are not limited to the workplace.

Time. The biggest challenge I face is lack of time. Because of my other responsibilities, I don't get to engage in photography as frequently as I would like. When I do have a project that requires my camera, I have to factor in time for set-up, photo shoot, breakdown and editing. Depending on the project, the editing can consume quite a bit of time.

Getting in front of the camera. When you are behind the camera taking photos you find that you are often not present in the photo. In order to be present, you have to opt for someone else taking the photo. For informal photos this requires coordination, which may not be worth it if you are trying to take a quick snapshot. It also requires finding someone who is comfortable behind the camera. I can be pretty critical about photos so I'm not always happy with the final product. The other option is to use a self-timer. Sadly for me, I'm horrible at positioning myself into the frame as I move from one spot to another. I'm often posing awkwardly or half-hidden behind someone. Nevertheless, I am determined to sort through my issues with the self-timer so that I can take part in group photos.

Expense. Photography can be an expensive hobby. One can easily get caught up in wanting to buy a lot of accessories (tripods, flashes, and lenses) and software for advanced editing. There's also the cost associated with printing photos. Regular prints are relatively inexpensive but when you consider the number of prints you make over time it quickly adds up. Costs grow exponentially for large format and specialty (canvas, wood or metal) prints. If you want to develop your skills by enrolling in classes, you will likely pay an enrollment fee.

Legal issues. Most libraries and organizations have policies pertaining to photography done by the media or members of the public. Many libraries will post these policies on their website. What is harder to find are photography policies related to faculty and staff who are employed by the institution but are not in the communications or marketing departments. My college, while having several public policies in place, has none for faculty and staff.

Policies vary from one institution to another. Policies may pertain to who can be photographed, what areas of the library can be photographed, how photos can be used, intellectual property, copyright, and ownership. These policies are in place to protect the subject of the photo, the photographer, and the organization (Greenberg 2015). I seek the help of our college photographer when I need professional quality, candid close-up photos of people in the library because I know all of the necessary policies will be adhered to and all required forms will be completed. General, wide-shot, photos of the library are within my rights to photograph. When in doubt, I contact the communications team for clarification.

Organizing and archiving photos. It does not take very long for amateur photographers to build reasonably large photo collections. The longer you shoot, the more photos you take. It's imperative that you keep your photos organized for easy reference. The day will come when you remember a photo that was taken several years ago that would be perfect for a current project and you will have no clue where to find it. In order to avoid this type of situation, develop a method for organizing and storing your photos.

- *Weeding.* Regularly review and delete duplicate photos and any photos that you will not use or need.
- *Storage space and software.* Unless you are producing high quality print projects, you do not need to take high resolution photos which result in larger file sizes. Taking photos in RAW file formats will consume lots of storage space. If you do opt to take high resolution photos, resize them to a smaller file size for long term storage. Determine what software is available to you. Does your organization have an intranet site with document storage options.
- *Photo sharing sites.* Sites like Flickr and Google Photos are great ways to store and easily share photos. They are free, with large amounts of storage options. Larger storage plans are available at affordable rates but consider long-term financial responsibility and commitments. You may consider setting up accounts for your organization if you will be working with large numbers of photos.
- *Archiving.* Back up photos to the cloud, DVD, flash or external hard drives. Your organization may have some archiving policies and procedures in place which apply to photos. Be sure to check with your organization about those practices.

Getting Started

If you would like to incorporate photography into your daily library activities but aren't sure where to begin, consider the following.

Take inventory of your skills. If you are new to photography consider what you can realistically do. Taking portrait photos may be beyond your comfort zone and skill level but perhaps photographing library materials is a less intimidating way to get started. You might also consider taking a beginner's course to help you determine if this is something worth pursing as part of your workday. For amateur photographers and hobbyists, consider the time you want to spend on these activities and the tools needed to achieve your goals.

Talk to your supervisor. Share your photography interest with your supervisor. Discuss ways you may be able to use your skills in the office. Discuss workload. It's important to be clear about how your work may be impacted by these additional tasks. Ask your supervisor to consider you when photography opportunities arise.

Equipment and software considerations.

- What do you have available to you at the office?
- What equipment do you own that you are willing to use at work?
- What equipment do you need? Items beyond your camera may include a tripod or flash. Do you have a safe and secure place to store your equipment?
- What software do you have to edit and store your photos once they've been downloaded?
- What type of costs will these items incur?
- Are there items worth having the department purchase? Several years ago, our library invested in a small, point-and-shoot, digital camera that faculty and staff can use to take photos around the library. I still opt to use my personal camera when I can, but it's nice to have the department camera available for unplanned photos.

Policies and procedures. Find out your library's policies regarding photography. What forms are you required to use? Are there restrictions on who, what or where you can photograph?

Network. Talk to your communications department and/or social media coordinator to see how you can contribute content. Follow social media accounts for your organization and those of your shutterbug colleagues.

Potential Projects for Shutterbugs

Here are a few activities and project ideas to incorporate photography into your professional life.

Find inspiration

- Follow library related accounts on Instagram. Many libraries have Instagram accounts that highlight the activities and collections of their respective libraries. Follow both local and (inter)nationally known libraries. You will find examples of the types of photographs being captured and shared.
- Read photography books. Browse photo books set in or focused on libraries such as *The Library Book* by Thomas R. Schiff (2017). How-to photography books help develop your skills. As you hone your skills, you will be inspired to exercise your new knowledge by putting them into practice.

Personal photography projects with a library theme

- Submit photos to LibrarianWardrobe.com. The site depicts various examples of librarian fashion in the workplace. Most submissions are selfies requiring little more than a camera phone.
- 365Project.org. This photography-focused social networking site encourages users to take one photo every day for a year. Projects can be random or based on a theme such as libraries. The site includes discussion boards and photo challenges as well as tips for improving your photography. This site is useful to both newbie users and professional photographers.
- Litsy Photo Challenges. Litsy is what you get "if Instagram and Goodreads had a beautiful, perfect baby" (Clarke Gray 2016). It is a social media app for bibliophiles. There are normally several photo challenges taking place on any given day. Since this app is geared towards book lovers and not photographers, the photography challenges are very accessible for all users.
- Contests and exhibits. Photo contests and competitions can be found locally and nationally with a simple internet search. Local organizations also host smaller, low-pressure contests. Review contest rules and requirements and submit your work.

Library marketing and promotion projects

- Provide content to your marketing department for use in promotional materials.
- Post and tag your photos on social media with designated hashtags used by your organization.
- Create a photo series that can be published on your library's blog. The series can be used to engage colleagues and users to submit their own photos.
- Volunteer to take photos of various events and activities.
- Volunteer to take headshots or candid photos for your colleagues that can be used as profile photos.
- Create Selfie Stations and related hashtags for users as part of events. These can be shared via social media.

Conclusion

There are many ways for academic librarians and staff to incorporate the fun and creativity of photography into their library work life. Work with your supervisor to determine tasks or projects and set reasonable expectations regarding workload and responsibilities. Your library or college marketing or communications department can provide input related to policies and procedures that must be followed. Take inventory of available resources such as equipment, software and supplies.

Be willing to share your talents in whatever ways are you able to within your comfort zone. Be open to sharing the photos that you capture, not only with your organization but with your colleagues. Although you can't charge a fee for your services, you can ask for photo credits if your photos are used in various places outside of your organization. This helps let others know of your talents and may lead to other opportunities in the future. Lastly, practice! Practice will help you become more comfortable behind the camera. When you are comfortable, you begin to test your boundaries by exploring the more advanced settings of your camera. You will be able to visualize the photos you want to take and capture them with more ease. Your photo collection will grow, giving you more options for projects. This will lead you to approaching projects with enthusiasm. That enthusiasm, sparked by your creativity, will lead to projects and work products that you enjoy.

REFERENCES

Clarke Gray, Brenna. 2016. "LITSY: If Instagram and Goodreads Had a Perfect Baby. "BookRiot. Accessed May 5. https://bookriot.com/2016/05/12/litsy-if-instagram-and-goodreads-had-a-perfect-baby/.

Greenberg, Ed and Reznicki, Jack. 2015. *The Copyright Zone: A Legal Guide for Photographers and Artists in the Digital Age*. Second ed. Burlington, MA: Focal Press. doi: 10.4324/9781315777016.

Schiff, Thomas R. and Manguel, Alberto. 2017.*The Library Book*. First ed. Aperture.

Artful Information

Lessons for Librarians from Visual Artists

TIM GORICHANAZ

Is being a librarian anything like being an artist? At first blush, it may not seem like it. The stereotypical librarian is strait-laced and reserved, while the artist is a freewheeling bohemian. But this characterization, as you might guess, overlooks the many similarities between librarianship and art-making.

In popular culture, we sometimes assume that artists are inscrutable geniuses, but the sociology of art has shown that art-making is a form of work whose processes can be analyzed. As it happens, these processes can be applied in other occupations, including librarianship.

In this essay, I reflect on the question of what librarians can learn from the work of visual artists. These reflections will be practical in nature. The conceptually-inclined reader may be referred to my paper "Understanding Art-Making as Documentation" (Gorichanaz 2017), where I broach this topic from the perspective of document theory.

Here I begin by reviewing some other scholars' work on the *art* of librarianship, and then I discuss findings from my own research. This discussion draws from my dissertation research on the information behavior of visual artists. In my research, I recruited local artists to each create a self-portrait and document their process along the way. In my analysis, I found a number of experiential techniques. I contend that these aspects of art-making can be harnessed by librarians. In this way, librarians can infuse their work with a measure of artistry.

Finding the Art in Librarianship

The end of the 19th century saw the first attempts to professionalize librarianship, which history is recounted by Matthew Battles (2015). This led to library schools finding homes within academe. Gradually, then, the focus of these schools shifted from skills training to conducting scientific research. Librarianship became a social science. The social sciences, like any science, work to observe and describe the world, and they value objectivity, replicability and prediction. This epistemology colors librarianship to this day. A small cohort of librarians and scholars, however, has begun to call this into question over the past several decades. Much can be said about this, but here I will focus on what this means for the *art* of librarianship.

As early as 1970, sociologist James March called for social scientists to infuse their work with artistry (March 1970). To turn "pedants" into artists, he sought to help social scientists see their analytical work as an art. He briefly outlined ways for paying attention to aesthetic excitement, creative imagination and unanticipated discovery when thinking about social phenomena. Regrettably, very few have taken notice of March's work. Still, similar ideas have begun to surface in the realm of librarianship.

Book artist and librarian Andrea Kohashi (2018) outlined the shared mission between book artists and librarians. First, both create points of entry. Book artists invite interaction through the book's form, and librarians make themselves available to patrons. Second, both provide tools for understanding. A book artist draws on the inherited tradition of the codex to bring the reader something new, and a librarian takes into account a person's current situation to help them effectively. And third, both inspire further inquiry. A book artist hopes to plant a seed of inspiration that will lead a reader to other books and artworks, and a librarian seeks to instill personal literacy skills.

Additionally, Rachel Clarke (2018) makes a case that librarians are fundamentally designers. She goes so far as to say that librarianship should not be considered a social science, but rather a design field. Whereas the social sciences have an epistemology centered on description and prediction, design epistemology is oriented toward problem solving and creation. Clarke presents elements of design epistemology and discusses how they manifest in librarianship. For Clarke, design epistemology is centered on three principles. The first is solving problems, generally oriented toward service and largely through the creation of artifacts. The second is generating knowledge through making, which involves iteration, reflection, and use of representations. The third is evaluating their designs through methods such as critique and rationale. Clarke argues persuasively that library education and professional development should be rooted in design epistemology. This is critical, she says, for librarians to remain relevant and be successful in today's changing environment.

In this essay, I build on these works. Though we don't typically think of artists as solving problems in their art-making, the epistemological tools of artists and designers are quite similar. Following Kohashi, I contend that librarians can improve their work by studying that of artists. And likewise with Clarke, I agree that librarianship is best considered a domain of creation. I contribute to this conversation by presenting aspects of the art-making experience that surfaced in my empirical study of visual artists. My participants were a diverse group of artists, ranging in age, gender, professionalism, artistic medium and more, suggesting that these aspects may be widely applicable. Even, I suggest, to librarians.

Thinking Through Working

It is said that Michelangelo saw human figures fully-formed within the stone and worked to set them free. This may give the impression that the artist begins their work with a very clear idea of how it will end. On this account, being an artist is simply having the skills to make that vision manifest.

However, for the artists in my study, this was resolutely not the case. These artists began working with only a general sense of how the piece would end up, sometimes in the form of a feeling. But they had to begin with a concrete step, and so they started where they could. One set off with a frame she found lying around. Several browsed through photos for inspiration—something to latch onto. They took their own photographs, several times until it was suitable, and they made small sketches and notes to work out the shape, layout and other aspects of the portrait. Through these tactics, the artists both produced and consumed various kinds of text and image, which together contributed to ideation. As the artists progressed, their work gradually took shape. Each action they took was the basis for further thinking and the subsequent action. For these artists, creating ideas was inextricable from creating artwork, and this was a process of active inquiry. "What next?" the artist asks.

Librarians can apply this insight to a wide variety of tasks, from writing grants, to organizing tables of printed materials, to designing programs. It is easy to get frustrated that our ideas aren't "good enough" or when we can't solve certain problems. But we must remember that ideas don't just spring up fully formed. Rather, they must be nurtured through engagement with the world. Just like the artists, librarians can work with different kinds of text and imagery, both actively and passively, in generating ideas. While you do need to have a general sense of where you want to end up, you shouldn't get bogged down about the details of where you're going. Instead, look around and see where you are, and then take the next step.

Listening to Mistakes

We do our work in the world, with all its constraints and dynamics, and so mistakes are inevitable. Given that artists think through working, this means that mistakes will happen as ideas are being formed. These mistakes, then, become part of the idea-generating process.

Almost all the artists in my study described mistakes they made, and how these mistakes changed the outcome. Some of them faced difficulties in rendering the proportions: first one feature was too big, then another. One found that she'd applied too much paint to an area. The artists worked to address these mistakes, but in general this was not a matter of undoing them as if on a computer program. Rather, they worked with what the mistake gave them, moving the piece forward, sometimes in a slightly new direction. Sometimes these mistakes produce an unexpected but desirable effect. For example, Brianna, one of the artists in my study, said, "And when I think I'm done, I realize the hands are way too big. It bothers me, but at the same time I like the distortion." She does not attempt to "fix" the hands, but rather riffs on that sense of distortion in the rest of the painting. So, clearly, it is not a matter of fixing mistakes, but of listening to them and embracing them. As Emily in my study said well, "Those accidents are the fun part, after all. It's completely unintentional, but it's intentional that I leave it."

This suggests that the word mistake is a bit of a misnomer. Mistakes don't have to be problematic. And while we shouldn't be careless in our work, the inevitable mistakes needn't exasperate us. They can be embraced. This goes for artists as much as it does for librarians. Mistakes are part of the conversation with the world that we take part in by being alive. We should listen to what our mistakes are saying.

Using the Whole Body

Our received wisdom on humans is that reason and emotion are housed in separate bodily compartments. Modern neuroscience, however, has demonstrated that this is not the case. It is, rather, as the philosopher David Hume wrote, that reason is the slave of the passions. Even decisions as seemingly purely rational as whether to buy this toothbrush or that one involve a medley of feelings. In everyday life we may wish to deny this, but the artist fully embraces it. The artist thus brings their full self to their work, melding their knowledge of facts and techniques with their feelings and memories.

Consonant with librarianship's status as a science, in the 20th century the notion of library neutrality predominated. This is clearly exemplified in Douglas John Foskett's 1962 booklet, *The Creed of a Librarian: No Politics, No Religion, No Morals.* This creed, however, has come into question. Increasingly librarians are positioning themselves as teachers rather than objective mediators of information, not to mention championing certain political agendas. There is not space to enter into a detailed discussion here, but interested readers can refer to Alison Lewis' (2008) book, *Questioning Library Neutrality.*

Artists also use their whole bodies in their work in a more literal sense. In this regard, my participant Brian gives a good example. His pieces are mixed-media pieces on large canvas, and he works on them with the canvas pinned up on the wall. To blend the colors at certain stages, he uses an old t-shirt as a paintbrush, using his whole body to move the paint. He once was an illustrator, but gradually he moved towards bigger works. Today, his paintings are life-sized. For Brian, art-making is a matter of being "invested and involved in the whole thing," and he hopes his eventual audience can have the same depth of experience with his finished works.

Librarians, too, can think of their work as life-sized—or even larger than life. Often we get wrapped up in details. This makes us go about our work with a magnifying glass. It also encourages us to be mentalistic rather than recognizing the role of emotion and bodily experience in our consciousness. All this gives us tunnel vision, and if we stay in that state for too long, we'll miss out on things. We'll lose the forest for the trees, as the saying goes. Throughout their work, librarians can ask themselves: How can I make this more whole-bodied? It may be a matter of going in person rather than sending an email. It may be redesigning a program to foster more in-person interactions. Or it may be reorganizing library spaces, from arranging furniture and shelves to arranging items on a table, to keep in mind how people will move through and interact with the space. After all, the people librarians serve are whole people as well.

Practicing Self-Efficacy

Another important theme in my study was the practice of self-efficacy. This is a person's sense of how well they can deal with a given situation. Of course moving through life is a matter of dealing with one situation after another. Many of these are not challenging in the least—at these times, we have high self-efficacy. Sometimes, we confront challenges that are more than we can bear—at these times, we experience low self-efficacy. There is evidence that we can improve our self-efficacy in certain situations. The specifics of this depend on the type of situation, but in general it is a matter of confronting gradually bigger challenges.

The artists in my study described doing this in their practice as artists. Little by little, they try out new materials and techniques. Insomuch as these are challenges, they help the artist grow. Moreover, they help the artist develop their own personal style. In the self-portraits they did for my study, the artists took on a range of challenges. One artist sought to ensure high self-efficacy by choosing a project they knew they could do well, while others worked to improve their self-efficacy by taking on a challenge. The former is comfortable, which can be valuable; the latter can be dubious, but when one succeeds it is quite rewarding. Many of the projects mixed challenge with comfort. Brianna, for example, found some aspects of her painting to be very challenging, such as rendering the details of her studded belt. All the same, on a day when she was having a difficult time at school and work, she was relieved to come back to her self-portrait in the evening "because this is something I can do." She, and indeed all the artists in my study, described feeling proud and accomplished after finishing their pieces.

Librarians can learn to consider the challenge level of the various situations they face at work. They can improve their ability to deal with situations by, when possible, scoping the challenge to an appropriate level, taking into account all that is going on in one's life at the time. Sometimes, this may be a matter of settling for good enough, while at other times striving for perfection. In other cases, it could be a question of setting time constraints, or working with coworkers versus working alone.

Taking Breaks and Stepping Back

While the image of an artist completing a piece in one manic, nose-to-the-grindstone session is romantic, this is not how art gets done. On the contrary, all of the artists in my study described taking breaks, from minutes to weeks, as part of their work process. This seems to be a method of gaining a refreshed perspective on the piece in progress, opening up new possibilities for moving forward with it. As Emily described, "When I take breaks and then come back, I have completely fresh eyes on the painting."

In addition to taking breaks, stepping back from the work was another tactic that most of the artists used. They did this physically. Seeing their work from farther away, or at a different angle, also gave them the fresh eyes they needed to see a new possibility. As an interesting twist on this, Tammy, one of my participants, took photos of her work in progress and then inspected the images on her phone. This helped her see things that needed to be fixed that were not apparent by just looking at the drawing.

Trying to complete something all in one go can be overwhelming, and it can also be ineffective. And almost paradoxically, if we take breaks while working on something, we'll often be able to get it done faster than if we hadn't taken any breaks. Taking breaks gives the body and mind time to relax, but also to digest what has happened. Returning to work later can show things that we could not see before. Not to mention that things happens in the interim, and these can shine new insights on the problem.

Stepping back, changing perspective, can also be useful. Librarians, like the artists, can often do this physically. To give a simple example, when we arrange books and other printed materials on a table, we should step back from the table every now and then. We may do this to some extent naturally, but doing so consciously can improve our work and our process. Taking a cue from Tammy, we may also find it helpful to photograph things and then assess the photos. When working on a text, be it a grant proposal or some signage, it may be helpful to print it out and look at it on paper during revision. Finally, another great (and sometimes overlooked) option is asking a colleague—they surely have a different perspective.

Conclusion

Throughout this essay, we have been considering how librarians can learn from artists to improve their work. Indeed, many aspects of artists' work process are applicable to the work of librarians—certainly more than we have reviewed here, and this could be a subject for future investigation. To close, we will reflect on how their motivations, too, are similar.

In my dissertation study, Jeannie mused on why she makes art. "It's some drive I guess," she said. "Some drive to make a difference in the world." She went on to tell me about a colleague of hers, a fellow painter. The two of them wonder aloud from time to time "what it's all about." The other woman often paints in public, and so a big part of her work is relating to the people who come up to her. "Where you see this person painting," Jeannie told me, "you can approach them. You can talk to them. And it's interesting because the number-one thing she does is pass out information to homeless people, about where to get help, where to sleep, where to get food. She's got all these things she gives to the homeless people because that's the main people that come up to her." This reminded Jeannie of an artist she once knew who was also a teacher. "And he would go out and sell his little paintings to the students," Jeannie said. "And I'm like, what's that about? But I noticed he was also sharing his philosophy and politics. And so there's a way for artists, as members of society, to get out there and meet people, and make a little ripple."

We may think of artists as eccentric, egoistic recluses, but that is not always the case. The purposes of artists and information professionals can be quite aligned: wanting to make the world a better place.

REFERENCES

Battles, Matthew. 2015. *Library: A Quiet History* (Reissue). New York: Norton.

Clarke, Rachel Ivy. 2018. "Toward a Design Epistemology for Librarianship." *The Library Quarterly* 88 (1): 41–59.

Foskett, Douglas John. 1962. *The Creed of a Librarian: No Politics, No Religion, No Morals*. London: Library Association.

Gorichanaz, Tim. 2017. "Understanding Art-Making as Documentation." *Art Documentation* 36(2): 191–203.

Kohashi, Andrea. 2018. "Blurring the Line Between Book Artist and Librarian: Special Collections Instruction as Artistic Practice." Presentation at the 2018 College Book Arts Association Conference, Philadelphia, January 4–6.

Lewis, Alison. 2008. *Questioning Library Neutrality: Essays from a Progressive Librarian*. Sacramento: Library Juice Press.

March, James G. 1970. "Making Artists Out of Pedants." In *The Process of Model-Building in the Behavioral Sciences*, edited by Ralph Stogdill, 54–75. New York: Norton.

Arts Enrichment
for a Working Artist Librarian

Yolanda Poston

I work as a Library Assistant in the Children's Department as well as the Gallery Curator for the newly added public art gallery at Scott County Public Library (SCPL). Both of these responsibilities propel me forward in my personal endeavor to continue my career as a working artist.

The Right Opportunity

Because the public interest for a gallery space was addressed through a library expansion, it became a priority for the SCPL director to find staff who knew how to network with visual and performing artists, run a gallery, and coordinate and host local art show openings. For these reasons, I was brought on board with the stipulation that part of my time would be spent working in the SCPL Children's Department. The whole package was a huge win for me!

Prior to working at the library, I had served on a local arts community board for about two years. This position led me to a fellow artist with whom I eventually partnered to open and run a local working artist studio gallery. Unfortunately, we were unable to keep the gallery open. So, into the work-a-day-world I returned. Thankfully, I was able to obtain this library position in which my creative instincts and skills could be utilized, as well as my past expertise of working as the Dean of Students for a private school. This opportunity could not have been more perfectly designed for me!

Incorporating creativity into working with children in the form of art class instruction and children's programming was a no-brainer. Additionally, I was able to expand children's arts education to include gallery exhibitions. Introducing children to art on a regular basis keeps creativity flowing in my personal artwork, forming new ideas and techniques for expression. Of course, being able to work with local artists on a regular basis also keeps up inspiration for honing one's own craft.

Juggling Two Worlds

Struggling to create original artwork is a natural part of being an artist. Being able to afford time for actual creation of art is one of the top challenges for artists, especially for those with the "day job" outside of art-related fields. There are some steps that can be taken to ease this difficulty. First, designate a special space; then use your current "nine-to-five" life to fuel your artwork; and finally, organize your own "hot-spot" arts community. Implementing these three suggestions could serve as personal encouragement as well as momentum for sharing your artwork.

Get a Room, Already!

In my opinion, the best designated art space is one outside the home. Finding a space outside the home is my number one choice because it sets you up to focus on creating art. You have a place to store your supplies, so items are less likely to get lost. This space can remain set up and you can be as messy as necessary for creation! Not to mention that being away from your home makes it easier for you to leave behind your "honey-do" list!

Not everyone can afford a space outside the home. The next best option is a less frequented area inside of your home, such as a spare bedroom, a utility room, or a garage that can be converted into a studio space. Make sure to schedule blocks of time to be in your space, especially if your family members know you are at home. Turn off your communication devices for the allotted time and let your family know not to bother you unless blood has been shed or death has ensued.

If you have a desire to create, you will do whatever is needed to make it happen! It is necessary to have a designated space, big or small. Currently, I am unable to make it to my studio space as often as I would like (that whole 9 to 5 thing). In order to keep myself motivated, I sleep with an unfinished piece at the head of my bed. The first thing I see every morning is this yet-to-be realized beauty. Believe it or not, I do work on it in spurts. Working sporadically is not my preference, But it's right there staring at me! That moves me to continue working.

Work Your Work Life

So, a space has been secured for creating visually. Next, take a look within your workplace. Every workplace is different, but each site has co-workers, an office space, and a day-to-day routine. This can become a fertile ground for the cultivation of original artwork. As constant students of human nature, artists literally "people watch" everywhere. Why not hold on to those moments from work? Just don't make it weird! Certainly, the way a co-worker uses her hands to talk; the tilt of a head in thought; or the office space itself can all provide inspiration for artwork and built-in models.

In my current position, I work with a lively team of independent, free thinking children's librarians. Definitely worth capturing in paint! So for their Christmas presents I decided to challenge myself by painting a small portrait for each of them. This forced me to schedule my painting time and to work toward a deadline (which I missed by two months, they received their presents on the following Valentine's Day). It was a complete joy and workout for my creative brain. Wherever you are, make it a point to somehow incorporate your artwork, if for no other reason, then for the practice!

Keep Track of Ideas

Note your ideas in a blank book or on a small spiral pad. I keep a pad in my purse at all times for such occasions. More often than not, I tend to use little random slips of paper that end up in a back pocket. The idea is to keep track of your ideas in real time, so that you can act on them later. I also keep a sketch pad on me at all times and again, I usually sketch on random slips of paper that prompt me to remember the relationships between thoughts I had during a day. Those notebooks tend to get used when I have a chunk of time to myself or in urgent moments when I definitely want to keep track of a visual or verbal train of thought. Take yourself seriously in these instances. Get into the habit of recording your insights!

Find Your Tribe and Celebrate!

The final situation to create for yourself, after establishing a creative space and selecting your work day experiences for inspiration, is to surround yourself with artists. Start with a fellow artist friend who is supportive of your work, one whose critique you invite and from which you can grow. Do not surround yourself with "yay" or "nay" sayers (i.e., people who only pour out nice banalities or people who only detract from whatever you create). Neither is helpful. Find those who will honestly give you feedback. Keep relationships with those artists who are not afraid to point out areas in which you need to grow and who also legitimately give praise when praise is due. This kind of critique is not easily found. For me, it was easier to start with the one "actively creating" artist friend I had at the time. This particular relationship encouraged me to deepen my commitment to art. We were fortunate enough to open the Georgetown Ice House Gallery, which allowed us to work regularly on our visual art in a shared space. It also allowed us to extend a platform to local artists in the Georgetown, Kentucky area. This gallery afforded us the opportunity to create open and mutually beneficial relationships with working artists in our area. In retrospect, this approach worked for me. For others, it may be easier to first join an art league in your community.

How you find a group of trusted fellow artists is not the important issue; the desired end is to establish this personal "hot spot." Within this group, create an open atmosphere in which thoughts can be tossed around and bounced of one another, without fear of competition or "stealing" ideas. Let the foundation be acceptable collaboration. If you participate in this kind of group work, your creative process will be boosted. Sometimes you just need a group in which you can brainstorm, fellow tribesmen who have an understanding of the process! An additional benefit is that your original works can be shared: the exhibition before an exhibition, if you will. This can be invaluable in your process for better understanding your own creation.

Water Your Networking Tree

Once you have established your networking tree of artists, water it by working together more intentionally. Create an atmosphere of inspiration for your group by hosting your own art shows. Encourage group members to do online investigation of art sites for contemporary knowledge of the art world to share within the group. Coordinate arts exploration trips that will not only lead to a more closely bonded group, but also a more informed group. These three suggestions are a good place to start for any aspiring artists not yet hooked into a gallery scene but who desire to have their artwork seen publicly and who want to continue to grow.

Do not be afraid of in-home art shows. It is a gentle way to push yourself and your group into the public eye. You have each other as allies and a built-in crowd starter! Each of you probably has a little different sphere of influence. Don't wait for "buzz" to happen to you, create it! Artists love getting together and chatting, but what if this chatting turned into an opportunity for each of you to take turns and attend an in-home show of one of your artist buddies? Bring your different spheres of influence together, paying particularly close attention to invite the individuals you each know to be appreciative of art. Rally around each other. Schedule a bi-monthly calendar in which all who are able to participate can do so and all those who are willing to host can open their homes. Is it a commitment? Yes! Is it worth it? Emphatically! I have seen and been a part of creating this kind of "buzz" within a group of my own. Devan Carpenter, an artist I previously mentored and taught, has become quite a prolific artist who desires to get her work into the public eye. She and other artists friends are continuing to enact this exact line of public exploration. Not only have they sold more art, they are actually building name recognition for themselves in our town and the surrounding areas. Buzz starts somewhere. Why not start it for yourself and your friends? Who knows how far it will reach into and outside of your town? I am happy to report that Devan has landed a couple of big community commissions as a result of this networking process. It has also built her confidence and solidified her commitment to being an artist. It all started with her artist friend base, and bonding while working.

There are some troubleshooting discussions your group should have before you have an in-home exhibition. The most important discussion to have is price range. Do online research to get a feel for the price range in larger cities for the size artwork and technique you are attempting to sell. I suggest watching the prices on sites like daily-painters.com, etsy.com, ebay.com and saatchiart.com; these are just a handful of sites that list prices. After you scroll through these sites and glue your head back on, do some down-to-earth calculating. How much did you spend on paints and materials? How many hours from conception to completion did you spend on birthing this baby? How much would you like to be paid per hour? Truly, what is reasonable? Then consider where you live and with what price you are willing to live. For myself, I did the calculations of these items after having done my online search. No one in my area would start off with prices similar to what I found online either, so I cut them down to about a third of what they might go for in a larger city. For example, if in Chicago a piece would sell for $1,000, I might move it at about $300 in Georgetown, and that is after several art showings.

Another sub-point to pricing is whether to make prints of your work. I have friends who are die hard "no to prints" people and I also know absolute "yes to prints" people. I fall in the middle. I don't want all of my works to have prints. Usually, I choose to print the ones in which I've invested more time and money. Because printing is another expense, I don't even want all of those works to be reproduced. Do what feels right to you. Keep track of works that are more popular amongst patrons. Which pieces have created their own "buzz?" Offer a couple of print sizes for these works. I like to offer a varied range of prices, so I offer the same piece in a smaller and a larger size, because where I live people are paying attention to all their pennies (as am I). Some of these people still like and want to support the arts, they just aren't going to engage at the upper end of the pricing scale. For me, it is not all about becoming rich or famous; it is much more about sharing ideas and poking people's hearts and heads. Buy, don't buy, but please pay attention is my feeling on the matter of purchasing. Each of you will have to figure out where you want to be on the pricing scale and act accordingly.

I suggest being very patient when it comes to sales. If your town is anything like mine, people have to become familiar with you and your work before they feel secure enough to invest in your talent. Seriously, enjoy your own good company, light refreshments (wine & cheese!), and get good at talking to people about why you create art and what specifically inspired you to create the pieces that are in front of them. I cannot stress enough the importance of making personal connections with patrons. People want to have a sense of who you are as an artist. You are your own best sales person. Time with you, the artist, is exactly what creates the "buzz!" There were many times a person walked into the Georgetown Ice House Gallery and stared at the same piece for hours because they were obviously drawn to it. The same person's attention, on the night of an opening in which they were fortunate enough to corner and question the artist, turned into a sale. Maybe they don't start off with the original work. Maybe they opt for a print. Either way, your work is out there in public and will be on display for people you have never met. Mission accomplished!

Pricing and prints are only two important discussions to have before opening your home for an art show. Other questions to discuss would be: How many pieces will be offered per show?; How will refreshments be handled?; Will music be used to set a mood ?; Is each show an individual endeavor to be attended by all within the group or is each show a "group endeavor" from start to finish?

Another area on which to focus is getting an understanding of what is going on in the art world at large. A good way to explore the greater art world is through the internet. Each person in the group could go hunting on his own for art sites that are of his own particular interest. Then there could be a routine arts education lunch or informal chat in which all members get to report the pros and cons of the information that has been discovered online. There are so many art sites being created, as individual artists decide to take the plunge and put themselves out there. I doubt that this kind of exploration could ever be completely exhausted. Again, I will use the example of my friend Devan Carpenter. She not only engaged in this kind of research (and sharing), but her research inspired her to put her artwork online. She first went looking for sites that displayed art and inevitably she became aware of the many artists who had their own sites. This finding caused her to warm up to the idea of an online presence. Her first personal engagement was on Facebook (Devan Ryan Carpenter Fine Art), followed by Instagram (devanryan-carpenterart). She now has her own website: dcarpenter.artspan.com. One of the more interesting endeavors that I have witnessed is her online art auctions that she holds on her Facebook page. She posts a date on which you can tune in for a certain selection of her artworks to be sold off in a first come, first serve fashion. She has experienced success in at least two ways: (1) She has moved more art in a more convenient way for her lifestyle and (2) She has gathered a following of people who look forward to viewing her work, so her name recognition as an artist has definitely gone up. A spin-off effect of her being online is that now she posts her pieces in progress and she has artists and patrons alike following her process which has been a source of great encouragement to her. I have also benefited personally from this "artist friend-sharing" situation. Devan has passed on valuable information to me that has resulted in me having an opportunity to display my art in a well-known community gallery. Information sharing works!

For some people, this line of exploration may not lead to an online presence, but doing a little detective work online could bring inspiration. Also, sharing what you have found online has the potential to enrich your group in unexpected ways. Get busy and dig in!

Finally, consider coordinating art exploration trips for yourself and your network group. The best way I know to be inspired as an artist is to see art. Take this seriously. Discover which art museums are in your immediate area, then branch out to surrounding areas. Aspire to visit places like the Smithsonian in Washington, D.C. Do not let money be an obstacle. Save individually and as a group. Set a time. Estimate the costs for larger trips and research cost-sharing to keep an arts trip affordable for all involved. The benefits of being in the presence of great artwork, whether of old masters or just-starting artists, are invaluable. You will be inspired and uplifted. It will affect you and your work. In the early 2000s I was fortunate enough to see a version of Monet's Water Lilies at the Boston Fine Arts Museum while visiting my friend in Massachusetts. I devolved into a puddle of uncontrollable, literal tears (I am not a crier). After getting over the shock to my system, I began to investigate the strokes, the color palette, the play of light. No book can take you into the overwhelming beauty of an artwork the same way as standing right in front of a piece can. Do yourself a favor, get in front of some art that is not your own. It will move you, it will push you in ways you cannot know, and it will pay in ways you cannot imagine.

P.S.: Enjoy the Ride!

Hopefully you create art because you love doing it. I have yet to find the magic wand that sprinkles stardust and teleports me to the top of the art world (whatever that is!). I'm committed to enjoying the ride! Although I did not attend an art school, I do think that would have suited me, had I been so fortunate. Maybe having gone to an art school would have drastically changed my creative trajectory. Who knows! My suggestions are for working artists whose paths did not go through art school doors, but they can be easily applied to all "working" artists.

If you are able to join with a close-knit group of artists, make the most of it. Push each other to explore new creative territory. Bolster each other's knowledge of art by planning trips to art galleries and museums. If trips are out of the budget, remember there are worlds of artists online waiting to be seen. Find online sites that deepen your understanding of art, artists, and the business of art in a practical and easy to use way. Always share new information and keep abreast of what's going on in the world of art outside of your immediate surroundings. Share information about how and which galleries to approach. Find creative ways to share your art experience inside and outside of your studio. You never know what artist associations might open up for you and your group. Go in the direction of whatever keeps you open to sharing your love of art and its creation!

PART VII

Partnerships, Collaborations and Networking

Finding Your Librarian Voice

*Creative Ways to Get Involved
and Share Ideas*

HOLLY MILLS *and* SHARON HOLDERMAN

Librarians are not limited to showing their creativity only in programming and patron services. There are many creative ways librarians can contribute to the profession including service to organizations and groups, presentations, and publishing. These creative outlets can help librarians find their niche and their voice in the profession by contributing in ways that match their personal and career goals.

Organizations and Groups

Being involved in organizations and groups and serving on committees is perhaps the easiest way to contribute to the library profession. Participation is often welcomed and voluntary, so there is a lot of freedom in choosing where to give time and effort. Starting locally is an easy way to find out where to be of use. It is up to the librarian how much time to invest and what type of benefit to seek. Here are some benefits of getting involved:

- Being involved in an organization will give the library exposure and become a source for assistance in getting programming off the ground, getting attention for services, and highlighting the library's future plans.
- Even if a person does not take a leadership position, being involved in committees and organizations provides the opportunity to lead discussions and engage in conversations with peers. Developing these leadership and social skills can also have a positive effect on both work and personal relationships.
- Meeting people in these settings leads to a greater opportunity for collaborating on services and special projects. Networking allows a librarian to learn from peers about activities and chances for professional development.
- Librarians elevate the profession by being involved in ways that bring positive and necessary change to libraries. Whether librarians stay local and boost their own library or get involved on a larger scale to affect change in other libraries, the profession benefits from forward-thinking and caring librarians actively working to improve libraries and library services.

How to Get Involved

There is so much a librarian can be involved in, and the beauty is that the level of involvement is easy to plan for and select. Community involvement will likely require less financial or travel demands than state, regional, or national involvement, but it could be more demanding in other ways. The basic levels of involvement are:

- Becoming a member of an organization and attending meetings, which can open a librarian up to ideas and issues. Much can be learned from watching meetings, listening to discussions, and reading information in group newsletters and forums.
- Being a participant, which may include donating time or money, joining committees, volunteering for events, leading discussions, planning, or sharing ideas. Whereas a member may simply attend and receive information, the participant takes attendance a step further and gets involved in the organization's activities.
- Creating or leading a group or organization, which is the highest level of involvement. This can range from chairing a subcommittee to being an officer in the organization. These leadership roles require the largest time investment but may yield a greater impact in the organization and the profession.

Types of Organizations and Groups

The library profession has many organizations, big and small, from local to international. Here are some places to get involved:

Local Community

- Friends of the Library. If a library has a Friends organization, get involved to understand what patrons are discussing, wanting, needing, and how they perceive the overall value of the library. This information can help inform choices and put a personal face to the library, both of which enhance interest and services.
- Businesses. Partnering with businesses can be a valuable tool in promoting library services and events. For example, if the library is hosting a maker event, asking local electronics or hardware stores to co-sponsor it will benefit those businesses in the form of advertising and will help make the library's event successful.
- Schools. Librarians are involved in education in K-12, colleges, and universities. A librarian could benefit by volunteering on committees connected to education, students, or curricula. It would be helpful to know what each librarian is expecting from patrons and what challenges are being faced. Librarians at every level can provide support and ideas, leading to a coordinated effort with educators in the area.
- Museums and archives. Local media archives, museums, and historians can be easily tied in with many library services and events. Keeping involved in any support or planning groups for these people and outlets will ensure that the library is meeting the needs of the community and supporting access at all levels.

- Local interest groups. Being involved in local organizations, even if they are not library-related, can keep the library relevant in the community. For example, a librarian could join the local camera club and use the library's photography resources and photographic archives to contribute to the club's mission. This gains exposure for the library and its services and will foster connections to the community.

State and Regional

- Library associations. State library associations may require dues, but they are an easy way to discover what is going on in libraries across the state. Also, many offer opportunities to present, publish, and serve on committees and in leadership roles.
- State libraries. Official state libraries may have support organizations or public interest groups or meetings, which would be excellent opportunities to support the state library and discover how it can support other libraries. Sharing of resources or even donating to collections between the state and other libraries could be beneficial.
- Consortia. A consortium often aids libraries in acquiring resources at a better rate, and being involved can help influence the choices the group makes which will benefit one's home institution. Another benefit of consortia is the ability to share resources between libraries, like OhioLINK.
- Regional associations. Some organizations serve a region across multiple states, like SELA, the Southeastern Library Association. These organizations often rely on involvement from state organizations, and like state organizations, they offer presenting, publishing, and leadership opportunities as well.

National

- Library associations and subgroups. The American Library Association (ALA) is the most widely-recognized national organization for libraries. Membership in ALA offers librarians educational materials, conferences, teaching, networking opportunities, and more. Furthermore, there are many subgroups targeting specific areas of librarianship including leading and managing (LLAMA), information technology (LITA), school libraries (AASL), and many others.
- Specialized associations and councils. Some organizations are specific to an area of librarianship and bring together librarians from across the nation. Knowing national trends, plans, and issues can help inform planning and management of one's home institution. Special associations cover topics like maps, Jewish libraries, and archives.
- Library of Congress. The Library of Congress is the authority and standard-bearer for library practice in the United States. It has many Support Friends groups, and it also provides a wealth of educational material about its services, initiatives, and special projects.
- Digital Public Library of America (DPLA). Archives, education, and technology are just three of the special interest groups in which one can be involved. In addition, librarians with a strong interest in digital preservation and access can seek to be involved as a content hub or a service hub, thereby directly contributing to DPLA content.

- National Library Week. Being involved in National Library Week is a great way to promote interest in the library and its services, and there are often local, state, or national planning committees looking for volunteers to make the week a success.
- National Library Legislative Day. This day allows librarians to influence legislation that affects libraries, library services, and patrons. Librarians travel to D.C. to meet with politicians and support libraries. Involvement can include planning activities supporting the effort or directly participating in D.C.

Librarians have the freedom to decide how involved to be in the library profession. Obtaining a library position is simply the first step; there are many outlets for service and many levels at which one can commit time and effort.

Presentations

Another way to be involved in the library profession is presenting. Just as with involvement in organizations and committees, presenting is also welcomed and voluntary, though there is a bit less freedom because presentations typically require approval. Still, librarians do have the ultimate freedom in where they propose to present, and there are usually a wealth of opportunities to do so. While presenting does take time, effort, and often money and travel, there are benefits including:

- Presenting at a conference provides the chance to attend other conference sessions, learn useful information, and discover new ideas. Whether the sessions are specific to the librarian's institution or not, there is usually a lot of information that can be gleaned about best ways to run a library and its services.
- Presentations allow the speaker practice, and practice improves confidence and speaking skills. Sharing information that may benefit other librarians and libraries gives one a rewarding feeling.
- During presentations, librarians have opportunities to start conversations and gain feedback. Other librarians will share their experiences, suggest ideas, and provide support. Feedback will help presenters understand how effectively they shared the information, as well as get ideas for future presentations.
- Getting feedback about a presentation is a form of networking. Speaking with other librarians who share similar interests and experiences opens the door for future collaborations and presentation opportunities. It also helps meet colleagues who can provide support and feedback during future professional endeavors.

Ways to Present

There are many ways to present, and there are different levels of difficulty related to preparation and skill. Here are some common presentation opportunities:

- Presentations. These effectively share information to a group, and they are easy to adapt to any time limit or subject. Using slides and visual aids can make presenting easier for the speaker and audience. For speakers, formal and informal presentations are an easy and expected way to communicate, and experience will further improve their skills.

- Webinars. Webinars are essentially presentations that happen online. They involve a similar amount of planning and preparation, but the presentation is delivered online and the speaker may not see or hear participants. Webinars usually have a wider reach than in-person presentations due to the online component. They have little to no impact financially and may be easily accommodated during work time.

- Posters. For librarians who do not enjoy speaking as much, posters are a great option for presenting. A working knowledge of how to use software to add and manipulate text and images helps create posters that are visually appealing and share the information effectively. In presenting the poster, prepared speeches are less necessary because discussions are often one-on-one and conversational.

- Roundtables/panel discussions. Discussions are led by a moderator and often do not require any formal presentation. Moderating or participating in discussions about library issues are great ways to have a conversation and share ideas and issues without extensive preparation. Being able to listen, communicate well, and keeping on track and on time is key. These discussions are most often found at conferences, though there are discussions that happen online.

- Workshops. Teaching a workshop is a wonderful option for topics that need more time. Workshops are best suited to new services with many components, training, research instruction, or any topic that needs more in-depth instruction or demonstration. Workshops get more in depth on a topic and can happen once or multiple times for maximum exposure. Workshops often involve learning objectives and activities for participants.

- E-Courses. Full courses offered online are the most time consuming in terms of planning, preparation, and time commitment. Participants are looking for in-depth information and practical help for a topic, so the presenter must be sure to cover all aspects of the topic thoroughly and provide ample opportunities for feedback, discussion, and involvement. These types of presentations may be paid or voluntary.

Presenting is an easy way to learn and share more about libraries and librarianship. There is a great variety in involvement, so librarians can choose how, when, and at what commitment level they are willing to participate. Presentations are also a way to show professional development and advancement, which is beneficial in the workplace.

Publishing

There are many publishing opportunities for librarians ranging in scope and formality. Librarians new to publishing can start with a more informal publication to ease into authorship. This helps them learn about publishing and become more confident in the process and their abilities. Aspiring authors should also learn from others who have published successfully because conversations can help authors develop their topics and find relevant publications.

General Publishing Process

1. Brainstorm topic ideas based on knowledge, experiences, and interests.
2. Search publications to learn what has been written and what is lacking on those topics to further develop ideas.
3. Find publications accepting submissions in those topic areas.
4. Become familiar with each publication in order to understand the scope, tone, and writing style.
5. Find the submission guidelines online or contact an editor to request them. These address scope, length, format, submission process, copyright, proposal requirements, turnaround time, and benefits.
6. Submit an article for publication. Follow the guidelines carefully and proofread thoroughly to increase the chance of acceptance.
7. Wait for the editor's response, and do not submit the writing to other publications.
8. If accepted, revise based on feedback and get published.
9. If not accepted, find another publication and/or change the article and resubmit.

Publishing has many benefits including:

- Authors can reach a wider audience than through presentations, yielding more recognition.
- Content is usually more permanent than presentations as most publishing platforms are long-term.
- Being a published author can create new collaborations and opportunities to review and edit other publications, especially as librarians develop relationships with editors and other writers.
- Sharing your knowledge and experience helps librarians with their careers and their libraries' services.
- Authorship looks great on a resume and can help with promotion and tenure if applicable.

Publishing has some drawbacks. Authors connect less with their audience than presenters, and the only way they receive reader feedback is if readers initiate contact. Publishing can be competitive, so most librarians will receive a rejection at some point. Not getting accepted does not equal failure but means the writing needs further work or is more appropriate for a different publication. The writing, submission, and publishing process can be very slow, which requires patience.

Not all publications are open source or open access. If a publication is not open source, it does not allow free access to all readers but requires a subscription. Librarians typically want to disseminate information as widely as possible, so they may desire an open source publication. Some open source publications charge the authors to publish since they do not require their readers to subscribe. These are important considerations for authors when they are selecting a publication. Charging authors for publishing has created an environment for predatory publishers, which refers to publishers who misrepresent their journal in order to get money from authors. They may claim higher prestige or other pretenses that are revealed as untrue only after authors pay. Librarians should talk to others and carefully research publishers to ensure the publications they select are trustworthy.

What to Write

- Book and media reviews. These reviews are a great way to break into the publishing arena because they are brief, and the subject content is clearly delineated. Reviewing can help librarians find items of interest to them or materials to add to their libraries' collections. Authors can write a review first and then submit it to a publication, or they can contact a publication first to determine what to review.
- Opinion pieces. Many authors find it easier to write about their opinions compared to other types of articles, which makes these a good option for new authors. Authors usually write in the first person and cover anything library related like collections, patrons, services, organizations, policies, or budgets. Not all places publish opinion pieces, so it is best to find appropriate publications by finding existing opinion pieces.
- Experience pieces. Librarians can write about their professional experiences like getting hired, managing others, attending conferences, mentoring, networking, or changing careers. The purpose of these pieces is to share experiences with librarians to help them navigate similar situations successfully or avoid potential pitfalls. Including lessons learned and improvements is especially helpful.
- Presentation content. Authors may take a previously presented topic and turn it into an article. Since the topic was already accepted as a presentation, it should appeal to the right publication. Authors should know if their presentation is already available to the public on a conference website so they can ensure the article offers more information.
- Best practices/case studies. These can be similar to experience pieces but usually have a more formal approach. These pieces often include references to other articles, requiring authors to research related literature and spend more time and effort. Ideally, readers will learn how to incorporate practices and services into their own libraries.
- Original research. These articles have a more extensive literature review and require authors to conduct their own research to obtain data. Gathering and evaluating the data and writing the article are much more time intensive than other types of articles. Analyzing statistics in depth may be difficult for new authors who have not conducted research previously, so co-authoring with a more experienced librarian can be helpful.

Where to Publish

- Blogs, vlogs, websites, social media. These types of publications can be more informal, but it depends on the publisher and the content tone. Many libraries and library organizations encourage submissions for their social media, and authors can always post on their own professional accounts like LinkedIn. Since many of these types of media are not edited or reviewed before publication, it is often easier to publish here. However, those same reasons may cause some people to see these publications as less prestigious.
- Organization publications. Many library organizations offer publishing opportunities. The more local the organization, the easier it may be to publish since there are fewer librarians in that organization. Many state and regional

organizations allow submissions from authors outside their areas, and authors rarely need to be members in the organizations to publish their articles.

- Conference proceedings. There are two types of conference proceedings. One type contains papers that were accepted for talks at a conference. Since the papers were submitted before the conference, there is minimal work required for publication. The second type contains articles that are based on conference presentations. These proceedings often have deadlines soon after the conference, and authors typically write the article from scratch. However, the workload should be manageable because the topic is familiar.
- Journals. These are common publication venues, and there are two main types of journals: peer-reviewed and non-peer-reviewed. Submitting an article to a peer-reviewed journal means the article is sent to multiple reviewers for feedback. The reviewers submit comments to the editor including whether it needs editing and is appropriate for the journal. Peer-reviewed journals usually have a lower acceptance rate, so they are considered more prestigious. Non-peer-reviewed journals are those where an editor works directly with the author to create the final product without reviewers. In either case, articles can be accepted "as-is," returned for editing, or rejected. Authors should not be discouraged by rejection because they can submit their article to other journals or other publication types.
- Books. Authors can write a book chapter or an entire book. Book editors will call for chapter proposals, much like presentation proposals, through email listservs and publishers' websites. The editor notifies authors whether or not they have been selected based on a chapter proposal. Publishing an entire book is a much more involved process. Often publishers want to see an outline and a few chapters to get a good idea of the concept and the authors' writing ability. A good place to start for writing books is the ALA Editions website because it specializes in library-related books. Authors may self-publish books as well, but those are not as prestigious as books accepted by established publishers.

The publishing field has production-related opportunities as well. Some publications require someone to facilitate the design, layout, and printing. This is a good opportunity to get some experience with publications without having already published. Librarians volunteering for these responsibilities should have some experience with the layout and design of newsletters, brochures, websites, or similar materials. Another opportunity is to review submissions for peer-reviewed journals. Journals usually have a number of reviewers and rotate submissions among them, so it does not require constant work. Librarians can volunteer to be reviewers by contacting the journal editor. The editor may only want published authors to be reviewers since they would be more familiar with the process, but it depends on the publication and editor. Some publications have committees to help guide the scope and content as well as selection of editors and reviewers. Librarians can volunteer to be on the committee and again may have better luck if they have already published. Lastly, volunteering to be an editor is a big commitment because the editor is responsible for the content and timely publication. The requirements to be an editor vary by journal and may favor previous publication committee work or reviewer experience.

Librarianship as a profession offers an open, welcoming environment that encourages and fosters collaboration and sharing ideas. Every librarian, regardless of their job, has many opportunities to be creative by contributing to the profession. The opportunities listed here offer many levels of options to get started and become further involved.

Collective Creativity

AMY GAY *and* KELSEY GEORGE

Access to art materials is no longer restricted to private collections or those who are able to travel to museums and other cultural heritage institutions. More than ever, cultural institutions are embracing the development of digital collections to bring art to a wider audience. Libraries and archives have become major stakeholders in the digitization movement, and, in turn, the roles of librarians and archivists have been impacted. This shift towards digital art collections in libraries has also affected the way that librarians interact with physical art collections. Librarians must be innovative and accurate in their presentation of art materials. This essay illustrates the symbiotic nature between collections and caretakers, including the workflows, collaborations, challenges, and experiences that come from involvement in these projects. Amy Gay, Digital Scholarship Librarian at Binghamton University, addresses the creativity involved in curating digital collections. Kelsey George, Cataloging & Metadata Strategies Librarian at University of Nevada, Las Vegas (UNLV), discusses how digital discovery impacts curation of materials and how working with art publications impacted her own art.

"*Collective creativity* is an approach of creative activity that emerges from the collaboration and contribution of many individuals so that new forms of innovative and expressive art forms are produced collectively by individuals connected by the network (Inakage 2007)." It encompasses both the scientific method, through the experimentation processes, and artistic processes through design thinking. In their 2011 book, *Collective Creativity: Traditional Patterns and New Paradigms,* Fischer et al. pointed out that "[a]ll creativity is collective. No creative person exists in isolation; all human beings, artists and scientists in particular, depend in their work and in their creative self-expression on the contribution of others…. Furthermore, all artistic creation aims at outside presentation and recognition in a process of collective reception" (Fischer et al. 2011). In other words, collective creativity is not just about the works of original creators; it also includes how the audience interprets the works. Collective creativity may start at an individual level, but it still grows as a collective of creative knowledge as others who are in contact with the work express it.

In this essay, Amy and Kelsey share their experiences working on creative collaborations in libraries. They each share an overview of a project they worked on, including its successes and challenges, and share details on the creative process that went into making these projects a reality. Both authors focus on the relationship between creativity and the ever-evolving role of library workers.

Digital Exhibitions (Amy Gay)

There are many ways of approaching digital exhibits. One is for institutions to band together to create a content management site that highlights collections from the various organizations around an overarching theme. Collaborating on these types of projects has many benefits, but it can also bring along difficulties for content management, display, and standardization. The collections on New York Heritage (NYH) research portal came from a variety of cultural heritage institutions. Each of these institutions are a part of a consortium, connected through one of seven library councils in New York State and Empire State Library Network (ESLN) members: Capital District Library Council; Central New York Library Resources Council (CLRC); Long Island Library Resources Council; Northern New York Library Network; Rochester Regional Library Council; South Central Regional Library Council; and Western New York Library Resources Council (New York Heritage, 2017). The portal serves as an access point to exhibits emphasizing the people, places, and institutions of New York State. Collections in NYH represent a broad range of historical, scholarly, and cultural materials held in libraries, museums, and archives across the state. Items currently exhibited include photographs, letters, diaries, directories, maps and books.

When the NYH site first launched, it looked cluttered and clunky. It was difficult to know where one institution's collection began and another institution's ended. Discoverability was not at its prime for NYH. The Councils joined together, led by CLRC, to redesign the NYH site for optimal searching, sharing, and accessibility. Around 2012, CLRC received grant money to help clean up NYH and set the redesign into production.

The major goal of the redesign was to provide better context for the institutions and collections in NYH. A secondary goal was to be relatively platform-agnostic. Members of ESLN designed the website so that all of the contextual content lives in an external database (built in eXist), while the display is constructed through Drupal, a content management system. All of this contextual information points back to the individual items that are still stored in CONTENTdm. Instead of users ending up on a page listing thousands of items, they would now have some context for what they're looking at first. Contributing institutions also have landing pages they can direct their patrons to view their individual collections.

While working on the New York Heritage project, through these networks, my colleague and I reached out to people who could assist us with understanding various collections, the creative process that went into building their collections, and the reasons they chose to share what they did as part of the larger New York State history on NYH. Since my colleague and I were also writing descriptions of these collections, these conversations helped us gain new perspectives and led us to devise new ways to write more enriched portrayals of collections from each of the institutions. Our goal was to help draw the connection between each collection and highlight these connections to our collective heritage as New York Staters. My colleague and I also wanted our descriptions and biographical context to be as verbally appealing as the collections were visually appealing. Since there were time constraints on the project implementation, we split up the collections based on councils, with each of us having three to start, and met twice a week to discuss any hiccups one of us had that the other might be able to resolve. We learned our individual strengths with various collection types. We each worked on the collections from our hometown institutions since we had knowledge of histories and personal connections to items in these collections; there was great value with having this internal collaboration.

Every image, whether it was a photograph or a written document, told a story; we wanted to share this story in the contextual information. We studied the pictures and documents looking, for names, places, events, time periods, descriptive details, or any other key elements. Since our content was focused more on collections rather than individual items, we needed to discover details that united the whole story. We researched these details and wrote the stories. We encountered some aspects, unfortunately, which were either unidentifiable or did not have much information on them. By producing contextual content we laid the groundwork for the process of creating this content on eXist and NYH.

Descriptions for the collections on New York Heritage were a challenge. Because each institution was submitting their own metadata for items, it led to inconsistencies in standards. To address that issue, a handbook was created for New York Heritage collections before I began my work there. It contained a section focused on specific standards for information display in each field. Still, collection metadata was not always correctly reflected in these formats. One task my colleague and I were specifically hired for was to work on the metadata cleanup. This became a challenge, because certain fields were either missing information or came with inaccurate data. For example, some items would have the date on which they were digitized listed as the date of their creation, when the creation date should have been the approximate origin date/time period for the item. Clarifications such as these needed to be made. CLRC asked my colleague and me to travel to participating institutions and train them on these standards as new collections were to be added to the project. Unfortunately, money for our positions ran out too soon, and CLRC was unable to attain additional funding to extend our contracts to complete these trainings. Currently, the councils work with their affiliated institutions to learn these standards and attempt to match the local metadata fields with the fields needed for the New York Heritage site.

Art and Exhibition Catalogs (Kelsey George)

The University of California, Santa Barbara (UCSB) libraries are home to many unique and diverse collections, including their collection of art exhibition catalogs (AEC's), which celebrated its 50th anniversary in 2017. The AEC collection holds over 90,000 titles spanning across four centuries. Works include rare and early-produced exhibition catalogs acquired from the collection of famous French curator, Marcel Nicolle. The breadth of this collection exemplifies the evolution of exhibition catalogs as a type of art publication: the transition away from simple yet practical inventory lists to illustrious designed catalogs with full color reproductions (UC Santa Barbara Library 1992). The Art Libraries Society of North America (ARLIS/NA) established best practices for cataloging exhibition catalogs. In the publication *Cataloging Exhibition Catalogs*, ARLIS/NA differentiates exhibition catalogs (works published to document an exhibition, and including a list of works exhibited) from art publications (works about art) and artist books (books produced by artists and intended as visual art objects) (ARLIS/NA Cataloging Advisory Committee 2008).

When the AEC's were first being collected by UCSB in the 1970s, the titles were brought into the library with accession numbers based on the order of their arrival to AEC collection (i.e., aec-1, aec-2, etc.) rather than Library of Congress call numbers derived from the title's subject headings. This was done to group all the works into one location to create a browse-able collection for students and faculty, so that this unique collection was more user-friendly. At the point of my arrival at UCSB, the collection had grown to almost 100,000 volumes, the Art Library had just moved into the main UCSB Library building as the Art & Architecture collection, and the library decided to transition away from this practice. New art exhibition catalogs were being integrated into the stacks alongside other art books on the same topics, with Library of Congress call numbers. The oversized art exhibition catalogs were being held in the "cage" for rare materials that did not fall under the purview of Special Research Collections or were awkwardly sized, and therefore did not physically fit in the stacks of the old Art Library. Now that the Art Library had moved to the new Art & Architecture space in the main library, there was room for the oversized materials to be on oversized shelves in the main art stacks.

The driving decision for this transition for the oversized materials and all newly acquired AEC's was to increase overall visibility and usability of the collection. With modern library catalogs, and use of the Library of Congress Genre and Form Term "Exhibition catalogs," users are able to identify these materials in ways that were not available when this collection was being first developed. Though the accession numbers kept the collection physically together, many exhibition catalogs were small or fragile print materials needing pam binding, resulting in shelves with thousands of grey folders, some with only an "aec-###" printed on the outside cover. This, when coupled with no context clues about content (such as neighboring related works) makes the collection more difficult to browse for new users. Due to the accession numbering and the size of the collection, there were frequent cases of duplication within the AEC collection and also the main art stacks. This issue was compounded by variation of cataloging description level throughout the collection, causing multiple OCLC records brought in for the same title, perhaps decades apart by different catalogers or in an automated batch process. Much of the deduplication cannot be done purely based on examining the records or running a job in the library system to match an ISBN (not all have one), exhibition title (try "Old Master Painters"), work title (some publications are just titled "Works"), institutional publisher (see the "Metropolitan Museum of Art"), artist (see "Picasso"), etc. Catalogers must physically compare items to see if they are the same or just similar publications.

Most of the duplications at UCSB were caught by users or our wonderful public services staff who would then send the copies to technical services. Technical services work does not exist in a vacuum. We heavily rely on user experience in our catalog to inform our work. When cataloging, we must be mindful of who our users are, how they search, and how we can combat our own biases as catalogers to describe the materials as comprehensively and accessibly as possible. UCSB Libraries, as a designated Name Authority Cooperative Program contributor, required that I do authority work for all artists and institutions represented in newly acquired art exhibition catalogs. In describing these objects, I was forced to think about the art beyond observation and deepen my understanding of different art movements.

One such movement was the Chicano Art Movement, which grew out of *el movimiento* (or the *Chicano Movement*) of the 1960s and consisted of Mexican American artists, poets, playwrights, musicians, and dancers who identified as Chicano/Chicana and incorporated the socio-political and cultural ideals of the Chicano movement into public art works. This movement is not currently reflected in the Library of Congress subject headings (LCSH), nor were there access points for "Chicano artists" or "Chicano art," despite there being a precedent set by the existence of the subject pattern heading "Chicano literature" as a cross reference for "Mexican American literature." UCSB is a major collector of Chicano artists and art resources, especially being home to Shifra Goldman's papers and many art book donations. It made sense for us to propose these subject headings. In October 2016, I worked with Catherine Busselen, now the acting Head of Content Management Services at UCSB, to create and submit updates to the Subject Authority Cooperative Program (SACO) for the entries "Mexican American artists"/"Mexican American art" to include "Chicano" cross references and submitted the "Chicano Art Movement" as its own subject heading. Even still, there is room for improvement, as the term Chicano is gendered "man," and does not accurately describe the work of Chicanas/Chicanx people.

In my current role at UNLV, I think a lot about how the way we describe objects impacts discoverability and how our lived experiences and biases impact our descriptions. This is not a unique line of thought; many inside and outside of our field have commented on the shortcomings of our existing controlled vocabularies. At Dartmouth College, the library worked with the Dartmouth Student Coalition for Immigration Reform, Equality and Dreamers to petition Library of Congress to replace the term "illegal aliens" in LCSH (Albright 2016). While not all proposals are going to be as imperative or politically charged, LCSH is undeniably incomplete and in many sections outdated. Description directly impacts discoverability and access. If our diverse collections are not being accurately described, are we not inadvertently suppressing their discoverability and censoring our materials?

The SACO proposal process is not restricted to librarians, and librarians are not always representative of the diversity of the community we serve. Our communities are filled with people with experience in a multitude of subjects. We have an opportunity to tap into that pool of knowledge to form relationships and enrich our work. Violet Fox, Editor of the Dewey decimal classification for OCLC, followed through on this idea when she developed *Cataloging Lab*, a "wiki where people can collaborate to construct subject heading proposals" (Fox 2018). Fox recognized that there were obstacles to submitting subject headings—whether a lack of knowledge, time, or resources—and found a creative solution that could allow anyone to overcome those obstacles. Technical services work can leave us feeling constrained and limited to the current established rules and standards set by our profession. Taking the time to collaborate with others outside of our departments, libraries, and institutions is necessary for our professional growth.

Role of Librarian Ever Evolving

The work of librarians is often shaped by the needs of the users. In the digital age, library workers no longer have the luxury of just working with our materials, we must also be teachers, curators, marketers, advocates, and magic makers. In order to challenge our users to interact with our collections in new ways, we curate book displays, physical and digital exhibitions, and library events. Now, more than ever, we must advocate for our collections and demonstrate their value.

Social media platforms are great to reach out to our communities and promote our collections. At both Binghamton University and the University of Nevada, Las Vegas, the libraries utilize blog posts, Facebook, Twitter and Instagram for sharing various collections added to our Special Collections, our institutional repository, and other areas of the libraries and campus. For example, Amy wrote a blog post about a photograph collection, "Guatemalan Forced Migration," by Oscar F. Gil-Garcia and Manuel Gil, and added a link to the blog post and collection to Facebook; within 24-hours, the post had been viewed close to 1,000 times (Gil-Garcia and Gil 2008).

One project currently in progress, specific to Binghamton University, involves the institutional repository serving as an access point to the Art Museum's digital images of their collections. BU's Library and Art Museum have partnered in order to showcase the museum's unique collections on a sustainable platform. Another goal was to reach a larger audience, since it was not widely known that there were vast collections within the Art Museum, or even that they had an Art Museum on campus. The goal of this project will be to increase awareness and discoverability, generating traffic to the institutional repository and visits to the Art Museum. Another art project in the works at BU Libraries involves their first interactive digital exhibit focused on the 1960s. The Dean of Libraries had an idea for the exhibit after receiving a generous collection donation by an alumnus. Amy and her team plan to build a site that will include books, photographs, video footage, oral histories, linked external resources, and a place for people to share their stories about being at BU during this time period. Currently, they are envisioning the layout and will do user testing over the summer. The first installment of this exhibit is planned to go live in September 2018.

Librarians and archivists are impacted by the collections we work with on a daily basis. There can be an added emotional weight for staff who work with materials documenting tragedy or dark subjects. Materials can also provide regular doses of inspirational energy for both the people processing and accessing. Amy felt that by studying the World War I and World War II propaganda posters she learned more about these time periods and society during the wars than she did within school classrooms. As she worked on the collection, she became more interested in the history and passionate about sharing this rich knowledge source with others. There is a sense of pride that goes into the completion of a project, when the final product is viewable and we can see the actual impact it then makes on patrons. The intricate details, language, and images within each item shared their own story of life during these wars.

Constantly working with art exhibition materials made the idea of participating in exhibitions more accessible and inspired Kelsey to continue to work on her own fiber art. When the opportunity arose to participate in call for artist books created by library workers, she had built up the confidence to submit a handwoven artist book. After two years of handling catalogs for art exhibitions almost every day, she took part in one of her first exhibitions, *Bibliothecarii et Glutinatores*, held at the Denver Public Library Central Branch from January 14 through April 15th, 2018 (Abecedarian Gallery 2017). The woven book, titled *The Dreaming Tree*, was inspired by the relationship between stories, lullabies, women's roles in protecting dreams, and what is traditionally perceived to be "women's work." The art piece was purchased by and now lives in the Special Collections of Baylor University in Waco, Texas.

Considerations for Library Professionals

Goals

As library professionals, we strive to make our collections as discoverable and accessible to as many people as possible. We want the content to be captivating, grabbing the interest of people viewing the content. However, we also need to make sure the content is legible, understandable. Explaining collections and items within collections in plain language is not as easy as it may sound. We also must decide what collections we can make available, especially in a world involving backlogs and limited resources. When planning to share these more creative, rare collections, it is important to keep the following in mind: How unique is the collection? Are there other institutions that have already made this collection digital? If so, see if your collection fills gaps that are missing in other collections and share links between institutions for further research. Points to address:

- What is the target audience of interest for the institution (i.e., is there an interest in getting more outside researchers to come to the institution)? Which collections would reach this audience and should be processed first? Once the audience is known, be sure to aim the content towards that particular focus group as well by using keywords, tags, descriptions, etc.
- How many items are in the collection, and approximately how much time is needed to process the collection?
- What are the needs of stakeholders versus wants for patrons? Where is the balance for both sides?

Funding and Staffing

For funding, it is important to keep the following in mind:

- Current and future budget (Are there projected cuts for the upcoming year?)
- If needed, what grants can be applied for and what are the conditions of the grants?
- What digital tools and equipment are needed to make the collection digital? Are there other nearby institutions or resources available to fill gaps here? Is there a sustainable content management system?
- Can your organization partner with others to pool resources to highlight related collections?

For staffing:

- What are the necessary hours to complete this project and the correlating staff requirements?
- Who are your stakeholders and how will communication take place between stakeholders and staff?
- What roles will staff play? Is there room for collaboration with others (especially if there is a particular area of expertise lacking)?

Memberships/Learning from Others

There are many committees and groups involved with creating digital art projects and sharing resources. At the national level, this includes Library of Congress, Digital Library Federation, Art Libraries Society of North America (ARLIS/NA), and Council on Library and Information Resources among others. Local organizations can also serve as resources for guidance or possible partners when curating digital collections.

Have standards. Document procedures for collection description and management, if those had not been already written or provided for the project. Refer to national or discipline-driven standards for description when applicable. Organizations such as ARLIS/NA and the Visual Resource Association put out standards for visual resource materials when cataloging in MARC or metadata respectively. Establishing preferred standard (such as LCSH or Getty Vocabularies) or locally controlled vocabularies for use when creating metadata can help get rid of some ambiguity when describing an item. Keep in mind that no controlled vocabulary is perfect or complete.

Tap into the power of collective creativity! Researching what other institutions have done and looking at exhibits with components that are being considered for your project are great places to start, but do not be afraid to try something new.

- Consider the greater context of the collection within your community. How does it relate to our lives? How can we relate to the materials in the collection?
- Collaborate with others, whether it be through a working group or crowdsourcing. Take these insights into consideration and view the project as a user, not just as a designer.
- Address internal biases. Drawing from a larger pool of experiences allows us to step back as librarians and approach our work as people.

REFERENCES

Albright, Charlotte E. 2016. "Students Persuade Library of Congress to Drop the I-Word." *Dartmouth News.* Accessed June, 2018 https://news.dartmouth.edu/news/2016/03/students-persuade-library-congress-drop-i-word.

ARLIS/NA Cataloging Advisory Committee. 2008. "Cataloging Exhibition Publications: Best Practices." Library of Congress. Accessed March 2018. Art Libraries Society of North America.

Fischer, Gerhard, and Vassen, Florian (eds.). 2011. "Collective Creativity: Traditional Patterns and New Paradigms." *Collective Creativity: Collaborative Work in the Sciences, Literature and the Arts.* eBook.

Fox, Violet. 2018. "Creating Change in the Cataloging Lab | Peer to Peer Review." *Library Journal.* Accessed June 2018. https://lj.libraryjournal.com/2018/03/opinion/peer-to-peer-review/creating-change-in-the-cataloging-lab-peer-to-peer-review/.

George, Kelsey Diane. 2017. The Dreaming Tree. Accessed April 2018. https://abecedariangallery.com/store/shop/kelsey-diane-george-the-dreaming-tree/.

Gil-Garcia, Oscar, and Gil, Manuel. 2008. "Guatemalan Forced Migration." Accessed April 2018. https://orb.binghamton.edu/guatemalan_forced_migration/.

Inakage, Masa. 2007. "Collective Creativity: Toward a New Paradigm for Creative Culture." DIMEA '07 Proceedings of the 2nd International Conference on Digital Interactive Media in Entertainment and Arts. Accessed May 2018. doi: 10.1145/1306813.1306822.

McConnell, Eric. 2010. "How to Set and Achieve Goals of a Project." May28. Accessed April 2018. http://www.mymanagementguide.com/five-essential-tips-for-managing-project-goals-how-to-set-and-achieve-goals-of-project/.

New York Heritage. 2017. New York Heritage Digital Collections. Accessed 2018. https://nyheritage.org/.

UC Santa Barbara Library. 1992. "Celebrating Diversity: 25 Years of UCSB's Art Exhibition Catalog Collection." Accessed March 2018. https://www.library.ucsb.edu/exhibitions/celebrating-diversity-25-years-ucsbs-art-exhibition-catalog-collection.

Around the State in Postcards

Creating Traveling Exhibits

RUTH ELDER *and* JANA SLAY

Technical Services departments and creativity are rarely thought of together. We "color inside the lines," but occasionally there are opportunities for us to use our creative sides and learn something for our own personal knowledge. One such opportunity occurred in the Troy University Libraries' Technical Services department in the form of creating two traveling exhibitions from an archival collection of postcards. The project called for us to develop working relationships with the grant funding agency, vendors outside the library world, and our graphic designer, as well as librarians and museum directors throughout Alabama.

Wade Hall Collection in the Archives

In the early 2000s, Dr. Wade Hall donated a collection of over 25,000 vintage post-cards to the Troy University Library Archives. The postcards were from every state in the union and many foreign countries. Many of the Alabama postcards were digitized and added to the state digital repository (Alabama Mosaic), but beyond that the collection was sitting unused except for occasional placement in a display case. This huge collection was an untapped resource for outreach, but at the same time finding a way to share it was not immediately obvious.

Research

Our research for this project did not follow the normally prescribed method of finding all the studies that have been done and going from there. Our needs were of a more practical than philosophical nature, so we focused on the "how to" literature that was available. Mark Walhimer's blog *Museum Planner: A Blog of Museum Planning by an Experienced Museum Planner* (Walheimer 2011) and in particular his post "Creating a Traveling Exhibition" provided good, but not overwhelming, amount of information to get us started. Angela Poulos's *Guiding Principles for the Design of Traveling Exhibitions* (Poulos 2008) gave us a more in-depth look into what we needed to know in order to create successful exhibitions. We also consulted resources from the Smithsonian Institution Traveling Exhibition Service (Smithsonian n.d.) and Common Approach to Scientific Touring Exhibitions (CASTEX) (Common 2004) to learn more about how to go about not only creating the exhibits, but getting them "traveling" to other venues.

Creating the Exhibits

Dr. Christopher Shaffer became the Dean of Libraries for Troy University in 2014. He is a strong proponent of library outreach through programming. His plan is for the Troy University Libraries to become more outward-looking as an organization and for the librarians to be actively engaged in the community and to build partnerships within and outside the University. In the past, this directive was aimed at public service librarians. However, Shaffer strongly encouraged all librarians to investigate activities, projects, and grants that would have a positive impact on our community.

Kansas City Public Library's award winning postcard exhibit entitled "Greetings from Kansas City" inspired Shaffer with an idea of how the library could share Dr. Hall's postcard donation. Because the technical services department was cataloging the postcards, we were the authority on the collection's content. Therefore, we were the ones tasked with investigating the feasibility of creating a postcard exhibit. This was a daunting task because neither of us knew anything about creating exhibits. However, when dealing with a job that seems overwhelming, break it down into manageable portions.

The first decision—overall subject matter—was easy since the Alabama postcards were the only ones digitized. Deciding the type of exhibit to create was also relatively simple because traveling exhibits could best accomplish our goal of promoting the Wade Hall Postcard Collection and raising the profile of Troy University across the state. In addition, a cursory examination of the collection led to the decision to create two exhibits, one focusing on main streets and the other on historical buildings. However, after we eliminated all items not picturing streets or buildings, we still had an unmanageable amount of cards. Consequently, our next step was to divide Alabama into geographical regions by counties. We arbitrarily chose the dividing lines for the regions. Keeping the four largest metropolitan areas—Birmingham, Montgomery, Mobile, and Huntsville—in separate regions was our only criteria. If we had to do this again we would not have put Tuscaloosa and Birmingham in the same geographical region. The cards from those cities make up ¼ of the Alabama postcard collection.

Once we had the themes chosen, it was time to decide how to design the exhibits and what to include. Even though we had no experience creating exhibits, we did have familiarity with exhibitions and knew what we wanted. For instance, an educational component was necessary because people visit exhibits to learn and Troy University is an educational institution. We also knew words were important, but the images had to be the most prominent feature. We also made a point of selecting postcards depicting large cities and small towns to give the exhibits wide appeal. Lastly, flexibility was essential so any venue could host an exhibit.

Organizing and categorizing the postcards is a simple task for technical services librarians because it is what we do. For each of the exhibits, the first step was to take the scanned images and put them into the six geographical regions. Second, we made sure that certain cities were included: Union Springs—Wade Hall's hometown, Tuscaloosa—

Wade Hall is a University of Alabama alumnus, and Troy since Troy University created the exhibit. Narrowing down the images from the major metropolitan areas was the third step. We did not want these cities to dominate a region. Lastly, we included towns because of their location and size in order to assure diversity. However, this still left too many images. This is where our expertise ended and we turned to a professional graphic designer.

Design

Dr. Shaffer recommended modeling the exhibits after the Kennesaw State University traveling exhibits, so we investigated the design companies they used. However, we ultimately decided to use a professor from the Troy University Department of Art and Design as our graphic designer for several reasons. First, we knew his work so we had confidence that the end product would be exceptional. Second, since he was on campus, we could work closely with him which gave us more control over the exhibits' content. Finally, he was a friend so we were comfortable working with him. Creating exhibits based on postcard images was new to all of us so working with someone we knew made the collaboration process go smoothly.

The designer helped us reduce the number of images based on their visual interest and the quality of the scans. He also directed us to the images that would impact viewers on an emotional level, allowing senior citizens "I remember when" moments and younger people glimpses of their hometown as it was "back then." Thus, for the streets exhibit we chose bustling streets, such as 20th Street in Birmingham, historic streets, such as Dexter Avenue in Montgomery, and small town streets, such as Front Street in Carbon Hill. The buildings exhibit was more difficult because the Wade Hall Postcard Collection has so many fascinating postcards of historical buildings. Our answer was to choose a sub-theme, non-commercial buildings, so we could narrow the focus. Therefore, only governmental, educational, medical, or religious buildings made the cut. The next step was choosing which courthouse, post office, school, hospital, or church to use so no one type of building dominated. For the colleges, we specifically chose historical buildings that were still being used. Troy is the exception because our students know what the current buildings look like, but not the original building. We also specifically included a lighthouse to remind people that a part of Alabama is on the coast

We worked together with the designer to create two eight-panel traveling exhibits. Our images and words combined with his colors, fonts, and arrangement resulted in two phenomenal exhibitions. The first panel for each exhibit has introductory information about postcards, as well as, a portrait and biographical information about Wade Hall. The last panel illustrates how postcards depict social history, their similarities to today's social media, and instructions for accessing the rest of the Wade Hall Collection. The other six panels include the fronts of eight postcards representative of the populace of that region along with descriptive captions. Panel two features postcard images from North Alabama. Huntsville, Gadsden, Florence, Athens, and Anniston are some of the municipalities represented. The third panel covers North Central Alabama, including Birmingham, Tuscaloosa, Talladega, Demopolis, and Sylacauga. For both exhibits, the fourth panel highlights Montgomery postcards. Dexter, Cloverdale, and Court streets are all included as well as historic buildings such as the Capitol, St. Margaret's Hospital, and the City of St. Jude. The cities of Union Springs, Opelika, Auburn, and Eufaula represent South Central Alabama on the fifth panel. Panel six covers municipalities in Southeast Alabama such as Troy, Enterprise, and Dothan while the seventh panel presents Southwest Alabama cities including Mobile, Evergreen, and Brewton.

The Wade Hall Digital Postcard Exhibit was the brainchild of the designer. When he saw all the remarkable postcards which could have been on the panels but would not fit, he suggested creating an online exhibit. Once again, we provided images and words and he crafted a web-based digital exhibit that complemented the physical exhibits perfectly. There is a special section for the postcards featured on the panels showing the fronts, backs, and captions to accord access for people unable to visit the physical exhibits. The "Wade Hall Postcards: Historical Scenes of Alabama" page (https://trojan.troy.edu/library/wadehall/) was added to Troy University Library website in June 2017.

As we said, the designer is a friend. There are advantages and disadvantages to undertaking an endeavor with a friend. We enjoyed the instant camaraderie and comfortability of working with someone we liked. Additionally, we never questioned his ability to do the job because we knew his background and that he did excellent work. We also knew he was absolutely trustworthy. However, the things we did not know led to frustrations. For instance, we did not know he had difficulty saying "no," which meant he always had several projects going at the same time. That resulted in many repeat conversations concerning the details of our project. We probably should have known he was a perfectionist because of the quality of his work, but we did not. Thus, we ended up with exceptional physical and digital exhibits that have received a myriad of compliments, but they took longer to produce then we expected. Because it is hard to push friends when you know how busy their personal and professional lives are, you end up with a digital exhibit available in June instead of January as expected.

Captions

We both have experience writing articles and doing presentations, but neither of us have experience writing for an exhibit. Interestingly, this kind of writing is a combination of both of those. As with an article, the writing has to be accurate and well researched, but also engaging like a presentation. However, the fact that the target audience is standing makes it very different. To test if the writing was concise and captivating, we were advised to read it aloud while standing. Doing this led to much shorter captions.

For each image, we wrote succinct facts about the town and a brief annotation concerning the scene on the postcard. We purposely stayed away from controversial and divisive subjects such as slavery, the Indian Removal Act of 1830, the Civil War, and civil rights and concentrated on finding little known snippets to add. All the writing on the panels was checked by an Alabama historian for anything misleading or inaccurate. We also had a team of proofreaders who looked for spelling and grammatical errors.

Neither of us grew up in Alabama so researching the towns for these exhibits was eye-opening. It is said you cannot truly know a new place until you understand its history—its origins, customs and rituals, and shifting ways of life over time. This is so true. For instance, we had no idea the Alabama settlers were Spanish, French, German, British, Italian, Scandinavian, Polish, Greek, and Czechoslovakian, as well as people from many regions of the United States. The state is also a religious melting pot with Catholic, Episcopal, Baptist, Methodist, Presbyterian, Universalist, Church of Christ, Quaker, and Mennonite congregations dating back to the 1700 and 1800's. We were amazed by the number of towns that started off as "planned private communities" or mill towns. Learning about the early educational institutions—many of which have closed or consolidated—was also fascinating. We have come to deeply appreciate the rich cultural heritage of our adopted state and we are pleased we can share this with the people of Alabama through our exhibits.

Budget

Before this project, the budgets we worked with from grants and our regular library budget were of the set amount kind, i.e., "You have $X. Spend it wisely." This was the first time we had the responsibility of creating a budget from scratch. In order to do this, we had to branch out from traditional library vendors to those in graphic design and commercial display printing. We learned about the different types of displays that were available, including the various materials that could be printed on. To come up with a budget for our grant application, we added our estimation of the library personnel time needed to develop the exhibits' content to the designer's estimate for design and the vendor's quote for printing of the panels, along with the cost of panel stands and cases. The grant we received was for ⅓ of the requested amount, but we were able to go forward with the project because the vast majority of the budget consisted of salaries for the library personnel's time. Overall, the creation of the budget was a positive learning experience for us, because now that we have done it, we have a template for our future grant applications.

Bookings

Despite the fact that we did not have any experience creating exhibits, both of the Wade Hall Postcard Traveling exhibits are essentially booked through December 2019—our target end date—in 45 unique venues. These include public libraries, academic libraries, community museums, community centers, and the Alabama State Capitol. In addition, the digital exhibit has had 3,547 page views (71 percent unique) from June 2017 through May 2018. So we obviously did something right. We credit the popularity of the exhibits to the following.

First, we generated interest in the idea of our Alabama vintage postcard project before we actually did any work. We did this by going to the 2016 Alabama Library Association (ALLA) annual convention and talking to many academic and public librarians. We also sent personal emails to numerous library directors across the state. Based on these conversations, seventeen venues expressed definite interest in hosting an exhibit like the one we proposed. We also talked with representatives from the Alabama Humanities Foundation (AHF) who thought this was a worthwhile project and encouraged us to apply for a grant.

These conversations led to our next decision which was to partner our exhibits with the public's nostalgic interest in postcards and the 2017–2019 celebration of Alabama's bicentennial. The themes for the three-year celebration are Discovering Our Places (2017),

Honoring Our People (2018), and Sharing Our Stories (2019). We felt our exhibits dovetailed nicely with these themes, and the endorsement from the Alabama Bicentennial Commission declares they agree with us. Part of the Commission's mission is to support and promote events and activities that tell the story of Alabama's path to statehood. They are encouraging all 67 counties to hold bicentennial events before the state's actual birthdate of December 14, 2019. Our traveling exhibits make it easy for communities to fulfill that request.

Which leads to the last reason why we feel our exhibits are so popular. We made specific decisions that made it easy for venues to host them.

First, we made the exhibits flexible in the following ways:

- The panels have no storyline so they can be set up in any order.
- The panels are single-sided so they can go up against a wall or sit back to back.
- No storyline also means it is easy to eliminate panels making it possible for any size institution to host.
- We only require venues to display the first panel, the last panel, and any regional panel(s) they want.

This flexibility gives host sites many different options for displaying the exhibits.

Secondly, we created lightweight and easy to manage panels. The panels are retractable fabric screens in bases approximately 34" by 9." They are freestanding and easy to set up. Moreover, they come in their own carrying cases and weigh approximately ten pounds so they are easy to transport.

Our third decision was to offer the exhibits to Alabama institutions free of charge. Since the exhibits were designed to increase Troy University's profile and as an outreach to the community/state, we wanted them available to all regardless of their financial resources. Our plan was for sites to work together on the pick-up and delivery of the panels to keep expenses down for everyone. Therefore, sites could incur traveling expenses, but we tried to keep these low by setting a traveling schedule with venues in relatively close proximity. In this way, the exhibits can be instruments for building partnerships throughout the state.

Finally, we did not ask the sites to fill out any reports or administer any surveys. That means we do not have statistics to share concerning the success of one site over another, but it made for happier hosts. We strived to eliminate as many barriers as possible so that anyone who wanted to host the exhibits at their venue could do so.

Although this undertaking was rewarding, it came at a price. Every part of this endeavor was time consuming but the communication component has taken and continues to take the most time. The exhibits themselves would not exist without the countless emails, phone calls, and conversations among everyone involved in the design process. Nor would there be any bookings without all the correspondence with interested venues explaining the content of the exhibit and answering questions about size, construction, scheduling, and how the transferring of panels worked. In addition, since these exhibits are booked through 2019, follow-up emails are necessary to make sure a venue remembers they are hosting and when. Add to this, the calls and emails necessary to firm up details concerning potential and definite speaking engagements. Institutional personnel changes usually meant the whole communication process had to start over again. We feel the personal emails and phone calls helped make this project successful. However, we also recognize that changes are necessary if we are ever going to do this again. For instance, developing a media packet to help sites promote the exhibit would be very helpful. Additionally, generating generic emails that give basic information about an exhibit and the logistics of hosting would be a time saver. A major effort like this does not need to be burdensome if managed correctly, and we are learning how to do that.

Presentations

Venues having events where they desired a speaker was something we had not anticipated, but it ended up being the component that had the greatest impact. We (the authors) are both introverts and do not enjoy public speaking, but we knew we were the most qualified. Our prior experience was in presenting at professional library conferences and giving bibliographic instruction sessions. The audiences for both of those situations are rather homogenous; at one we had librarians and the other traditional college students. However, the audiences for the exhibits presentations were diverse because the talks were open to the general public. The target audience may have been a college history class or high school students fulfilling a history assignment. Generally, it was members of historical societies or senior citizens' groups. Nevertheless, keeping the presentations adaptable was challenging.

In as much as I (Ruth Elder) was the main researcher and writer of the exhibits and thus knew the most about them; it only made sense for me to give the talks. It would have saved a great deal of time if I had just prepared two presentations—one for the streets exhibit and one for the buildings—and gave them whenever a site requested a speaker. However, that is not what I would want if I were a member of the audience. Therefore, I tailor each presentation to the area of the state where I am speaking. When I gave a talk at the University of South Alabama, I talked about Bishop Michael Portier, Spring Hill College, the Cathedral of the Immaculate Conception, the Sand Island Light and the first Mardi Gras. In Florence and Athens, I talked about the settlers in the northern part of the state and the Military Road. The Montgomery talks included stories about how the city was formed from the merging of East Alabama Town and New Philadelphia and the creation of the Alabama Department of Archives and History. Thus far, I have given sixteen presentations and have several more booked for 2018 and 2019. Although I still get very nervous each time I give a speech, I know the most current presentations are more creative than the first ones I gave. I have also learned new PowerPoint techniques that use graphics instead of words to make my point. I will never hire myself out as a speaker, but I do know I have gotten better with time.

Conclusion

This project has allowed us to step out from our normal technical services duties and into public outreach. Our goal was to bring quality exhibits to audiences across Alabama. By creating traveling and digital exhibits about the social and cultural history of postcards, we encouraged visitors of all ages to learn more about themselves and their communities. The process of developing these exhibits called for creativity that we are not always able to express in our daily work; i.e., it mattered whether the colors on two adjacent postcards would clash, but we have never taken into account the color of a book when we were ordering or cataloging it. In addition to learning how to create the exhibits, we became more knowledgeable about successfully applying for grants which will serve us well in the future. In the end, we learned a great deal about our adopted state, including a few quirky stories that will probably never appear in history textbooks.

REFERENCES

Common Approach to Scientific Touring Exhibitions. 2004. CASTEX: Guidelines for Touring Exhibitions in Europe. Accessed June 27. https://museumplanner.org/wp-content/uploads/2011/10/Guidelines-CAS-TEX.pdf.

Poulos, Angela. 2008. "Guiding Principles for the Design of Traveling Exhibitions." Accessed June 26. http://travelingexhibition.blogspot.com/.

Smithsonian Institution Traveling Exhibition Service. n.d. "Show Off Your Story: How to Create an Exhibition." Accessed July 2. https://museumonmainstreet.org/sites/default/files/how_to_create_an_exhibition.pdf.

Walhimer, Mark. 2011. "Creating a Traveling Exhibit." *Museum Planner: A Blog of Museum Planning by an Experienced Museum Planner.* October 17. https://museumplanner.org/traveling-exhibition/.

PART VIII

Budget Matters

Creative Problem Solving in Libraries

Budgets, Staff and the Lack Thereof

NORA FRANCO *and* MARLA LOBLEY

Introduction

Librarians have many opportunities to use creativity to address complex problems. The familiar problems libraries face—budget cuts and limited staff—are made even more complex by the need to continue to serve users with reduced resources while simultaneously working to restore funding and staff to sufficient levels. While the issues libraries face are often similar, the solutions are not as universal. Each library must solve problems according to their community's needs, using tools that will empower library staff to contribute to a creative solution.

This essay reviews three major problems that frequently occur in libraries—budget cuts, understaffing, and reorganizations of staff. Presented with each problem are examples of creative solutions from other libraries, exercises to help encourage a creative outlook, and activities to facilitate the creative problem solving process. Some general tips from the literature for achieving creative solutions to many kinds of issues in libraries include:

- Collaborate with staff and stakeholders to form solutions (Frank and Henry 2016, 117–121)
- View the problem in terms of stakeholders' priorities (Murray 2017, 254–256)
- Be transparent with stakeholders about the complexities of the problem—they may be more willing to compromise to reach a solution (Robertshaw, Willi Hooper, and Goergen-Doli 2017, para. 4)
- Use relevant data to justify potential solutions (Frank and Henry 2016, 126–128)

Viewing serious problems with a silver lining can be challenging. It can help to remember that limitations require decision makers to identify and prioritize what is absolutely essential. In this way, limitations bring librarians closer to users' needs. The following exercise and activity illustrates how limitations can be facilitators of creativity.

Exercise

Instructions: Do not read the next step until after you have completed the first step!

1. Draw a picture.
2. Now draw a picture using only circles.
3. Now draw a picture using only 3 circles of different sizes.

Debrief:

- Which exercise was the easiest?
- Did the extra limitations help you focus your drawing?
- If you did this exercise in a room full of people, which set of instructions do you think would produce the best results?

Just as the limits in the exercise helped focus the drawing, so can external limitations help focus library services. However, it is not sustainable for libraries to continue "doing more with less." Libraries must keep in mind the need for long-term solutions.

Activity

1. Individually or as a team, list the limitations your library is facing. Beside it, list how these limitations are helping bring the library closer to users' needs.
2. Could any of the ways the library is learning more about users be the foundation for a long-term solution?

Budget Cuts

Insufficient budgets affect every aspect of library operations, and therefore every staff member has an opportunity to contribute solutions. While administrators work to influence decision makers to increase library funding, front line staff strive to keep usage numbers up to support the argument for a budget increase. New initiatives can help increase usage numbers and may persuade decision makers. Even though it seems counter-intuitive to try something new when resources are limited, implementing a new service that aligns with stakeholder priorities could help secure full funding for the library (Murray 2017, 254). There is an opportunity for creativity in this three-way intersection with

- learning stakeholder priorities
- developing a new service that advances stakeholder priorities
- staying within the limitations caused by a lack of funding

Libraries often serve a diverse group of users with varied priorities. It may seem daunting to craft a service that meets such disparate, and sometimes opposing, needs. As the exercise in the introduction section demonstrated, limitations can be a catalyst for creativity. The following exercise shows creativity's role in finding similarities in seemingly incongruent ideas.

Exercise

Instructions:

1. Ask another person to participate in this step with you. One person thinks of an animal and the other person think of a genre of music. Discuss and try to find at least five similarities.
2. After your conversation, try to find at least five more similarities between the animal and the genre of music by yourself.

Debrief:

- What surprised you about this exercise?
- Did having a conversation partner in Step 1 impact your perspective in Step 2?
- If you had done the steps in reverse order, do you think you would have had the same results?

Trying to create a service that meets diverse or opposing needs may seem impossible, but this exercise suggests that including someone else's perspective can help find the commonalities among more disparate needs.

Activity

- What stakeholder priorities is your library struggling to meet?
- How can engaging with the stakeholders produce ideas for meeting their needs?

Once a common need among stakeholder priorities is determined, there is still the problem of finding a way to meet the need with limited funding. Volunteers, donations and grants are often used to fill the gap caused by funding issues, however, these solutions come with their own set of problems. Volunteers must be managed, donations may not include what the library really needs, and grants are often limited in what can be purchased. Applying a creative twist to these familiar solutions can yield some more effective options. The following ideas can help jumpstart your imagination to create a solution that works for your library.

Volunteers

CREATE CROWDSOURCED VOLUNTEER OPPORTUNITIES

Not everyone can commit to volunteering a few hours a week, but there may be people interested in making small contributions to a larger project. Check out the Library of Congress Beyond Words project and the examples below for inspiration.

- Make a sign suggesting mental break activities for students that includes straightening the chairs, tables, or shelves in their area.
- A Storytime leader can instruct guardians how to help their toddlers learn the alphabet by picking up board books off the floor and putting them in the right letter bin.
- Occupy bored patrons by having a duster with a magnet and a small sign instructing patrons to dust one or more shelves and then leave the duster in the place where they stopped dusting.

CREATE INTEREST-BASED OPPORTUNITIES

Provide a service to patrons and complete a much needed project by letting beginners learn or practice a skill. Alternatively, increase the engagement of an existing program by encouraging users to give back to the library. For example,

- A group attending a web design class works together to build a new webpage for the library.
- A class of students from a local school completes a service learning project by planting a new flower bed.
- A book club dedicates a portion of their meeting time to planning book displays.

TAKE ADVANTAGE OF EXISTING PATRON BEHAVIOR

Volunteering can be as simple as turning the behavior of one patron into something that can benefit all.

- Create a "What's Hot" display of books that were recently checked-in, no shelving required!
- Peruse your library's reference question database for inspiration for a social media post. Turn "Where do I find the book for BIOL 2043?" into "Looking for your required textbooks? Search our course reserves here: [link]."

Donations

ORCHESTRATE WAYS TO FIND WHAT YOU REALLY NEED

- Organize a supply swap with other local libraries or organizations. The abundance of supplies left over from a long-ago grant may be exactly what another organization needs, and maybe they will have something that your library needs.
- Voice specific requests to your community, such as asking for replacements of particular popular books or for a certain type of toy for the children's section. People may be willing to part with an item if they know it will be put to good use.

FIND FREELY AVAILABLE RESOURCES

- Search professional associations' websites for free webinars and listservs.
- Search Open Educational Resource databases like California State University's MERLOT to substitute for materials your library may not be able to purchase.
- Use free advertising available through social media, press releases, and word of mouth. Teach front-line staff to "upsell" services and programs to maximize word of mouth advertising.
- Host no-cost or low-cost programs such as discussion groups, career fairs, coffee/tea socials, or work with local nonprofits, such as therapy dog organizations.
- Host "Bring Your Own…" programming. Patrons could bring unfinished scrapbooks or knitting projects to work on during an "Un-Finished Object (UFO) Night." Or host a competition for structures built of canned goods supplied by patrons and then donated to a local non-profit.

Grants

SHARE THE RESPONSIBILITIES

- If a lack of time to manage a grant is hindering your library from applying, try collaborating with other organizations to share some of the responsibilities.
- Ask other organizations or departments within your institution about their current grant projects and see if there is an opportunity for the library to participate.

RE-THINK YOUR NEEDS

- Grants are often about programs that provide a service or opportunity rather than about capital improvement or replacing needed resources. If your library can't find a grant that will fund your needs, then create a program or service that will involve the purchase of the needed objects. For example, if you need new computers, create a weekly program for job hunters that's taught by local community leaders and uses the computer lab.
- Be willing to compromise in order to gain more in the long run. If a grant isn't available for a large project, start with a smaller project that can build up over time.

Short Staffing

Short staffing is an issue libraries face for many reasons, such as decreased sources of funding, a lack of staff retention, and attrition. Library administrators in all types of libraries have the opportunity to focus on the empowerment of employees rather than assignment of tasks to nurture staff creativity. All library employees, including librarians and support staff, have a role in facilitating creativity among their co-workers. Administrators and staff can work together to

- prioritize the services necessary to keep the library open
- collaborate for efficient workflow
- boost morale in the library

Prioritizing services is the first step in tackling problems related to limited personnel. Organization leaders and employees may have different perspectives on which services are essential. Conflicts may arise when combining staff departments and people have not yet had time to understand each other's perspectives. The library that clearly states its mission and priorities will empower staff when encountering these issues. When everyone understands the mission, they can assign projects or tasks even in the face of disruptions. The following exercise aids in including all voices when setting priorities.

Exercise

Instructions: On an index card or sticky note, identify a critical area of operation, the number of staff needed to complete, and the amount of time needed per day, week, etc.

1. Repeat for a total of no more than 3 critical services.
2. Ask each staff member of your department to do the same.

3. Group the cards into the following:
    a. Low maintenance (requires few staff and little time to complete)
    b. Medium maintenance (requires more staff or much time to complete)
    c. High maintenance (requires many staff and much time to complete)

Example:

Critical Area of Operation	*Number of Staff Needed to Complete*	*Amount of Time Needed to Complete*
Interlibrary Loan	• 1 Librarian to maintain software, troubleshoot issues, and communicate with vendor • 1 Paraprofessional staff to process incoming requests • 1 Paraprofessional staff to process outgoing deliveries	Daily • 4 hours Librarian • 16 hours Paraprofessional

Debrief:

- What were the similarities and differences in the 3 services each person chose?
- How does identifying the maintenance level of the services impact their ranking in the list of priorities?
- What high maintenance services can be made more efficient?

Limiting the number of services each person can identify as critical provides insight into their perspective. Understanding others' mindsets along with noting the additional criteria of low, medium or high maintenance can help start conversations about how to collaborate for efficient workflow. Staff may start this discussion by looking to other organizations where short staffing is common, such as hospitals, for inspiration in making sure essential services are always covered. When discussing how to improve workflow, it is equally important to consider morale. The following lists provide ideas for administrators and staff to work towards boosting morale and improving processes.

Boost Morale

- Create a list of each staff member's birthday or work anniversary. In lieu of a party, grant a day off for each, separate from vacation or flex-time balances.
- Create a place for staff to leave shout-outs to each other; examples include a whiteboard in a breakroom or a staff only online discussion board.
- Take time to acknowledge the extra duties staff have taken on and express appreciation. Consider creating an infographic highlighting notable statistical data or a kudos board as a means of encouragement.
- Create a place for staff to post photos they take of their favorite places in the library or to answer prompts such as "Take a picture of something that makes you enjoy your work" or "Post a picture of something funny you've run across in the library this week."

Collaborate for Efficient Workflow

- Designate time for staff to reflect on one another's workflow and make comments or suggestions, thereby offering them the opportunity to guide their peers using the skill sets they hone in their "home" departments. This also highlights the value of their unique perspectives and original input.

- Focus on departments of your library that work in similar areas; i.e., systems/electronic resources and collections/purchasing. Reorganize their work spaces, whether on a trial or more permanent basis, in order to facilitate easier flow of communication between these two groups.
- Crosstrain in other departments' procedures, to prevent tasks from building up if a staff member needs to take time off work.
- Create succession plans to prevent issues if a staff member leaves their position.
- Delegate separate times for focused work and patron interaction. For example, incorporate opportunities for meeting more patrons while working reference shifts, such as "coffee time with a librarian" or, in the case of virtual reference shifts, displaying librarians' virtual chat hours with creative, graphic displays around the library.

Reorganizations

Reorganizations may occur due to budget cuts, a need to update outdated models, and staff attrition, among other reasons. It is best to begin a reorganization by creating a concrete strategic plan, including your staff in the process, and making it publicly available, to provide an easier transition. Casey (2015) noted that library staff accepted undesirable changes due in large part to the transparency of the priorities stated in the strategic plan and the alignment of their jobs to it (11). Transparency involves communicating each step of the plan clearly, not only to staff but also to stakeholders.

Equally important as creating a strategic plan is explicitly stating the value of the individuals who work in your organization. Conveying the value of staff strengthens the team and creates or opens communication lines. While the directors or managers of the reorganization may feel accomplished with achieving their goal of budget reduction or staff allocation, the staff likely experience the change from a completely different perspective (Lockwood and Papke 2017, 120). When leaders empathize with their staff, they take a step toward measuring and understanding their organizational empathy, described by Lockwood and Papke as "an attribute of culture demonstrated by the ability of its people to relate to and experience the emotion of others" (88). By practicing organizational empathy, leaders may be able to better identify barriers that occur between their units during the change.

Strategic plans and organizational empathy represent what must be balanced to create an effective reorganization—organizational priorities and individual staff preferences. Encouraging creativity at all levels of staff can help decision makers find a balance. The following exercise facilitates creativity by encouraging participants to reflect on their values and expand their listening skills.

Exercise

Instructions (modified from Franklin 2014, 152):

1. Create a sample memo regarding a change in procedures. The memo may be silly, such as changing the positioning of ice cube trays in the freezer, but employees' responses will provide insight into their style and adaptability. Some might focus on how the previous system worked fine and should not

change, while others see the change as allowing for more space in the freezer.

2. Ask employees to write down their important takeaways from the memo, then ask them to write down unimportant takeaways.
3. Discuss which takeaways were essential and which were unimportant.
4. Ask staff to compare their interpretation of the memo with the intended message.

Debrief:

- Do you feel your important takeaways are essential to functioning or are they your opinion?
- Did you feel resistant to the change?
- Could you see how the change would create an improvement?

Once a team has collectively reflected on the varying communication styles and values within the group, they can start finding productive ways to use their differences rather than letting them be obstacles. The following ideas can help teams collaborate to design and implement a reorganization that balances the needs of the institution with those of individual staff members.

Empower Each Staff Member with a Voice

- Separate each piece of the hierarchal organization chart into a linear model, using titles instead of personal names. Ask staff to rearrange the chart into a hierarchical fashion according to how they see the library structure working most efficiently. Debrief with staff about how the input will be incorporated into the planning process. If any input is not able to be included, explain why.
- Ensure your planning meetings include diverse staff voices. Open meetings for people of color and LGBTQIA individuals to discuss how the reorganizations affect them and provide an avenue to report their discussions to administration.
- If input is lacking, suggest or assign particular areas for staff to comment on, such as outreach or instruction.
- If administrators have not included staff in the planning process, they may wish to organize on their own. Collectively, the group may determine creative solutions to providing input and addressing the management. The collaboration of the group could range from formal to informal, including
  - holding meetings to identify any barriers in the new reorganization or strategic plan
  - creating a private, collaborative internal web page or shared drive for Q&A about the process
  - placing comment or question boxes around the library for anonymous questions
  - supporting one another when approaching administration with difficult topics.

Consider the Impact of Change

- Structural changes may also create cultural changes. Leaders should plan for the type of culture they would ultimately like to see.

- Everyone expresses and interprets changes differently. Communicate with employees about how the change affects them/their department, how the reorganization will solve current problems, and provide detailed examples of new opportunities for the library and its staff (Franklin 2014, 152).

Let Staff Explore and Express Their Strengths

- People often leave positions when they cannot fulfill their personal passions due to the outline of their job descriptions. A reorganization provides an opportunity for leaders to design jobs that utilize employees' strengths and mesh their individual interests with the essential functions of role. Supporting your employees in this manner allows people to feel a sense of pride and satisfaction in their work (Goler, et al. 2018).
- Have employees take a values or personality assessment. Facilitate regular discussions about how they incorporate their strengths into their position and how their personality or values impact how they relate to their co-workers.

Be Transparent with Data and Decisions

- Communicate with staff about the ways workloads are being examined and how they will shift. Inform staff about which personnel will be impacted the most and the least by the change.
- Explain what stakeholder groups' needs may be left unmet or underserved.
- Use tables to illustrate workloads in order to balance the distribution of service, volunteering, and job responsibilities. For example,

Wren B., Librarian / Education Department, XYZ University Library

Internal Library Committees	Administrative Issues Committee, Budget & Fiscal Affairs Committee
Other Committees (University, Board, etc.)	Diversity Committee, Faculty Orientation Committee
Institutional groups, organizations, or initiatives affiliated with	LGBTQIA Affinity Group for XYZ University
Community groups, organizations, or initiatives affiliated with	Local Chapter of Quilt Historians & Makers
Volunteer Service not listed above	Fridays & Saturdays–Soup Kitchen
Professional Development/Continuing Education Activities not listed above	Submitted Data Management poster to Local Library Chapter Conference; Enrolled in Information Literacy MOOC

- Gather data on how essential functions are completed, in order to have a baseline to compare to once the change is implemented. It will likely be necessary to measure continually (Franklin 2014, 262–263, Appendix 4).
- Share data after the reorganization is completed to celebrate improvements and call for ideas for areas that did not improve.

Conclusion

Library employees have many opportunities to use creativity, especially when over-coming issues with limited funding, insufficient staff, and departmental reorganizations. When stakeholders and library staff are included in forming solutions, challenges can become opportunities to improve library services, restore funding and staff, and bring the library closer to users' needs. In the face of these restrictions, libraries may find re-aligning and viewing their issues from a creative lens allows for renewed sense of purpose, self-motivation, and commitment. Creative exercises allow leaders and staff to engage in personal development and join forces in designing a vision and plan to pave the way to their organization's success.

References

Casey, Anne Marie. 2015. "Strategic Priorities: A Roadmap Through Change for Library Leaders." *Library Leadership & Management* 29, no. 2: 1–16. https://journals.tdl.org/llm/index.php/llm/article/view/7085.

Frank, Cindy, and Henry, Christine. 2016. "How the University of Maryland Architecture Library Avoided Closure and Emerged as a Professional Library." *Art Documentation: Bulletin of the Art Libraries Society of North America* 35, no. 1: 114–129. doi: 10.1086/685980.

Franklin, Melanie. 2014. *Agile Change Management: A Practical Framework for Successful Change Planning and Implementation.* London: Kogan Page. EBSCOhost eBook Collection (Academic).

Goler, Lori, Gale, Janelle, Harrington, Brynn, and Grant, Adam. 2018. "Why People Really Quit Their Jobs." Last modified January 11, 2018. https://hbr.org/2018/01/why-people-really-quit-their-jobs.

Library of Congress. n.d. "Beyond Words." Accessed February 2, 2018. https://labs.loc.gov/experiments/beyond-words/.

Lockwood, Thomas, and Papke, Edgar. 2017. *Innovation by Design: How Any Organization Can Leverage Design Thinking to Produce Change, Drive New Ideas, and Deliver Meaningful Solutions.* Wayne, New Jersey: Career Press. ProQuest eBook Central.

California State University. n.d. Multimedia Educational Resources for Learning and Online Teaching (MERLOT II). Accessed December 21, 2018. https://www.merlot.org/merlot/index.htm.

Murray, Tara. 2017. "An Unlikely Collaboration: How Academic and Special Libraries Can Help Each Other Survive." *Journal of Library Administration* 57, no. 2: 249–258. doi: 10.1080/01930826.2017.1281667.

Robertshaw, M. Brooke, Willi Hooper, Michaela, and Kerri Goergen-Doll. 2017. "Finding the Silver Lining in the Serials Budget Crisis." *Against the Grain* 29, no. 2: 16–18. https://ir.library.oregonstate.edu/concern/articles/gh93h320j.

Beyond the Boot Camp

No-Cost Conferences

HEATHER C. SEMINELLI

Disclaimer*: The views expressed here do not necessarily reflect the views of the United States Military Academy, the United States Army, or the United States Government. The author is not involved with any of the companies mentioned and holds no interest in recommending any particular application.*

The United States Military Academy Library serves 4,400 undergraduate students, as well as approximately 600 staff and faculty members. We are open 103.5 hours per week during the academic year with no student workers, and a librarian on duty during every hour we are open. We have 15 librarians who serve as departmental liaisons to each of the academic departments at USMA, as well as the Departments of Military Instruction and Physical Education. Our liaisons' main positions include reference librarians, cataloguers, archivists, and administrative leadership; their responsibilities also include supporting their academic department.

Background

Over the last several years, the liaisons conducted a summer program. It has gone through various iterations, being called a "Boot Camp," and with varying objectives. The types of programming included inviting librarians from another local college to come talk about their personal librarian program when we were in the process of starting our own program, or librarians giving summaries of talks they heard at a conference they had attended during the previous year.

Last spring, the head of the liaison program and the communications librarian decided that the summer liaison workshop should be a more organized and longer program. While we are fortunate to be at a library that supports professional development, not everyone gets to attend a regional or national conference every year. Some staff members are unable to travel. Those of us who had attended conferences recently wanted to recreate that rush of creativity and productivity that we felt when we came back, but within our own library, and with the advantage of all of our colleagues feeling the same way.

The practical concerns for producing this workshop were that with the various responsibilities that the liaisons have during the academic year, it is difficult to get everyone in the same room at the same time to share information. Many of our academic year meetings are more informational than interactive. From talking to our coworkers, we knew there was a desire to share our experiences and learn from each other. The summer workshop became the mode for this interaction to happen. During the initial planning, knowing that we were deviating from what had been done before, we decided what we would like to accomplish for this event to be successful. Our goal became to produce a positive and productive gathering of the liaison librarians to share ideas, successes, and failures to improve the program.

Calendar

The first challenge during the introduction of a newer, longer summer workshop was to determine when our 15 liaisons would be available to attend. Previous iterations of the summer Boot Camp had been held earlier in the summer, so we continued that pattern. We thought that June would be a good time to do it because the academic year was over, there was less demand for reference during summer school, and most people took their vacation later in the summer. One challenge we did not take into account was that we still had extended hours in June 0700–2100. That meant we had staff members participating in the workshop who also had to close at night. In the future, we will either hold the workshop later in the summer when we do not have extended hours, have staff who were not participating work the closing shifts, or ask volunteers to work those nights so that no one feels like they were forced to be at work for more than a normal work day.

To help decide when to hold the workshop, we created a Google form and sent it out to our colleagues with the following questions:

1. What week do you prefer to participate in a liaison workshop? (Can select multiple weeks)
2. Are you unavailable for any of the following dates? (Check only if cannot attend)

This method allowed us to take into account preferences (question 1), and the dates that would not work (question 2). We wanted to have buy-in for this event, and getting input on when to hold the workshop was the first step to involve other people and help them feel like this was their event. Everyone responded within a week of sending the form out.

We were fortunate that all but one person voted for the first week in June, and no one said that they could not attend that week. This level of agreement made the decision of when to hold the workshop easy, and the leadership shared with their staff that they would be expected to participate. We also shared the date with the staff not participating because they would be helping to cover the service points while the majority of the reference librarians (who are all liaisons) were busy with the workshop.

Planning

Once the timeline was finalized, we began our planning. A small group of 4–6 librarians comprised the committee to plan and execute the workshop. We had a shorter timeline for planning than would be ideal for an event like this and are going to have a longer planning cycle in the future. We set the dates for the workshop to be held on June 6–8th.

There are pros and cons of having a small planning committee. Relying on a smaller group, especially with such a short timeline, made communication easier. However, it also meant that a small group of people did an incredible amount of work to make this a success. In the future, we want this workshop to represent a larger proportion of the staff. We also want to create ways for people who don't want to attend every planning meeting to be involved. For example, someone could be responsible for a game or break. This would take pressure off the core planning group and increase involvement and buy-in of all participants.

Activities

When we started planning, we had a lot of ideas and needed to organize those thoughts. We asked everyone who had an idea for a session to fill a form with the following information:

- title of session
- session lead: name of person leading/coordination the session
- target audience (ex. liaisons, all library staff, reference librarians, personal librarians)
- description of the session content
- time and date (left blank during initial planning)
- location of the event
- reasons for doing the session
- format of the session (e.g., lecture, panel, small group discussion)
- length of the session
- supplies needed (e.g., paper, pens, white board, computer and projector)
- homework: are participants expected to bring information with them, read an article, or do anything else to prepare?

Each member of the planning committee brought in these forms to the next meeting, with as much information filled out as we knew. We wanted a variety of content types to keep it interesting. We included icebreakers/games, small group discussions, keynotes, internal topical discussions, a panel, and guest speakers. Creativity and using the resources available at our college were key to having this variety of activities without a budget.

Once we identified the desired sessions, we used these forms to organize the schedule. We designed the table with three sections—one for each day. If, for example, an outside speaker gave us one option of time they could participate, that was filled in first. There were sessions we wanted to have at the beginning or end of the workshop, so those were filled in next. We even included games, meals, and breaks in this rough outline of the schedule. The fourth iteration of the schedule became what we executed. We created the schedule using one page for each day, recording the times, titles, descriptions, and staff responsible for each session.

Icebreakers and Games

We wanted this workshop to be positive, so we felt that having some fun would keep everyone awake and upbeat. Our first activity was "People Bingo." One of our planning committee members made a bingo card with little known facts about other library staff members. These facts included information about staff who loved camping almost as much as shoes, could fly a helicopter, and had a registered clown face. This was a fun way to learn new things about each other. This activity was so well received that even staff members who were not participating in the workshop wanted a copy of the bingo card to play. The winner got bragging rights for days. We also played the librarian version of "Cards Against Humanity" called "Cards Against Librarianship" (Lloyd, 2014). We made a G-rated version of the game, and also added some cards with our local peculiarities, which were quite popular whenever they were played. We also prepared a word search race. We planned it for a day when participants would be broken into two teams, and each team would be charged with helping their scribe find all of the hidden words. We used a word search creator online (A to Z Teacher Stuff) to make a custom word search with library words and local words that the staff would be familiar with (ex. database, reference, abstract). This activity was cut because we got behind on the schedule, but having it prepared in case we needed an injection of energy was still useful. If you want to create this activity, here are some word search suggestions: abstract, bibliography, catalog, circulation, citation, curriculum, database, delimiter, digital, engagement, exhibit, graduation, information, instruction, interlibrary, liaison, literacy, loan, manuscript, marc, millennium, reference, resource, scholarly, and serial.

Keynotes

We used online videos of keynotes. We watched the 2017 Coalition for Networked Information keynote by Alison Head on "What today's students have taught us" and the TED talk by David McCandless on "The Beauty of Data Visualization" (Head, 2017) (McCandless, 2010). Colleagues who had attended conferences (CNI 2017 and ACRL 2017) and heard these speakers in person recommended these keynotes. We could not send our entire staff to these conferences, but the staff who did attend brought back recommendations for how to share the experience within our own building.

Small Group Discussions

We did not have a large group (15 attendees), but we wanted to avoid group discussions becoming dominated by a few people. We chose to introduce small group discussions so that more opinions could be heard. We broke up into the small groups for about 2/3 of the discussion time, then came back together for the final 1/3 to share the best of the small group discussion with the entire group. Our discussion sessions included one based on a roundtable at ACRL 2017 called "Confessions of a teaching librarian: Teaching anxiety, growth mindset, and resilience for Library instructors (Brillat, Lafferty, Jimenez, Del Castillo, & Hammill, 2017)," liaison work, and the future of the library. We had discussion questions planned to get the conversation started, and to keep the groups talking about parallel topics. This also helped guide the discussion when the entire group came back together. It is useful to have printed copies of the discussion questions ready to hand to each group so that they can be referred to if they are leaving the large group area. We had feedback that someone felt the discussions weren't focused enough, even though our goal was to get the conversations started and to follow up on any good ideas outside of this event. If you want the discussion to truly lead somewhere, consider printing an end state for the group to work towards. For example, we discussed our discovery layer and how to improve it. The end state was to decide what changes to the settings on the discovery layer would make it easier to use for the coming academic year, and we actually made those changes the week after our workshop. You may also want to consider where the small groups are talking. It would be ideal to have a room nearby for those discussions so that the group doesn't have to worry about disturbing library users.

Guest Speakers

In addition to our "keynotes" via YouTube, we chose to utilize the talent that we had on campus and invite faculty to speak. We invited the Head of the Department of Behavioral Sciences and Leadership to talk about student engagement and techniques to use in our work with cadets. We also invited a small panel of faculty to help enhance our understanding of what skills our students need to have to be successful, and how we can support the development of those skills. We invited faculty who taught core courses and electives, military and civilian faculty, and faculty from different humanities departments. This gave us a broader view of what we could do to support the academic programs. The final guest was the Dean of the Academic Board. She had a very good discussion about what she expected from the library, librarians had a chance to tell her what we were doing, and what type of support would make us more effective.

Inviting guests from the campus has multiple benefits. We did not have to pay outside speakers. Our local faculty had an easier time squeezing in our event between their other commitments. It was also good for the faculty to see that we were serious about our liaison work, having committed so much staff time to a workshop designed to make us think about what we were doing and how to make it better. Just like identifying an outside guest to come and speak, it takes time to research potential good guest speakers within the college. There is a librarian liaison assigned to each department who collects the scholarship created by our faculty for a separate event we host each semester, the Dean's Celebration of West Point Authors. This collection process helps us see what our faculty is working on, and what they are presenting or writing about that might be good for our staff. We attend the summer faculty orientations with our departments, and see many presentations as part of that program that could also be applicable to the library. We are also on the email distribution lists of our departments so that we can see who is invited from one department to talk to other departments. These interactions give us our starting points to brainstorm who we can invite.

Ideally, guests are identified early in the planning process. This planning process was on a compressed schedule, so by the time we identified some speakers we were interested in, they already had other commitments and had to decline. In other cases, we had last minute scrambling as we changed our schedule to accommodate our guests' schedules. This led to a late distribution of the event schedule to the librarians attending, and did not support predictability of the event. In the future, we will plan to invite local guests no later than six weeks prior to the event. We also conducted final coordination with the guests at least one week prior to the event so that they knew when and where to be. We took care of any support they needed, such as printing handouts or having slides already up on the computer when they arrived. We wanted to make their experience as painless and enjoyable as possible. We also had backup plans in case a guest could not come. This can be as simple as talking to the person leading the last session of the day, and making sure they can be prepared earlier in the day. This backup plan works best with a session led by someone in the library.

Internal Library Programs

In addition to inviting outside "keynotes" and guest speakers from the college to inspire us, we also had to talk about the actual work that we needed to do to prepare for the next academic year. These events included presentations or working sessions led by our liaison librarians on internal college topics that were a necessary part of what we wanted to accomplish, so that all the reference and liaison librarians would start the following academic year working toward the same goals. We found that it was better if these sessions were spread out. The first day was very heavy on these types of programs, and it was not as successful as on the days when they were interspersed with others.

Classroom Assessment Techniques

A secondary goal during the planning was to practice different classroom assessment techniques to make the staff comfortable with them, and then use them during the academic year for library instruction. Librarians leading the sessions could choose one method from a list of classroom assessment techniques. We found these exercises were effective to introduce the techniques, but trying to do them during every session took time that we had not planned for. If you want to utilize an activity like this, plan for it to take longer than expected.

Timeline

During our initial planning, we decided to hold this workshop over three days, approximately six hours per day. This was to allow additional time during the work day if staff members had other work that had to be accomplished. We also wanted to keep the length of the sessions under an hour, and to allow 10–15-minute breaks between sessions. We scheduled lunch for an hour each day. In our post-event survey, 90 percent of our staff said they liked the length of the workshop. Of those who choose to answer the questions about the length of sessions and breaks, almost everyone said that they were a good length. We found that it would be better to lengthen lunch to 90 minutes. That would give adequate time for setup and teardown for any group lunches, and for staff to check their email or take care of anything that comes up during the day.

We also found that it was good to be flexible. Some of the sessions ended up being longer or shorter than planned. We wanted to stay on schedule, but not at the expense of ending a very productive discussion early. We did have a staff member identified as the time keeper to give time warnings, and to help steer a session back on topic if it got off track. This person was also empowered to make judgment calls about letting a productive session go a little longer or to end a session that had culminated early. We stressed that patience and flexibility were going to help make this a successful event, and most staff members worked together to keep us on schedule. The time keeper also made note of the actual start and stop times of each session, break, meal, etc., so that we would have that record to help us plan for the workshop next summer.

Technology and Space

Due to other events scheduled in the library, we had to change rooms during the workshop, so we experienced how this event worked in a small conference room, large classroom, and a tiered computer lab. A medium sized room that just fits all of the attendees seemed to work best for us. When you have a small group of attendees, people can get lost in a large room or quiet staff members may not speak loud enough for everyone to hear. The small conference room was a good place for an icebreaker on our first day. There were no extra seats, so we all had to sit next to each other and look closely at who was speaking. The tiered room was a little more comfortable, but harder to have conversations in. We also found that when the computers were put away, we had a much higher quality conversation. If technology was necessary, we tried to encourage everyone to just look at the projected screen instead of using individual computers.

Food

We are not allowed to spend library funds on food. Therefore, there was no budget to provide food or coffee. However, sitting in a room for 18 hours together meant that some sort of nourishment was required to make this experience more enjoyable. We chose to solve this dilemma by sharing the load. The majority of snacks were provided by members of the planning committee and the library leadership. Any contributions were completely voluntary. On each day, we did something different including lunch on our own, a potluck BBQ, and one day we each chipped in to buy pizza as a group. If someone wanted to bring their own lunch, they were invited to eat with us because we wanted their company in a more casual setting. Next year, we plan to do a very similar setup. Our hope is that some of the people who did not want to be on the full planning committee might take charge of a potluck meal or a break time. This would solve the challenge that occurred when the person responsible for the session after lunch was also the person cleaning up the break room. Food was great for bonding and keeping everyone's energy up. Even if trying to serve food with no budget was a challenge, for us it was worth doing.

Post-Workshop

After the workshop, we sent out a survey to all participants to record their feelings about the event. We also did a comprehensive after-action review to record issues, discussion, and recommendations for the major parts of the workshop. This helped us remember what we did right and want to continue, as well as things we could have done better.

Post-event Survey Questions

1. Prior to the workshop, did you feel like you had enough information to be prepared? (multiple choice answers)
2. How far ahead of the workshop would be ideal to get the schedule, homework, and any other information for the workshop? (multiple choice answers)
3. Was the workshop length too long, too short, or about right? (multiple choice)
4. Was the length of the sessions and breaks appropriate? (pick all that apply)
5. How helpful was the content presented at the workshop? (Likert Scale)
6. Were the icebreakers, games, and lunches a good use of time during the workshop? (Likert Scale)
7. Were the small group discussions valuable to you during the workshop? (Likert Scale)
8. Were the "keynote" videos valuable? (Likert Scale)
9. Were the library internal discussions valuable? (Likert Scale)
10. Were the guests valuable? (Likert Scale)
11. Are there other topics that you would want to be covered during another liaison workshop? (or during future meetings this year) (short answer)
12. Are there other guest speakers you would like to invite? If so, please list. (short answer)
13. What did you like about the workshop? (short answer)
14. What did you dislike about the workshop? (short answer)
15. Is there anything else you would like to share about the workshop? (short answer)

Most of our liaisons enjoyed having time to set aside daily duties and focus on what we do and how we do it. We received feedback from several liaisons that they would like these types of discussions and events to continue throughout the year instead of just during the summer. In our library, this took the form of adding an extra meeting to our meeting cycle. These "Special Topics" meetings have taken different forms throughout the year. Examples include inviting the head of our local Academic Library Consortium (ConnectNY) and the West Point Writing Center to speak to us about their programs.

As we move forward, we believe that this workshop was worthwhile to host. In the future, we want to expand the scope beyond the liaison librarians. We gained enough momentum moving forward that we have other divisions of the library wanting to participate, including non-liaison librarians, paraprofessionals, and administrative staff. After this workshop, the liaison librarians were excited and motivated to improve our program, and we want that enthusiasm to spread throughout our entire staff and go straight into the academic year, ready to greet our students and faculty with improved programs.

REFERENCES

A to Z Teacher Stuff. n.d. "Word Search Maker." Accessed March 2, 2018. http://tools.atozteacherstuff.com/word-search-maker/wordsearch.php.
Brillat, Ava, Lafferty, April, Jimenez, Christopher, Del Castillo, Melissa, and Hammill, Sarah. 2017. "Confessions of a Teaching Librarian: Teaching Anxiety, Growth Mindset, and Resilience for Library Instructors." *ACRL 2017*. Baltimore. March 23.

Head, Alison. 2017. "What Today's Students Have Taught Us." Filmed April 2017 at the Coalition for Networked Information. Albuquerque. Video, 1:13:41. https://vimeo.com/212821471.

Lloyd, Emily. 2014. "Cards Against Librarianship: Let's Play!" Last modified January 21, 2014. Accessed March 2, 2018. http://shelfcheck.blogspot.com/2014/01/cards-against-librarianship-lets-play.html.

McCandless, David. 2010. "The Beauty of Data Visualization." Filmed July 2010 at TED Global 2010. Video, 18:11. https://www.ted.com/talks/david_mccandless_the_beauty_of_data_visualization.

About the Contributors

Paula **Archey** is the Teaching and Learning Librarian at the University of Virginia. Prior to that she served as the Research Assistant for Medical Education at the University of Virginia School of Medicine. She holds degrees in education and psychology from Wheaton College in Massachusetts and library science from Southern Connecticut State University. She is a graduate of the Association of Research Libraries Digital Scholarship Institute. Her work is focused on student and community support and engagement.

Robin R. **Breault** obtained her Ph.D. in rhetoric with an emphasis in organizational management from Georgia State University. She has been an action researcher and educator for 25 years in classrooms from pre–Kindergarten to Executive MBA. She lives in Tucson and works with Lead-Local to help professionals in schools, libraries, and cultural institutions navigate institutional change and build organizational leadership capacity.

Michael P. **Buono** is an adjunct lecturer at CUNY Queens Graduate School of Library Science, speaker and a library leader in Suffolk County, New York. He received his MLS in 2012, and his masters in human resources management in 2015. His writing has appeared in *Young Adult Library Services*, *Library Services for Multicultural Patrons*, the YALSA blog, and PMLIB.org. You can read more about him on www.michaelpbuono.com, and you can follow him on twitter @MichaelBuono.

Mary Todd **Chesnut** is an associate professor/lead faculty member for Northern Kentucky University's Library Informatics Program, teaching five courses. She was the Online Faculty of the Year in 2012, is a fiction reviewer for *Library Journal* and an instructor for an online ALA course: Adult Readers' Advisory Services. She is certified as a Quality Matters Peer Reviewer. Her research interests include information literacy, online learning, and academic philanthropy. She obtained her MSLS from the University of Kentucky.

Kathleen **Christy** is a manager of the Information Services Department at Blount County Public Library in Maryville, Tennessee, where she has worked for 13 years. Although she started her library career as the library director at a technical college in Ohio, she enjoys public librarianship.

Ruth **Elder** has been the Cataloging Librarian at the Troy campus of Troy University since 2009. Prior to this, she was the Technical Services Librarian at Taylor University Fort Wayne in Fort Wayne, Indiana, for over 25 years. She received her MLS in 1985 and a Specialist Degree in library and information in 2000, both from Indiana University. Her research interests include cataloging practices and accessible digital collections.

Christine R. **Elliott**, Learning Services & Assessment Librarian at Juniata College in Huntingdon, Pennsylvania, obtained her MLIS from Valdosta State University in Georgia. Her interests include universal accessibility, library marketing, innovative technologies, information literacy instruction, and makerspaces. She has published in *College & Undergraduate Libraries* (2018), *Teaching Technology in Libraries* (2017), and the *Discovery Tool Cookbook* (2016). She is a coeditor of the 2018 LITA Guide on Augmented and Virtual Reality in Libraries.

Erin **Elzi** is a Design & Discovery Librarian at the University of Denver, where she also held the position of as Cataloging & Metadata Librarian for three years. She worked in art libraries in the New York City area for several years, including at the Bard Graduate Center, Pratt Institute, and the Frick Art Reference Library. She is a photographer and holds degrees in art history and philosophy.

Rachel K. **Fischer** is a Metadata Librarian and assistant professor at the University of Alabama. She has a MLIS from Dominican University and a MS in management from Minot State University. Her memberships include ALA and ALCTS. She has previously contributed articles to the *Public Library Quarterly, Reference and User Services Quarterly*, and *Library Journal*. Her advice to new librarians comes from prior experience as a recruiter and as a tenure-track librarian.

Nora **Franco** is an Embedded Clinical Medical Librarian at the University of Missouri–Kansas City. She earned her master's in information science with a concentration in health informatics from the University of North Texas. Her previous employment includes time as an Interlibrary Loan and Reference Librarian at Sul Ross State University (Texas), a Library Research Assistant at the National Library of Medicine's Disaster Information Research Center, and a Web Archives Assistant at the Library of Congress.

Shelia **Gaines** is the Head of Circulation at McWherter Library, University of Memphis, Tennessee. She obtained her MLS degree from the University of Tennessee, Knoxville. She holds a BS in business education from the University of Southern Mississippi. Her research interests include customer service and the library as place. Her memberships include Tennessee Library Association and Association of Christian Librarians. Her work appears in *Tennessee Libraries, The Christian Librarian,* and *Carson-Newman Studies.*

Amy **Gay** is a Digital Scholarship Librarian at Binghamton University, Binghamton, New York, She obtained her MLIS degree from Syracuse University. She is a member of Library Leadership and Management Association (LLAMA), American Library Association; Society of American Archivists, and SUNY-LA. She is a former National Digital Stewardship Residency (NDSR) fellow, D.C. cohort of 2016. She has presented at the 2017 NDSR Symposium and at DigiPres 2017.

Kelsey **George**, Cataloging & Metadata Strategies Librarian at the University of Nevada Las Vegas, received her MLIS from Syracuse University. She is a member of the American Library Association, Library Information Technology Association, Association for Library Collections & Technical Services, and the Nevada Library Association. She has written for InfoSpace, the official blog of the Syracuse University iSchool. She is passionate about accessibility and metadata.

Tim **Gorichanaz**, Ph.D. candidate at Drexel University, conducts research at the intersection of art and information. His work appears in many journals, including the *Journal of Documentation* and *The Library Quarterly*. His professional experience includes advertising and teaching English as a second language, and his educational background includes Spanish literature and linguistics. In 2017, he received the Litwin Books award for ongoing dissertation research in information studies.

Vera **Gubnitskaia** is an art fellow at Crealdé School, Winter Park, Florida, with library degrees from Moscow Institute of Culture (Russia) and Florida State University. She has worked in public and academic libraries in Russia and United States, and contributed chapters to, coedited anthologies and created indexes for ALA, Bantam, McFarland, and Rowman and Littlefield. She has published book reviews in *Journal of International Women's Studies, Small Press Review,* and the *Florida Library Youth Program Newsletter.*

Sharon **Holderman**, an associate professor and coordinator of public services in the Volpe Library at Tennessee Tech University, received her MLIS from Kent State University and is pursuing a doctorate in leadership from Creighton University. She has appeared in *The Journal of Academic Librarianship, College & Research Libraries News, Library Leadership & Management*, and *Tennessee Libraries*. Her areas of interest include financial literacy, policies, copyright, and library career services.

Jim **Jipson** is a professor of art at the University of West Florida in Pensacola, Florida. He received a BFA from Wayne State University, and an MFA from Michigan State University, in printmaking and drawing. He has exhibited his work at national and international galleries and museums. He teaches Advanced Ideas and Concepts, a conceptually based art course dedicated to helping students expand their creative potential, for the UWF Art Department.

Marla **Lobley** is the Public Services Librarian at East Central University in Ada, Oklahoma. She graduated with her MLS from the University of North Texas. She is the Vice-Chair for the Community of Oklahoma Instruction Librarians (COIL) and is a member of the Oklahoma Library Association. She has presented at the Texas Library Association Conference and the Oklahoma Library Association's iCon conference. She has also worked as a Children's Librarian in a public library.

Addison **Lucchi**, Instructional and Research Librarian at MidAmerica Nazarene University (Olathe, Kansas), obtained his MLIS from Simmons College (Boston). He is a member of the American Library Association and Association of College and Research Libraries and has worked as an Information Literacy Fellow at the University of Missouri–Kansas City, and as an instruction librarian at Davidson County Community College. As a librarian and creative writer, he is passionate about demonstrating the connections between professional and creative work and helping other librarians grow creatively.

Jack **Maness** is the Associate Dean for Scholarly Communication & Collections Services at the University of Denver Libraries. He spent a decade at the University of Colorado Boulder as a science librarian, and has worked in public and special libraries. He has won awards for research in the curation of scientific data from Johns Hopkins University Press and the International Earth Data Alliance, and in historical fiction from the Colorado Endowment for the Humanities.

Courtney **McAllister**, Electronic Resources Librarian at Yale University in Connecticut, obtained her MLIS from the University of South Carolina, Columbia, and holds an MA in international performance research from the University of Warwick in Coventry, England. Her interests include change management, service design, and usability. Her publications include *Technical Services* (forthcoming chapter) and a guide on change management practices for library technologies and systems (LITA, forthcoming monograph). She is the associate editor of *The Serials Librarian.*

Michelle P. **McKinney** is the Reference and Web Services Coordinator at the University of Cincinnati Blue Ash College Library. She earned a BS in communications from Ohio University and an MA in Library and Information Science from the University of South Florida. Her responsibilities include overseeing research services, website management, marketing and promotion via the web, and coordinating diversity and inclusion training.

Holly **Mills**, an assistant professor and Public Services Librarian in the Volpe Library at Tennessee Tech University, received her MSIS from the University of Tennessee at Knoxville after earning English and education degrees. She has previously worked as a school librarian and a media specialist. She is involved with the Tennessee Library Association as well as faculty senate and many university committees. Her areas of interest include information literacy, technology, presentation instruction, and library marketing and promotion.

Maggie **Nunley** is the Teaching and Learning Librarian for the School of Engineering and Applied Science and was formerly the Student Academic Support Librarian at the University of Virginia. She holds a BA in English and creative writing from James Madison University and a MSLS from the University of Kentucky. Her work is focused on engineering education, information literacy, and critical librarianship.

Astrid **Oliver**, Collections and Electronic Resources Librarian and associate professor at John F. Reed Library, Fort Lewis College in Durango, Colorado, obtained her MSIS from the University of Texas, Austin. She has written a variety of articles for publication in peer-reviewed journals, almost all stemming from the real-world activities happening in libraries on a daily basis. She has enjoyed a varied career in academic libraries, having worked in Access Services, Library Administration, Collection Management and Electronic Resources.

Erin E. **Pappas** is a Research Librarian for the Humanities at the University of Virginia. Prior to that she held the position of Librarian for European Languages and Social Sciences at Georgetown University. She holds degrees in anthropology from Reed College and the University of Chicago, and in library science from the University of Kentucky. Her research interests include emotional labor and reference work, digital pedagogy, and the future of area studies librarianship.

Casey **Parkman**, Reserves Room Coordinator at McWherter Library, University of Memphis, is an MLIS candidate at the University of Tennessee, Knoxville. He oversees course reserve items and manages the library's circulating technologies and their application. He teaches 3D printing workshops, makes promotional videos for the library, and loves graphic novels and talking endlessly about them. He also is a former cartoonist of his alma mater's newspaper, a position once held by Eudora Welty, as he often points out.

Robert **Perret** is a First-Year Experience and Reference Librarian at the University of Idaho (Moscow); he obtained his MLS from the University of Denver. His memberships include the Idaho Library Association and the John H. Watson Society. His professional writing has appeared in *Libraries and the Academy, Reference & User Services Quarterly, The Journal of Academic Librarianship,* and *Victorian Detectives in Contemporary Culture.* He is also a fiction writer of minor repute.

Joy M. **Perrin**, associate librarian at Texas Tech University Libraries, Lubbock, obtained her MLS from the University of North Texas. Her memberships include the Texas Library Association, and the American Library Association. Her work has appeared in the book *Digitizing Flat Media,* and the journals *Library Management, The Reference Librarian, The Electronic Library,* and the *Journal of Academic Librarianship.* She has served as the DLF AIG User Experience (UX) Working Group Chair and is a Certified User Experience Professional.

Yolanda **Poston**, Library Assistant and Gallery Curator, Scott County Public Library (Georgetown, Kentucky), has a BS in psychology from Freed-Hardeman University (Henderson, Tennessee) and served as Dean of Students at Hillview Acres Non-Public School, Southern California. With a fellow artist, she jointly operated the Georgetown Ice House Gallery. Her artwork has been exhibited at Art Space Gallery (Lexington, Kentucky) and has been highlighted on "Secrets of Chefs of the Bluegrass" (Georgetown, Kentucky.) She has produced artwork with the public for Kentuckians for the Commonwealth, a grassroots social justice organization.

James (Jamie) **Ritter** is the State Librarian for Maine. In this role, he works with Maine State Library staff to build a greater culture of creativity and innovation, and strives to break down organizational silos and enhance problem solving skills for all staff. With prior corporate experiences, he challenges how libraries tackle traditional structural, operational and organizational management practices. He holds a Master Degree in Library & Information Science, and Creativity & Innovation from Drexel University, Philadelphia, Pennsylvania.

Bruce R. **Schueneman**, Library Director at Texas A&M University–Kingsville, obtained his MLS from San Jose State University. His memberships include the Music Library Association and the American Liszt Society. His work has appeared in various journals and books, including *Music Reference Services Quarterly* and *Fontes Artis Musicae,* as well as *Giovanni Battista Viotti* (2006). He participated in a Kennedy Center podcast on football songs (2010) and has written numerous CD essays for Naxos Records.

Heather C. **Seminelli** is the Assistant Director for Communications and Assessment at the United States Military Academy Library, West Point, New York. She earned her MSLIS from the Pratt Institute School of Information, and also completed a MS in geological engineering from Missouri University of Science and Technology. Before becoming a librarian, she flew UH-60 Blackhawk helicopters.

Brooke McDonald **Shelton** is the former CEO and co-founder of LeadLocal, a think, learn and do tank based in Tucson, Arizona. As an experienced designer and facilitator, she has worked with dozens of schools, libraries, and cultural institutions to create learning experiences that are human-centered, equitable, and fun. Providing individuals with tools to lead from "where they are" is essential to her philosophy. She holds a BS in health and human services administration from the University of Arizona, Tucson.

Jana **Slay** has been the Head of Technical Services at the Troy University Library in Troy, Alabama, since February 2007. She previously worked as Collection Development Librarian at the Troy University Rosa Parks Library and the University of South Alabama Biomedical Library. She received her MLIS from the University of Southern Mississippi in 2000. Her research interests include workflow efficiencies in technical services and e-book usage compared to print usage in academic settings.

Carol **Smallwood** received a MLS from Western Michigan University and a MA in history from Eastern Michigan University. Her library experience includes school, public, academic, special, as well as administration, and library systems consultant. She has edited, coedited several dozen library anthologies by ALA, Rowman & Littlefield, McFarland, and others. Her most recent book is *Patterns: Moments in Time* (WordTech Communications, 2019). Hundreds of stories, essays, poems, reviews have appeared in *RHINO* and *World Literature Today*, among others. A multi–Pushcart nominee, she has founded humane societies.

Rochelle **Smith** is the Humanities Librarian at the University of Idaho. She is a graduate of Rutgers University and the University of Pittsburgh. She has worked as a public librarian, and currently serves as chair of the board of trustees for her local county library district. She is a published poet and essayist with an MFA from the University of Idaho.

Kellie **Sparks** is the Evening Reference Librarian at the University of West Florida Libraries in Pensacola. As the Psychology Liaison Librarian and co-chair of the libraries' marketing and outreach committee, she has a deep interest in the psychology behind creative insight. As a librarian who has personally struggled with sustaining creativity, she enjoys delving into the latest secondary research and applying it to her daily library life.

Anthony **Stamatoplos**, Student Success Librarian at the University of South Florida St. Petersburg, received his MLS from Indiana University. He is active in ACRL and serves on the editorial board of *College & Research Libraries*. He has published on a variety of topics in LIS and higher education journals.

Carrye Kay **Syma**, assistant academic dean and associate librarian at Texas Tech University Libraries, Lubbock, obtained her MLS from the University of North Texas. She began her career in 2005 as an assistant librarian and achieved promotion to associate in 2011; in 2017, she was promoted to assistant academic dean. Her memberships include the Texas Library Association; American Library Association; Sigma Tau Delta, Alumni Epsilon Chapter. Her work has appeared in *Reference Services Review* and *College and Research Library News*.

Deb Biggs **Tenbusch**, Master of Arts (Library Science), University of Michigan, is an account manager at Gale, Cengage Learning. Previously, she has held challenging positions in librarianship, such as a reference/instruction in academe; marketing/promotions for a bibliographic database management company; special library development work; directing a national clearinghouse for instruction librarians; and coordinating and promoting a statewide digital library. In 2018, she received the Michigan Association for Media in Education Lifetime Membership Award for contributions to the profession.

Shannon **Tharp**, Collections & Content Management Librarian at University of Denver Libraries, earned her MLIS and MFA in creative writing from the University of Washington. She is the author of the poetry collections *The Cost of Walking* (2011) and *Vertigo in Spring* (2013). With Sommer Browning she is the coeditor of *Poet-Librarians in the Library of Babel: Innovative Meditations on Librarianship* (2018).

Dana E. **Thimons** is an assistant professor and Health Sciences Librarian at the University of Nevada, Las Vegas, and serves as liaison to the School of Dental Medicine and School of Medicine. She received her MLIS from Florida State University and her MS in health law from Nova Southeastern University. She has worked in a variety of libraries across the U.S., including a community hospital, private university, for-profit college, and public library.

Anastasia S. **Varnalis-Weigle** is an assistant professor in library and information science at the University of Maine in Augusta. She obtained her MSLIS in archives management from Simmons College in Boston and is a Ph.D./LIS doctoral candidate at Simmons. Her memberships include the College Book Arts Association, Art Libraries of North America, New England Archivist, and Maine Archives and Museums. Her work has appeared in *The Journal of Contemporary Archival Studies*.

Silvia **Vong** is the Head of Public Services at John M. Kelly Library, Toronto, Ontario, Canada. She obtained her Master of Library and Information Science degree from Western University and a Master of Education degree from York University. She has published in *Communication in Information Literacy* on zine-making and reflective practice with undergraduate students and presented a poster session on zine-making and information literacy at ACRL 2017. Her research interest is the intersection between critical reflection and information literacy.

Leslie A. **Wagner** is an Associate Archivist at the University of Texas at Arlington Libraries and holds a master's degree in history from the same university. She is the Chair of the American Library Association's Mapping and Geospatial Information Round Table, Past Chair of the Texas Library Association's Archives, Genealogy and Local History Round Table, reviewer for the Society of American Archivists' *Practical Technology for Archives*, coeditor of *Spoken Memories: Reflections on Dallas Jewish History*; and the author of LibGuides on genealogy, Texas history, and local history resources.

Laura **Wimberley** is the Assessment Librarian at Oviatt Library at California State University Northridge, where she also serves as the liaison for Geography, Recreation & Tourism Management, and Government Documents. She earned her Ph.D. in political science from the University of California San Diego, and her MLIS from San Jose State University. Her previous work has appeared in the *Journal of Academic Ethics*, and work is forthcoming in *Practical Academic Librarianship*.

Index